Lean Leadership for Healthcare

The second edition of this Shingo Prize-winning book builds and expands on the first edition. When originally published over ten years ago, there was a need to understand how to lead process and cultural transformation within the healthcare industry. The perfect storm of rising costs, decreasing reimbursements, substandard quality, a shortage of resources, and a new run of better technology and electronic health systems requires leadership to navigate in a different environment.

Since the original book, lean improvements have been made to the governance of process and quality improvement programs, and to the management of operations using the daily management system. The core of the book remains the same; however, the results have been updated and made more current, given access to better data and enhanced use of the electronic health record. Extraordinarily good advice is given throughout this book on best practices of what to do and what not to do in leading large-scale change based on another ten years of hands-on experience of the author working in large and small healthcare systems across the country, including case studies that share the time-tested insights of healthcare team members and leaders. The book outlines a management system for sustaining lean improvements and provides the lean leadership approaches, thoughts, and visual tools needed to guide organizations along the path toward world-class healthcare performance. It walks the reader through developing an improvement strategy, laying out a detailed transformation roadmap for initiating, accelerating, and sustaining lean improvements and delivering world-class improvement of outcomes and culture, discussing leadership behaviors necessary for success, and closes with actions that can be used to mitigate risk. It reviews the fundamentals of lean and explains how to link a strategy of continuous improvement to corporate strategy to achieve operational excellence. The book also describes how to mitigate the risk of failure when undergoing large-scale corporate change, including what can go wrong and how to prevent these failures.

Updated and refreshed, *Lean Leadership for Healthcare* remains the gold standard for end-to-end delivery of lean transformation in healthcare. This book is ideal for leaders in the healthcare industry looking to initiate or accelerate lean improvements to clinical and non-clinical processes.

Ronald G. Bercaw is the President of Breakthrough Horizons, LTD, a management consulting company specializing in World-Class Improvement through the application of the Toyota Business System, or "lean." With over 38 years of experience in operations, his hands-on, lean management experience was gained through multiple enterprise transformations in different industries including custom packaging, power reliability electronics assembly, and test and measurement products. Educated at Purdue University, he learned the details and disciplined applications of lean principles, habits, and tools from both the Shingijutsu Sensei and their first-generation disciples. Since leaving industry, Ron has consulting experience in the healthcare sector (U.S. and Canada health systems including primary care, acute care, and community applications of both clinical and back shop operations), the commercial sector (administration, manufacturing, distribution, supply chain, and engineering), and the public sector (U.S. Army, U.S. Navy, U.S. Air Force including Depot Repair Operations, the Pentagon, and Surgeon General Assignments). Ron is also a recognized author with the release of four books, including Shingo award-winners entitled *Taking Improvement from the Assembly Line to Healthcare*, and *Lean Leadership for Healthcare*. He is a co-author of *The Lean Electronic Health Record*, along with Susan Snedaker and Kurt Knoth, as part of the HIMSS book series.

Lean Leadership for Healthcare

Approaches to Lean Transformation

Second edition

Ronald G. Bercaw

Routledge
Taylor & Francis Group

A PRODUCTIVITY PRESS BOOK

Designed cover image: Shutterstock
Second edition published 2025
by Routledge
605 Third Avenue, New York, NY 10158

and by Routledge
4 Park Square, Milton Park, Abingdon, Oxon, OX14 4RN

Routledge is an imprint of the Taylor & Francis Group, an informa business

First edition published by CRC Press 2013

ISBN: 9781032873404 (hbk)
ISBN: 9781032871035 (pbk)
ISBN: 9781003532132 (ebk)

DOI: 10.4324/9781003532132

Typeset in Garamond
by Deanta Global Publishing Services, Chennai, India

In the final days of completing the manuscript for the publishing of this book, my oldest sister, Lisa Hankins, passed away suddenly and at the way too early age of 62 years. She was able to donate her liver and will be survived by the organ recipient and her children and grandchildren.

Lisa worked many years in the healthcare field working with disadvantaged youth, seniors, and those struggling with mental health and addiction issues. This book is dedicated to her memory. She has left a hole in our hearts but will not be forgotten.

Contents

Foreword

The challenges facing healthcare organizations today are very similar to the challenges facing the industry when this book was first written. While the COVID-19 pandemic put the industry under a microscope, highlighting supply chain challenges (among other things), the underlying problems of declining reimbursement rates, an aging population, and provider burnout continue to be a burden on our industry. Another thing that has been amplified since the pandemic has been the exodus of experienced providers and staff from the healthcare industry. Their jobs were hard enough before the pandemic, but now they can sometimes seem downright unbearable. This has made it even more critical for organizations to use lean thinking to make dramatic improvements in productivity and quality with the same number or fewer employees. Those who are students of the Toyota Production system know this is not achieved by spending exorbitantly on technology or asking people to do more with less. It's about engaging the people closest to the work to help identify and eliminate non-value-added activities, using a structured approach to make certain that everybody feels a part of the change and not having the change "done" to them. These statements sound obvious and should be considered "common sense," but it's a lot harder than it seems and this approach is *not* commonplace in our industry. That said, I'm hopeful that if you are reading this book, we are making progress toward a brighter future in healthcare that includes lean leadership.

Lean Leadership for Healthcare has been used by practitioners and leaders alike for the past decade to drive improvement across their organizations. Ron has taken his Shingo Prize-winning book and managed to make this classic even better. This is not a book about what could be, or what should be, rather it's a field book that takes the reader through the steps needed to truly transform their organization. This edition adds new A3-based strategy tools, additional details around the governance structure, and new tools to lock in your improvement via robust Managing for Daily Improvement boards at the front lines. If you are searching for the roadmap to your organizational True North … making improvements to patient outcomes, cost, and the engagement of your providers and staff, this is the book for you!

Kurt A. Knoth

VP, Performance Improvement (Retired)
Corewell Health
Grand Rapids, MI

Preface

In 2011, I completed the manuscript for my first book titled *Taking Improvement from the Assembly Line to Healthcare* (CRC Press). This book was my personal translation of the application of lean within the healthcare industry. At the time, lean quality and process improvement was gaining momentum, but was misunderstood and even misapplied and I was attempting to send a simplified message on how to do lean in healthcare. While not everyone was able to figure out what the assembly line had to do with improving healthcare, the book's title was an homage to the greatest management system in operation across the world today, the Toyota Production System. As a result of this effort, I was fortunate to be recognized for advancing the lean body of knowledge and was awarded a Shingo Research award.

Before the book was published, I had a chance to reflect on the message I want to convey to the many dedicated healthcare professionals, providing a wide spectrum of medical and preventative services to patients. The book was a comprehensive approach to lean improvement. Topics included understanding the fundamentals of lean improvement, understanding the tools and applications of these tools to "see and eliminate" wasted time and activity in the healthcare setting, and a review of several case studies of lean in practice. The case studies demonstrate that meaningful change in performance and culture can occur when a focused team of individuals properly applies the Toyota Production System in the healthcare setting. I included the necessary steps an organization should take prior to applying the lean model and closed with a chapter on leadership behaviors essential for success.

Throughout the development of *Taking Improvement from the Assembly Line to Healthcare*, I continued to operate my consulting practice. My company, Breakthrough Horizons LTD, services a wide range of clients in creating a culture of improvement through the application of the Toyota Production System, commonly known as lean. A portion of this consulting base consists of healthcare organizations all along the continuum of care. The healthcare client base consists of large and small healthcare clients including private, not-for-profit, government-funded, socialized medicine, union, non-union, U.S. based and international, etc.

While critical to our consulting practice that we teach organizations the tools and techniques for improvement, we were spending a large amount of time teaching organizations how to lead change, and our efforts were increasingly focused on leadership development. This formulated my hypothesis that the most important part of creating a culture of improvement is "leading" the change. Despite this fact, at that time, there were few resources available to help develop these skills at various management levels. This book, which you are about the read, *Lean Leadership for Healthcare*, was created to provide healthcare leaders with a comprehensive resource on how to *lead* transformation improvement within the healthcare industry.

Why leadership? Why not management? I frequently hear in my work that "our organization needs to do a better job of managing improvement." Organizations certainly spend a lot of time on management development, and universities and public workshops teach a myriad of management courses. Fewer university curricula and public workshops are dedicated to leadership, and organizations often spend on leadership development than management development. But what's the difference?

Management is the set of work processes that keep a complex organization – one filled with departments, people, processes, and technology – operating effectively and efficiently. There are many aspects to management including planning, budgeting, staffing/scheduling, and controlling. Organizations spend a lot of time and resources on these management systems. *Leadership* is the set of processes that creates organizations and then helps these organizations change to meet ever-evolving business conditions. The key aspects of leadership include creating a future vision (the direction of the organization), aligning the resources to meet the vision, and then inspiring people to realize this new future.

In creating a culture of improvement, are we trying to create a management system to plan, budget, organize, control, and staff our way to improvement? Or are we trying to create a new direction for the organization, aligning the resources and then inspiring people to realize this vision in spite of the obstacles we are sure to encounter along the way?

In reality we do need strong management systems to be successful. I will discuss many of the management systems, tools, ideas, and behaviors necessary to foster a culture of improvement. However, we also need a heavy dose of leadership. This book will provide you with many lean leadership approaches, thoughts, tools, and applications to put your organization on its way toward world-class performance and culture.

For most of you, this is a place where you have never been, and any transformation will require great leadership. Done well, you can create an environment where world-class healthcare quality and outcomes, patient safety, and customer service are the norm. The workplace can be transformed into one where medical staff are engaged in their work and inspired to do better and be better every day. You can lead and shape a healthcare system that delivers more "value." Value from a healthcare system performance is broadly defined as outcomes divided by cost. My goal in this book is to help your organization create a healthcare system that, through your people, continually improves outcomes and lower and lower costs.

There are plenty of skeptics out there and perhaps some of you who are reading this book are already skeptical. This is ok, no one should ever take things at face value. Do your homework and ask a lot of questions. But before you dismiss lean as an improvement system. Keep in mind that "lean" is not common sense; rather, it is counterintuitive. It takes many years to learn lean and a lifetime to master. But those organizations that have applied lean thinking to their processes, with the diligence of effective management and strong leadership support, are already realizing the benefits of their efforts. Many of the benefits far exceed what was possible from benchmarking just a few years ago. If you speak with a lean leader, a lean healthcare service provider, a lean hospital, or a lean clinic, they will tell you the reward far exceeds the efforts. To be successful, these leaders and organizations had to provide leadership to design and then create their future. I hope to leverage their leadership stories, successes, and failures, plus a few of my own, to help you transform your healthcare organization.

As a second edition, I hope to add more detail to the tried-and-true leadership practices necessary to get the best outcomes with the least risk to your organization. Of note in this book is the update and detail on the governance of the improvements necessary to deliver and sustain world-class rates of improvement and culture. Having systems in place to ensure improvement stays on track is another essential ingredient to successful transformation.

Acknowledgments

The first edition book was reviewed, enhanced, and critiqued by Scott Brubaker. He invested many hours into this process and added many valuable inputs to the book. His help is greatly appreciated. Scott also said that this story needed to be written. At the time there were few books for leadership on transforming healthcare through the application of lean. The attempts to translate the first edition book from random musings to a manuscript with structure, grammar, and readability go to Heather Wood. Over the course of 10 months, we had many back-and-forth moments improving the copy. A special thanks to Heather. I want to thank Kurt Knoth for writing the foreword for this book. I have known Kurt for over 20 years, and he has decorated career filled with lean accomplishments. Kurt and I have also collaborated on a different book, *The Lean Electronic Health Record* (CRC Press).

Taylor & Francis Group senior editor, Kristine Mednansky is another valuable partner in the book-writing business. Kristine breaks down the publishing business into understandable parts and helps navigate the timelines to ensure timely completion and launch of the book.

I would like to acknowledge the over 300 hospitals, systems, and clinics I have had a chance to work with over the last 20 years. Whether it was through refining the improvement standard work, providing wisdom and experience in the healthcare setting, or contributing case studies and graphics to the book, all of these experiences and products contributed to the completion of this book. I'd like to think that we learned from each other.

For the many organizations that are using lean management, you have my respect. Creating a lean enterprise and sticking with it is very difficult. I know this personally from having gone through this as a leader with four organizations and having helped dozens of organizations over the last 20 years. I can promise you that if you stay true to lean principles and avoid taking shortcuts, your organization, your staff, and your patients will all be rewarded or continue to be rewarded for your efforts. I know it doesn't always feel that way during the process but doing things the right way and for the right reasons will always be rewarded.

Finally, to my wife Darlene, thank you for being the best part of my life and giving me the wiggle room to write this book.

About the Author

Ronald (Ron) Bercaw is the president of Breakthrough Horizons, LTD, a management consulting company specializing in delivering world-class improvement through the application of the Toyota Production System more commonly known as "Lean." With over 35 years of experience in operations, his lean management experience was gained through multiple enterprise transformations in different industries including packaging, electronic power reliability assembly, test and measurement products, and agriculture.

Educated at Purdue University, Bercaw learned the details and disciplined applications of lean principles, habits, tools, and applications from the Shingijutsu Sensei and their first-generation disciples. Working in shop floor, engineering, and administrative areas, he vigorously strived to remove waste from organizations through the involvement and ideas of the world's greatest experts, those people doing the work.

Bercaw has consulting experience in the healthcare sector (U.S. and Canadian health systems including primary care, specialty, care, acute care, and community applications of both clinical and administrative improvement), the commercial sector (administration, manufacturing, distribution, supply chain, engineering, sales, marketing, finance, etc.), and the public sector (U.S. Army, U.S. Navy, U.S. Air Force) including maintenance, repair, and overhaul (MRO) assignments, Pentagon, and Surgeon General assignments, the Veteran's Health Administration including central office administration and medical center clinical and administrative processes and Public Health.

He is also the author of four previous books including *Taking Improvement from the Assembly Line to Healthcare*, first and second editions, and *Lean Leadership for Healthcare*, first edition, and *The Lean Electronic Medical Record*. Bercaw is a two-time recipient of the Shingo Research and Professional Publication award for advancing the body of lean improvement knowledge.

Chapter 1

Lean at a Glance

What Is Lean Healthcare?

Lean Healthcare is a business system, built upon decades of development of the Toyota Production System, which is used to deliver continuous, world-class quality, outcomes, access, and customer service to patients, caregivers, and their surrounding communities. The Toyota Production System, most commonly known for producing personal transportation in the form of cars, trucks, and sport utility vehicles, is the comprehensive business approach and corresponding culture Toyota embraces toward continuous process improvement to deliver compelling value to their customers. The words "Lean" and "Toyota Production System (TPS)" are used often synonymously; however, I will use the term lean going forward. Before I describe what is meant by continuous improvement, it will be helpful to better understand a few essential lean terms. After we understand some fundamental lean concepts, we can more easily define lean Healthcare.

Value Added

Lean improvement is based in its entirety on two themes: continuous elimination of wasted time and activity (a different way to state continuous improvement) and respect for all people as shown in Figure 1.1.

To understand the first theme, continuous elimination of wasted time and activity, it is necessary to understand the value-added/non-value-added

DOI: 10.4324/9781003532132-1

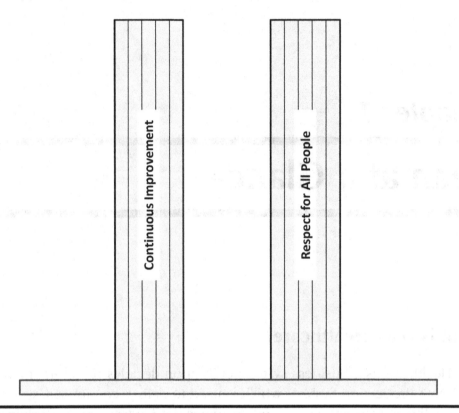

Figure 1.1 Themes of lean improvement.

principle. Every activity that occurs in any organization falls into one of two categories: value adding or non-value adding. Although the idea of what a value-added activity entails is easy to grasp when producing a physical product, the concept becomes less clear when applied to the service industry. A value-added activity is any action (either product or service related) that a customer is willing to pay for; activities that change the form, fit, or function of the product would be considered value added. An industrial example of value-added activity might include drilling, painting, heat treating, or assembly of a product. Within the service industry, a value-added activity might include help desk services offered on the telephone.

Non-value Added

Non-value added is by default, the opposite of value added; it is any activity that requires time, space, or resources, but does not directly change the form, fit, or function of the product. Alternatively, it is also an activity that the customer is not willing to pay for. Examples of industrial non-value-added activity include conveying a part from one machine to the next or the counting of inventory items to ensure accuracy of on-hand quantities.

Every industry has activities that are required by law or required by business requirements (accreditation or third-party certification). Such activities may include Occupational Safety and Health Act standards (OSHA), adhering to ISO standards, or Generally Accepted Accounting Principles (GAAP). While it can be tempting to classify these as value-added activities, at the end of the day, many of these activities are usually non-value added to the end customer. Sometimes in "lean-speak," organizations will refer to this set of requirements as non-value added, but required.

In healthcare, the perception of value is slightly different. A value-added activity is any activity that *directly* meets the needs of the customer. In order to determine if a step is value added, you need to clarify two things: First, who is the customer, and second, what are their needs? Many times, in healthcare the dialogue jumps from the customer being the patient and/ or the caregiver, to the customer being the provider, or the customer being administration, etc. It is helpful to remember value is always specified by THE customer. And there can be only one.

The way I find it easiest to determine the true, single customer is by answering the following question: Who is creating the pull for the services needed? So, if we are trying to figure who the customer is in a surgical procedure, we try to understand where the pull for the service comes from. Since we would not need a surgical center, sterile processing, materials, supplies, equipment, surgical staff, a surgeon, a billing department, etc. without a patient needing surgery, the patient is the customer. In this surgical procedure, value will be specified by the patient, so value-added and non-value-added activity is based solely on the patient perception. The second decision we need to make is *to clearly identify the needs of the customer.* Healthcare professionals are experts in this area and possess extensive knowledge, which can be very helpful in determining customer needs. However, it is not exclusively the role of the staff and provider to specify the customer's needs, nor is it the insurance company's role, nor the administration's. With information available at the click of a mouse, many customers (patients) are quite capable of specifying their needs. As I often tell healthcare professionals, when I work with engineers who are designing new products, they are quick to articulate that the consumers do not know what they want/need. As highly skilled engineers, they have to make those decisions for the consumers since they have technical expertise. I think everyone as a consumer can determine the features and benefits they are looking for in a new product or service. It would be expensive, and quite impractical, to drag an engineer around with us every time we shopped for a product. As consumers, we have no problem specifying value-added and non-value-added activity within our purchases. This same theory holds true with most patients when they seek medical services. Even though you may be the healthcare "engineer," the patient is generally quite capable of determining their needs. Your job as the service provider is to identify the activities that directly meet those needs, as those are the value-added activities.

To further illustrate the differences between value-added and non-value-added activities, let's discuss the front-end processes of getting a CT scan. Being an outdoor enthusiast, let us assume you fell while skiing during a recent snow skiing trip, and your knee is hurting. Your primary care physician provides an examination and gives a diagnosis of a potential ACL injury. To further refine this diagnosis, he or she orders you to get a CT scan. When one gets a CT scan, one will likely need to schedule the exam date and time, register with someone when you arrive, and complete some paperwork. While all of these front-end activities are common during a typical CT exam experience, none of them will directly meet your needs. So, the collection of all of the pre-CT scan activities, as described, would be considered non-value-added activity.

To summarize, in order to determine the value-added activity, we need to identify the customer, specify their needs, and determine which activities directly meet those needs. The customer of this process is you, the patient needing the CT exam. The needs you need to be met include the examination and the corresponding results. The value-added activities would be the actual exam (which takes minutes), and the actual reading of the exam (which also takes minutes). But what about registration, the preparing for the exam, the transcribing of the results, the charting of the activities, the sending of an invoice, etc.? Using the value-added/non-value-added definition, these are all classified as non-value-added activities. These steps take time, space, and resources, but do not directly meet the customer's needs. The understanding of value-added (VA) and non-value-added activity (NVA) is the first lesson that must be learned in improvement, and it is not always an easy lesson to understand. When we can understand both VA/and NVA activity, we can start to look at the ratio between the two activities. This ratio informs us of our improvement potential. A typical process, regardless of industry, is 95% NVA to 5% VA

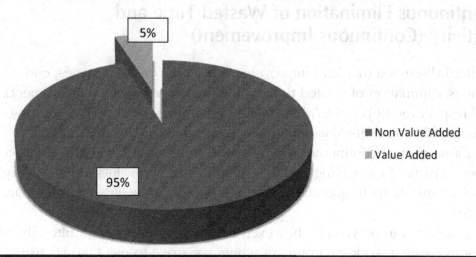

Value Added versus Non Value Added

5%

■ Non Value Added

■ Value Added

95%

Figure 1.2   Value-added/non-value-added principle.

as shown in Figure 1.2. World-class organizations understand this and take advantage of the insight this ratio provides as a means quantifying the improvement potential of a process.

Improvement using lean fundamentals involves the identification and elimination of non-value-added activity. Another term for non-value-added activity is "Waste". When 95% of the activity is non-value added that leaves a *lot* of room for improvement. Focusing on non-value-added activity provides two benefits. First, the improvement potential is much larger. Would you rather pay attention to the 95% opportunity, or the 5% opportunity? This is why lean organizations can and do routinely show 25 to 50+% improvements. They understand the value-added/non-valued-added principle and they choose to play in the 95% space. Secondly, the cost of the improvement is significantly less. When we focus on eliminating non-value-added activity, we are in essence "stopping" some kind of work. How much does it cost to stop doing something? The definition of non-value-added activity is an activity taking time, space, and resources, but not directly meeting a patient's needs. So, if we eliminate non-value-added activity, then we free up time, space, and resources! These newfound resources can be used to add even more value to our customers, increasing access, improving quality, improving the patient experience, and lowering costs.

The First Theme of Lean Improvement – Continuous Elimination of Wasted Time and Activity (Continuous Improvement)

Earlier I discussed that lean improvement is based on two themes, continuous elimination of wasted time and activity (continuous improvement), and respect for all people. We just spent a fair amount of time discussing value-added and non-value-added activity. Understanding this concept is the foundation of continuous improvement. In the simplest terms, improvement consists of identifying and then eliminating non-value-added activity. Lean organizations frequently shorten this phrase to "seeing and eliminating waste."

Continuous improvement, however, has two other tenants. Culturally, we want to create a work environment where we strive to meet targets using *courage* and *creativity*. Courage implies making individual and team decisions in the best interest of serving the customer. For example, clinic hours of operation may best serve their customers with operating hours from 1.00 pm to 9.00 pm. We have been comfortable working from 8.00 am to 4.00 pm for years. A courageous decision would include altering work hours in the best interest of the customer. Creativity entails using new approaches and techniques in lieu of adding resources and capital costs. A term used by lean practitioners is "creativity before capitol." This implies generating solutions that take minimal resources to implement before making a significant capital investment in equipment, IT, space, and facilities or hiring additional staff. Remember, if the solutions implemented involve eliminating non-value-added activity, then by design, additional time, space, and resources have been freed up.

Another tenant of continuous improvement is the concept of Genchi Genbutsu, loosely translated as "go to the source to find facts." When problems arise in the workplace, how would a manager traditionally respond? Many organizations would schedule a meeting, get a small group of knowledgeable experts together, and try and solve the problem in a conference room. To illustrate my point, if you are a manager/leader in healthcare, I would be willing to bet the majority of the time you spend each day is either attending a meeting (virtual or face to face) or traveling from one meeting to the next. A lean company views problems as treasures of information, telling a story in plain language where the current process is not adequate. A lean manager will always go to the area where the problem occurred and observe the process to see if the source of the problem can be identified. This is tremendously different from the traditional approach. Not going to the area where the problem occurred is the equivalent of a police investigator not going to the scene of the crime to uncover forensic evidence. How effective would investigations be if the standard approach to crime solving involved scheduling a meeting at the police office and bringing in some experts to try and solve the crime? The healthcare example I like to use is let's assume we had an instance where a dose of medicine was missed. This resulted in a poor outcome, that while not catastrophic, warranted further investigation. The question I'd like you to ponder is, "how many missed doses occurred in the conference room?" We need to go to the source to find facts.

The Second Theme of Lean Improvement – Respect for All People

From a global perspective, respect for all people means having a purpose for improvement. How can improvement in healthcare benefit our patients, our staff, our physicians, our community agencies, and our service providers? How can we improve our local community, our country, and the world as a whole? From an individual and organizational perspective, showing respect for people comes in the form of understanding each other. What work do I do and what work do you do? Together, how do we build a foundation of mutual trust? Respect is also demonstrated in taking individual and team responsibility. Are we doing the right thing, every time? Are we following the known best, evidence-based method? Are we putting forth our best effort? As an organization we want to optimize both team and individual performance. Additionally, we must also ask ourselves if we are sharing opportunities for personal and team development.

A lean organization is not excited by benchmark performance and peer comparisons; rather, a lean organization gets excited about knowing they are making a difference in the world. Maybe they are not directly affecting the entire world, but most certainly their community and customers (patients). This organization's staff knows that they are continually providing better and safer care, reducing lead times for services thus increasing access, and continuously lowering the cost of services increasing the value of the healthcare that is delivered. This relentless pursuit of perfection is how respect for all people is realized.

The Seven Wastes

As we discussed earlier, non-value-added activity and waste mean the same thing. The early founders of the Toyota Production System spent a lot of time observing waste. Because of the repetition of certain forms of waste, it proved helpful to put the waste into common categories. As detailed in Figure 1.3, the major forms of waste found in operations became known as the seven operational wastes; I will provide a brief discussion of each below.

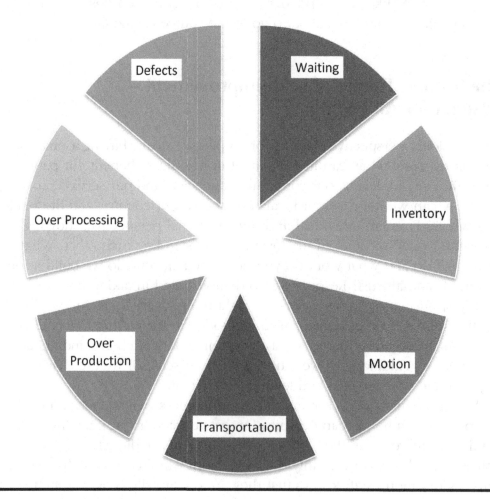

Figure 1.3 Seven wastes.

Over-production

Over-production is producing too much stuff or producing stuff too early. Let's say we were unable to use a pre-mix IV and our current process mixes this IV solution in the pharmacy. Subsequently we delivered two days' worth of this mixture to the unit where the patient was being treated. At the end of the first day following the delivery of this solution, the patient was discharged home. Since the remaining solution would now need to be returned to the pharmacy and likely disposed of, we over-produced. When over-production occurs, we have expended labor to mix IV solutions that can never be recovered. Additionally, the excess corresponding solution now has to be disposed of, another unnecessary and unrecoverable expense. Over-production is often referred to as the worst waste. Generally, when you observe over-production it spawns other waste. Notably, it will almost always lead to inventory and waiting.

Waiting

Waiting causes a disruption to workflow. This disruption can result in idle resources, stopping and starting of work, and time delays for our customers and stakeholders (patients or staff). Within healthcare, we can experience waiting for service providers, diagnostics, information, equipment, and materials. Waiting is the largest single waste within healthcare. It is easy to measure because it is measured in increments of time. Recall non-value-added activity is anything that takes **time**, space, or resources but fails to directly meet a customer's need. For service providers that work in the Emergency Department or a clinic, I'm sure you can recall an occasion where a patient or family member verbally expressed disappointment with the time they were spending in the waiting room, or in an exam room with little activity happening. Staff members do not always see waiting as a waste. If a therapist walks to a patient's room to provide some therapy and the patient is not present, then the therapist likely would not wait. The therapist would simply go to their next patient. So, since the therapist is not idle and is now adding value (providing therapy) to a different patient, the waiting was not considered wasteful. I would like to point out that this argument is flawed on two fronts. First, waste was created when the therapist walked to the patient's room only to find out the patient was not present. This walking to a missed appointment would be a waste of motion (motion consumes both time and resources). But more importantly, remember that waste is always viewed from the customer's perspective. For the therapist to not see the missed therapy session as wasteful is looking at the waste from the wrong pair of eyes. The patient is the customer, and it is that customer that is *waiting* for their therapy. Even though 95% of the activities going on around us are non-value added, it still takes time and practice to be able to see waste. Understanding the seven key wastes is a good start to being able to identify waste in your organization. I do find it humorous that oftentimes in healthcare, the waste of waiting is easy to spot. In fact, the waste is clearly labeled in plain sight. Do any of you have a *waiting* room?

Over-processing

Over-processing is a waste generated by performing work in excess of value. While this may be hard to believe, it is possible to do *more* work than the customer values. For example, many administrative and support staff use spreadsheet solutions on a daily basis. Software solutions are invaluable; they enable us to sort numerical data, determine averages, sum column totals, and quickly build charts and graphs. Have any of you ever considered the work that went into the engineering process of these solutions? You have the ability to do conditional formatting, data validation, pivot tables, and logical formulas in a matter of moments. It is my belief that you could spend years trying to learn all the functionality of this type of software, but 99.9% of us will never use greater than 10% of this capability. From the customer's perspective, this product is over-engineered; it has capabilities far beyond what the customer values. It is important to note, however, that other people may find these many features beneficial. Thus, from their perspective, the product does not appear to be over-processed.

As an example of over-processing within healthcare, we might consider inter-professional assessment. A complex patient might be assessed by multiple nurses, multiple physicians, and several members of the allied health team. While each team member is looking for different pieces of information, relative to their expertise and scope of practice to provide the best possible care, a patient might be asked the same question by two or more people. Many of you in the course of your work have heard from patients, "I've been asked this five times already. Do you people that talk to one another?" Again, from the patient's perspective, as an organization, you have over-processed. The redundancy in questioning creates work in excess of value. The over-processing waste scales when each member of the care team records the questions and/or result of the question in the health record.

(There is more on this topic in the book *The Lean Electronic Health Record: A Journey Toward Optimized Care,* CRC Press, 2018.)

Inventory

When we think of inventory, we think of supplies. Everyone, whether in a production environment or a service environment, can relate to the disruption in work when we run out of materials and supplies. The opposite is also true; when we have too many supplies, this excess can lead to damaged products, obsolescence, and time wasted on inventory management. This excess of inventory also adds strain to the overhead budget, and none of these activities meet the needs of the customer. Inventory consumes space and resources while failing to directly meet the needs of the customer.

In healthcare, however, there are other forms of inventory present. One inventory that we do not frequently think about is patients waiting for services. Patients could be waiting for an admission, waiting for an in-patient bed, waiting for an appointment, waiting for test results, etc. But the collection of these patients is inventory as they are queuing up, and occupying space. A simple definition of inventory is "things" (people, items, information) waiting to be worked on. Another form of inventory is things waiting in your inbox. Moving beyond the inventory of patients, within administration, there are lots of places where work queues up. Bills waiting to be paid, charts waiting to be coded, invoices waiting to be processed, e-mails waiting to be answered, performance appraisals waiting to be completed, payroll waiting to be processed, supplies waiting to be ordered, financial reports waiting to be generated. The backlog of these items is inventory.

Inventory is another waste that generates other waste. When administrative work (inventory) backs up; typical solutions include prioritizing the work, sorting the work, reporting on the backlog, etc. All of the additional administrative work is non-value added. None of the subsequent work caused by the queue directly meets a customer's need. Clinical backlog is prioritized, and supply chain excess is counted and rotated. All of this work is also non-value-added.

Motion

When we speak of the waste of motion, we are talking about "people" movement in excess of that required to create value; this movement is from the staff and providers. One form of motion is present we walk from one area to the next looking for supplies and equipment. A simple example of wasted motion occurs when we have to walk an extra ten steps to get to the hand sanitizer because the dispenser is not located at the point of use. I often hear the argument that it is "healthy" for the staff to be active. I agree that it is healthy to have an active lifestyle, but unnecessary movement in the workplace is wasteful. The following example demonstrates how easily wasted motion accumulates in the workplace.

One organization, I'll call them "St. Gerard," did an extensive study of the waste of motion for their in-patient nursing staff. They used a stopwatch to record the percentage of time that a nurse spent walking during their 12-hour shift. The results of the study revealed that 53% of the time, a nurse was walking from one point to the next. That is more than half of their total time working. This organization had over 800 full-time nurses on their staff across the hospital. After some simple mathematical calculations, this would imply that over 400 nurses were being paid throughout the week to walk from one point to the next. If this organization could reduce the nurse walking time across the organization by 25%, that would be the equivalent of getting an additional 200 nurses (25% of 800 nurses = 200 nurses). Can any of you use 200 nurses? For free?

I'd like to use artificial intelligence, spreadsheets, and benchmarks to help all healthcare organizations improve. But what I really enjoy is the elegance of lean. In this case, we can make a substantial gain in nurse productivity, timeliness of care, patient satisfaction, and nurse satisfaction by determining how to eliminate this waste of motion through nursing assignment optimization, supply storage optimization, and charting location optimization. In my 20+ years working as a lean Sensei, I have never seen, create additional nursing capacity by reducing the waste of nurse motion as a strategic initiative. Think of the power of this activity. And it can be done with minimal investment!

Defects

Defects create waste because they result in work needing to be redone or corrected. Before we get too far into the waste of defects, we need to differentiate between a defect and an error. Any work that is completed by humans is subject to errors; an error is a mistake in the execution of a task. An example of an error is a paper physician order for a medication that was inadvertently not signed. Regardless of how well-trained people are, how often they complete a given task, or how diligent/conscientious they are, errors will be made. However, an error need not turn into a defect. A defect is an error that makes its way to the customer and results in work needing to be completely redone, corrected, or clarified. In healthcare, defects frequently appear in the form of missing information, incorrect information, or information received in the wrong format. But defects can also be clinical in nature and appear in the following ways: The wrong test could be ordered; the wrong diagnosis could be made; patients can be harmed through infections acquired at the hospital; recovery can be lengthened by not following evidence-based best practices.

Regardless of the type of defect, these wastes are of critical importance to see and eliminate in any process. It doesn't matter how fast work is performed if it isn't right. I often hear that people are so busy. "I had to rush to keep up," or "I didn't have the time to get the proper information." My response to these comments is the same as what I was taught 30 years ago. "If you don't have the time or methods to do work right the first time, when are you going to find the time to do it right the second time?" Defects can lead to a loss of staff productivity, create delays in treatment, decrease patient satisfaction, and in some instances even harm the patient. Defects are also a source of management, staff, and clinician frustration.

Transportation

Transportation is the conveyance of materials, equipment, information, and patients through an organization. From the patient's perspective, rarely does the movement of items or information create value, thus transportation is considered a waste. Said differently, my hurt knee doesn't feel better because you moved from point A to point B. Transportation consumes staff resources, and also takes time, while failing to directly meet the needs of the customer. Motion is different from transportation in that motion involves the movement of staff, while transportation is the movement of items. Consider a patient that shows up for a surgical pre-admission visit. This patient must first be registered. Next, the patient has to go to the lab for a blood test, followed by walking to diagnostic imaging for a chest x-ray. Finally, the patient returns to the clinic for a nursing screen and pre and post-surgical education, followed by a trip to a different office for a meeting with the Anesthesiologist. While we have optimized the utilization of the staff, and leveraged the footprint of the facility, we have created a lot of transportation for the patient. Consequently, the customer perceives the visit as a nuisance rather than as an efficient process engineered to benefit the customer. And a one-hour visit has now turned into a four-hour visit because we designed our process around department optimization and not the patient experience.

Great organizations work relentlessly to identify and eliminate waste. To summarize, operational waste presents itself in seven common forms. The seven common wastes again are over-production, waiting, over-processing, inventory, motion, defects, and transportation.

As a practical exercise, pick any area in your organization. Find 30 minutes in your workday and walk to a place where work is being done. Stand in a single spot and observe. Look for waste. In this time period, you should be able to complete a large portion of this waste chart. This waste identification challenge is invaluable in teaching leaders, staff, and physicians how to see waste. In 30 minutes many people can identify 50 or more wastes. These wastes can be documented on the 7 X 7 waste chart shown in Figure 1.4. The best way to identify waste is to "see" waste. Going to the workplace and observing the seven operational wastes will lead you to dozens of opportunities to eliminate non-value-added time. If you personally can find fifty forms of waste in 30 minutes, how many forms of waste do think the people that do the work can identify?

Two Additional Wastes

There are two other types of waste that show up within organizations that are not operational in nature: the waste of unused human capital (creativity) and the waste of organizational design. From an improvement perspective, the focus is generally on process and the seven wastes will show up when we

Type of Waste	Inventory	Motion	Transportation	Over-Production	Over-Processing	Defects	Waiting
Instance 1							
Instance 2							
Instance 3							
Instance 4							
Instance 5							
Instance 6							
Instance 7							

Figure 1.4   Seven by seven waste chart.

study the process in detail through either direct observation or time observation (we will cover both direct observation and time observation in a future chapter). The waste of unused human capital and the waste of organizational design do not generally present themselves when studying a process, but they can be present and do generate some of the common wastes we just discussed.

Unused Human Capital

This waste presents itself when we fail to take into consideration and utilize all the talents that people have. I believe that every staff person, administrator, and physician wants to do great work; the challenge is creating the structure to enable this great work to happen. Many organizations are top-down in their approach with a command-and-control management structure. With heavy amounts of firefighting that occur each day, it is difficult to even find the time to empower and engage staff and medical staff. Without daily formal and informal mechanisms to engage and empower, opportunities for process improvement and personal growth are missed. These missed opportunities are the unused human capital. Sometimes in healthcare we believe that when we underutilize a clinician's scope, we are wasting human capital. An example of this would be paying a nurse to perform stocking or housekeeping tasks. While this might be frustrating to the clinician, this is *not* always an example of unused human talent. Without getting too technical, sometimes given the frequency of the task and the cycle time to complete the task, this clinician is the appropriate resource to complete the activity. For those of you who are lean technicians, there are instances where in order to balance the work to the takt time, non-clinical tasks need to be loaded on the clinician. The loading diagram or cycle time/takt time bar chart would be the tool you would choose to help make this decision.

The loading diagram is used to show the relationship between the workload of each team member (known as manual cycle time in lean circles) and the frequency with which a process must be completed (loosely known as takt time) to meet the customer demand. In a simple example shown in Figure 1.5, a nurse needs to see a patient every fifteen minutes. The physician also needs to see a patient every fifteen minutes to maintain a steady "flow" within the clinic. The nurse's work content consists of ten minutes of work per patient, meaning that the nurse has five minutes of idle time between patients. While we would prefer this work to be professional in nature, this specific clinic is not providing that opportunity at this time. To be efficient, we should have the nurse perform additional tasks; these

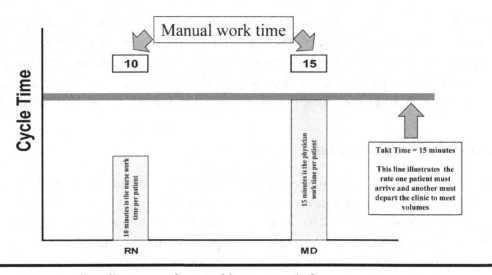

Figure 1.5   Loading diagram and unused human capital.

tasks could include re-stocking the rooms or cleaning the rooms between visits. Is this unused human capital? It would be even more wasteful, and disrespectful to the additional resource, to have a different resource provide these services when idle capacity exists. Worse, this often causes further delays in waiting for the second resource to perform the required task.

The Waste of Organizational Design

Can the management structure and design for your organization create waste? One of the common problems we find in healthcare is that many of the departments operate in silos. Each department has its own budget, management, staff, patients/services, and measurement targets. Is this bad? Let me provide an example of silos outside of healthcare. One of the things that people in the manufacturing sector learned long ago is that optimizing a department can have negative effects on a system. For example, if a machining department is operating without concern for the downstream welding department, then many wastes can be created. The machining department could outperform the welding department, creating **inventory** between the departments. The inventory would need to be transported. When the inventory is **transported** it can become damaged, creating **defects** and corresponding rework. Since the machining department will try to optimize its department targets, the typical day consists of long runs of parts. This ensures good productivity. However, this can have negative effects on the downstream welding department that might need two different parts to make their subassembly. This can lead to downtime in the weld department **waiting** on pieces from machining, while machining is meeting their budget and operating targets. Actually, the Toyota Production System evolved by solving these exact types of problems.

But what about healthcare? Patients frequently encounter more than one department during a visit. Let's take a simple visit to an urgent care clinic for an ankle sprain. During this visit, the patient would likely encounter the following departments:

■ Registration
■ Urgent Care Services (primary care nurse, and physician)
■ Diagnostic Imaging (x-ray technologist, radiologist)
■ Support Services (portering)
■ Billing

There are also a host of other departments that are indirectly involved with the patient. Minimally, this includes environmental services, infection prevention and control, and materials management. Do you think that all of these departments have aligned goals? Or perhaps I should ask a different question, such as "Do all your departments have aligned goals?" What waste is present when the goals of the departments are not aligned? Can we find rework, transportation, over-processing, and inventory?

When waste is present within the organizational design, you see extra hand-offs of patients and information, lots of reporting requirements and data collection that doesn't add value to the customer, and layers of management with politics between departments that make it more difficult than it should be to provide high quality, patient-centered care. The organizational design and management of this design can and does generate wastes within your entity. Now that we have a working definition of the seven common forms of waste (with the addition of two others), we will discuss some tools to help us identify and then eliminate this waste.

Principles of Improvement

The value-added/non-value principle claims that 95% to 99% of the work we observe is non-value added to the patient. After you practice identifying waste over a short period of time and get comfortable with the concepts of value added and non-value added, waste will start to become obvious and abundant. The harder of the two tasks is eliminating the waste. Before we discuss how to eliminate waste, we must first understand some improvement principles to help guide our thinking in designing and optimizing our processes in pursuit of eliminating waste and creating more value. Every time we want to eliminate waste, we should use these principles as the foundation. These principles are flow, pull, defect-free, visual management, and kaizen are shown in Figure 1.6. Let's review each of these in further detail.

Flow

The place we almost always want to begin when making improvements is by creating flow. (Flow and defect-free are kind of 1A and 1B when it comes to importance). The anaolgy for flow is often the waterfall that is shown in Figure 1.7. People often think of flow as a means of lining up work activities

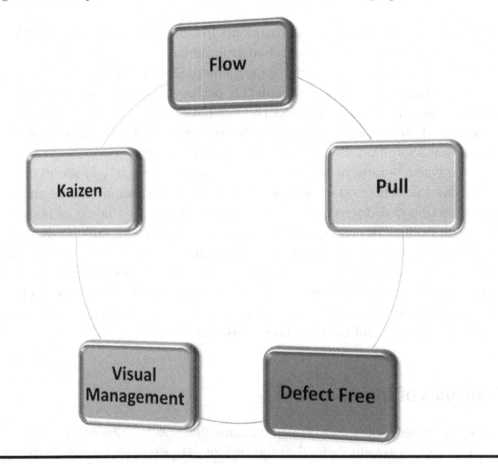

Figure 1.6   Principles of lean improvement.

Figure 1.7 Flow.

to be completed one after another in a continuous manner. In healthcare, we want to "flow" patients through our healthcare system. Lining up all of the activities to occur one after another would be a great improvement, albeit very difficult, to accomplish. However, the concept of flow is more than just the continuous processing of tasks. The lean definition of flow is completing *value-added* tasks in a continuous flow, at the rate of customer demand in a standardized way.

By linking only the value-added steps together, this implies that we have eliminated the non-value-added activity between the steps. It would not make sense to link all the tasks, both value-added, and non-value-added tasks, together in a continuous flow, as it is obvious that we want to avoid expending resources completing non-value-added work. Let's imagine that we have eliminated some waste and now we have linked the value-added tasks together. For an x-ray procedure, assume that the x-ray technologist can per-form the exam and **immediately following,** have the exam read by a radi-ologist. The result is now available for review by the ordering physician. This would be flow in practice. Now we need to ensure that this new process is capable of meeting customer demand. If this process can be repeated 28 times in an eight-hour shift (4 exams per hour), but we have a patient demand of 36 exams per shift, we still have not satisfied the principle of flow. A process meeting the spirit of flow has to be paced to the rate of the customer demand in the process. Finally, let's assume we have now lined up the value-added steps and have a process capable of meeting customer demand. However, due to variations in the process, we get varying outcomes. If we fail to perform the activities in a standard way, and continue to get consistent outcomes, we still have not met the spirit of flow. A process flows when the value-added activi-ties are lined up one after another with no waiting or inventory between each step. The process will be capable of meeting the customer demand, and the work is being done in a standardized way with consistent outcomes.

Pull (Figure 1.8)

Sometimes it is not possible to create continuous flow between all of the steps. Constrained resources, or resources used very infrequently, can make continu-ous flow very difficult. An example of this would be a patient arriving in the ER after being struck in the mouth by a hockey puck during an adult league game with considerable trauma. This patient now needs a dental plastic sur-geon. How many ERs have one of these on staff? So, the work will come to a halt while the referral is made, and a response is received. The principle of pull is what enables areas of continuous flow to be linked together.

The concept of pull comes from the supermarket, the same supermarket you buy your groceries from. How does the grocer know when to re-stock the shelf? The answer is when there is an empty space. How did the empty space get there? A consumer puts something in their grocery cart to take to the

Figure 1.8 Pull.

register for purchase. The signal to re-stock the shelf comes from the consumer removing an item. The item has been **pulled** from the shelf, creating a signal to replenish. This simple concept is the basis for pull. Without a signal to replenish, what could happen? We could run out of product, causing a loss of sales, or we could overstock the area leading to spoilage or obsolescence (think about meats, dairy, and produce). Over-stocking the area causes us to waste time, space, and resources while failing to meet the customers' needs. This is the waste of over-production, and pull was designed to prevent over-production. Conversely, under-stocking creates wasted motion and unnecessary waiting.

Pull in its simplest form is a signal to do work. In the case of the grocery store example, consumption is the signal to replenish. In lean terms, the principle of pull implies that we would only perform work when we have a true need from the customer. To satisfy the principle of pull, the signal should contain certain attributes in its design. First, we'd like to standardize the signal to one type. Although there are multiple ways to trigger any form of work, we would like to have a single trigger. Other attributes of a good pull system included words such as seamless, no gaps, no over-production, no asking, no searching, no clarifying, and synchronized.

We will first discuss the standardization of a trigger signal. As an example, let's talk about referral workflow in healthcare. On an in-patient medical floor, let's assume we need to trigger a respiratory therapist (RT) to perform an assessment. To trigger the assessment, we could page the RT, call the RT, send an e-mail, or chat message, do a face-to-face request, trigger the referral in medical rounds, or place an order in the electronic health record. A great lean organization has a *single*, authoritative way to trigger the referral. Pick the best one for your organization, but only pick one. We don't want to consume organizational energy deciphering signals to do work.

Once you have standardized the signal to perform work (trigger), then we want to find one, single way to respond to the signal. How do you acknowledge the referral? Again, we could acknowledge by calling, emailing, etc., but a great pull system employs a single method in response to a trigger. In healthcare, an example of a good pull signal is flagging a physician when a patient is ready to be seen. There is one way to trigger the work: flipping the doctor flag lets the physician know the patient is ready to be seen. Subsequently, the physician can flag the nurse when the patient is ready to be sent to check-out as shown in Figure 1.9.

Assuming the physician has other responsibilities besides seeing patients, the response time to see the patient once ready to be seen, can be standardized to get us near continuous, but not full, continuous flow. Interestingly, these flags currently cost about US$50–$70 today. Most organizations will utilize an electronic signal through the electronic medical record system for their pull system to notify staff. What do you think is the difference in cost? Which one is more effective? The key point here is the pull signals do not need to be expensive. They just need to have the following characteristics:

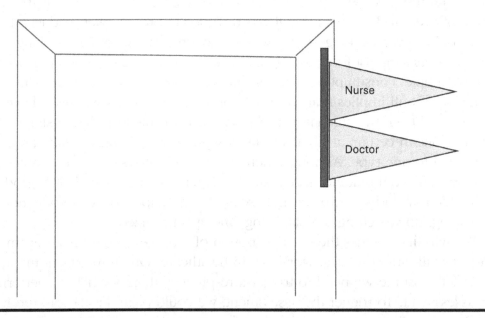

Figure 1.9 Pull signal.

- One organizational way to signal
- One organizational way to respond
- Standardize the response time between signal and response

Additional examples of where pull signals have been utilized in healthcare include:

1. Using the supermarket concept to trigger supply replenishment of medicine, supplies, and equipment
2. Triggering that results are available so re-assessment can occur
3. Triggering a consult for a specialty service not always in-house
4. Triggering a service referral for home care
5. Using a visual queue to know when to porter the next patient for a procedure
6. Triggering a room clean following a discharge
7. Triggering the build of the next two hours of OR case carts

There are literally thousands of examples, and a great lean organization utilizes the principle of pull to link steps together in a standardized way, every single time that work cannot flow continuously.

Defect-free

Let's assume now that we have begun to design our work process and we have been able to implement pockets of continuous flow, and where we couldn't create continuous flow, we have been able to implement pull systems that link our areas of continuous flow together. So far, so good! Will it matter that the work flows continuously and is closely linked with pull systems if the outcomes are wrong or inconsistent? Definitely not, and bad outcomes in healthcare can be very serious. In fact, our first mission in healthcare is to do no harm! We use Figure 1.10 on medicine administration to highlight the importance of defec free processes.

To prevent bad outcomes, we utilize the principle of defect-free. In lean terms, defect-free means doing the work in a way that meets customer-specified quality requirements the first time. This implies that as the work moves from step to step, quality is designed into the process so the outcomes are consistent, meet customer requirements, and can be completed without rework and inspection. Some of the attributes of defect-free work would include no errors, no rework, standardized, quality at the source, non-personality based, and no over-processing or redundancy.

Figure 1.10   Defect free.

Expanding on the defect-free principle, there are several design approaches to allowing value to be delivered defect-free. Let's review a few of the more common tools and concepts of defect free in the Table 1.1.

Table 1.1 Defect-Free Concepts

Concept	Description
Successive staff checks	Each staff member checks the previous work before adding their own value. This ensures that work is not completed in addition to previous work that may have a defect.
5S	A management system for creating a high-performing work area that designs the work space, tools, supplies, equipment, and information in a way that enables the work to be done defect-free.
Operational methods sheets	A visual tool that explains the work to be done at the task level, defines the quality specifications of the work, and shows the checks the staff member must take to ensure the work is defect-free. This approach ties closely with Successive Staff Checks. The operational methods sheet is sometimes also known as a Key Points Sheet.
Andon	Andon loosely translates to stopping the line. This is a management principle where the staff stops performing work when a defect is found and will not begin performing work again until a countermeasure is in place to prevent further defects. This creates time to identify the root cause of the problem, allowing for a permanent solution to be found.
Poka Yoke	Poka Yoke loosely translates to mistake proofing. This concept is in action when work is designed to make it impossible to do the work improperly. A simple example would be designing a date field so that the field has to be filled out in a computer screen before going to the next field. This mistake proof's leaving the field empty, preventing an error from occurring.
7 quality tools	The seven tools include the cause and effect diagram, the check sheet, the control chart, the histogram, the Pareto diagram, the scatter diagram, and the flow chart. These tools are used to explain what is happening in a system and are used because they do not require a lot of statistical training for the user. They are used frequently in healthcare to explain and interpret data.
Cause and effect diagram	Expanding on one of the seven quality tools, the cause and effect diagram, or Ishakawa diagram, or fishbone diagram is used to determine causes of problems and helps sort the problems into useful categories.
5 why's	This is a technique used to determine the root cause of a problem. By asking Why five different times it is possible to get to the underlying source of the problem so a solution can be identified that permanently solves the problem. Beyond impacting the principle of defect-free, "5 why's" is also a technique used to develop people.

Philosophically, we need to move beyond the thinking that staff need to be "careful when they work to prevent errors. As humans, we simply aren't wired to be error-free. When we repeat tasks hundreds of times our brain starts to map to this reality. If we inadvertently make an error, our brain is used to believing things are correct like they have been all the other times. If you challenge people and ask if they have made a mistake, they will vehemently deny the question. Does this imply some people are better than others, more conscientious or diligent? While this is possible, I think that thinking is a stretch. Rather, it implies we are human and humans are prone to making mistakes. The defect-free concepts of mistake proofing, and successive checks help overcome our human deficiencies. We would be far better served by the staff, physicians, patients, and leaders to put our energy into designing out the ability to create defects. This eliminates the need to worry about errors.

When designing processes to eliminate waste, the first three principles of flow, pull, and defect-free are utilized. In doing so we can dramatically reduce the waste of inventory, motion, transportation, defects, waiting, over-processing, and over-production. Once the system is properly designed, we need a way to manage our systems. This is where visual management comes in.

Visual Management (Figure 1.11)

A lean system is designed to be managed visually. Visual management allows everyone to distinguish easily and quickly normal from abnormal conditions. What kinds of things are we interested in managing visually? Anything you can imagine! Are we ahead or behind in the schedule? Is everyone following the standard work? Is all of the necessary equipment, materials, and supplies available? Is it time to re-order? Do we have a home for everything? What are the top three problems we are working on? Who is responsible for the corrective actions? When will they be completed? What have the results been for the last month? Are we on budget? All of these types of scenarios can be managed visually.

There are a few attributes we like to see in a lean visual management system. First, we need absolute transparency; this means that everyone has the ability to see normal from abnormal in five seconds or less. We shouldn't need to run a report or open a drawer to see the status of normal from abnormal. Let's discuss a very simple example of transparency.

Figure 1.11 Visual management.

Figure 1.12 is a picture of an appointment card used to create transparency for an in-patient diagnostic imaging test. The card has two sides, a red side and a green side. The red side shows that an exam has been scheduled. It also shows the patient's room and bed, patient's name, and appointment time. When an exam is scheduled, the card is filled out and placed on the appointment board. Thirty minutes before the exam, the nurse will prepare the patient for the exam and when complete, turn the card over showing the green side. The green side highlights the steps for preparing the patient to eliminate portering delays and time waiting in diagnostic imaging. The porter will arrive fifteen minutes before the exam and transport the patient to the appropriate test location, properly prepared, and on time, allowing for a seamless transition into the testing process. Prior to this visual management system, patients would be delayed upwards of an hour for their exams, and in some cases the exam would be canceled, leading to delays in diagnosis, treatment, and discharge.

Another attribute of visual management is that it must trigger an action. Part of the system is to see normal from abnormal; the other part is doing something about it when the abnormality is discovered. If we are behind,

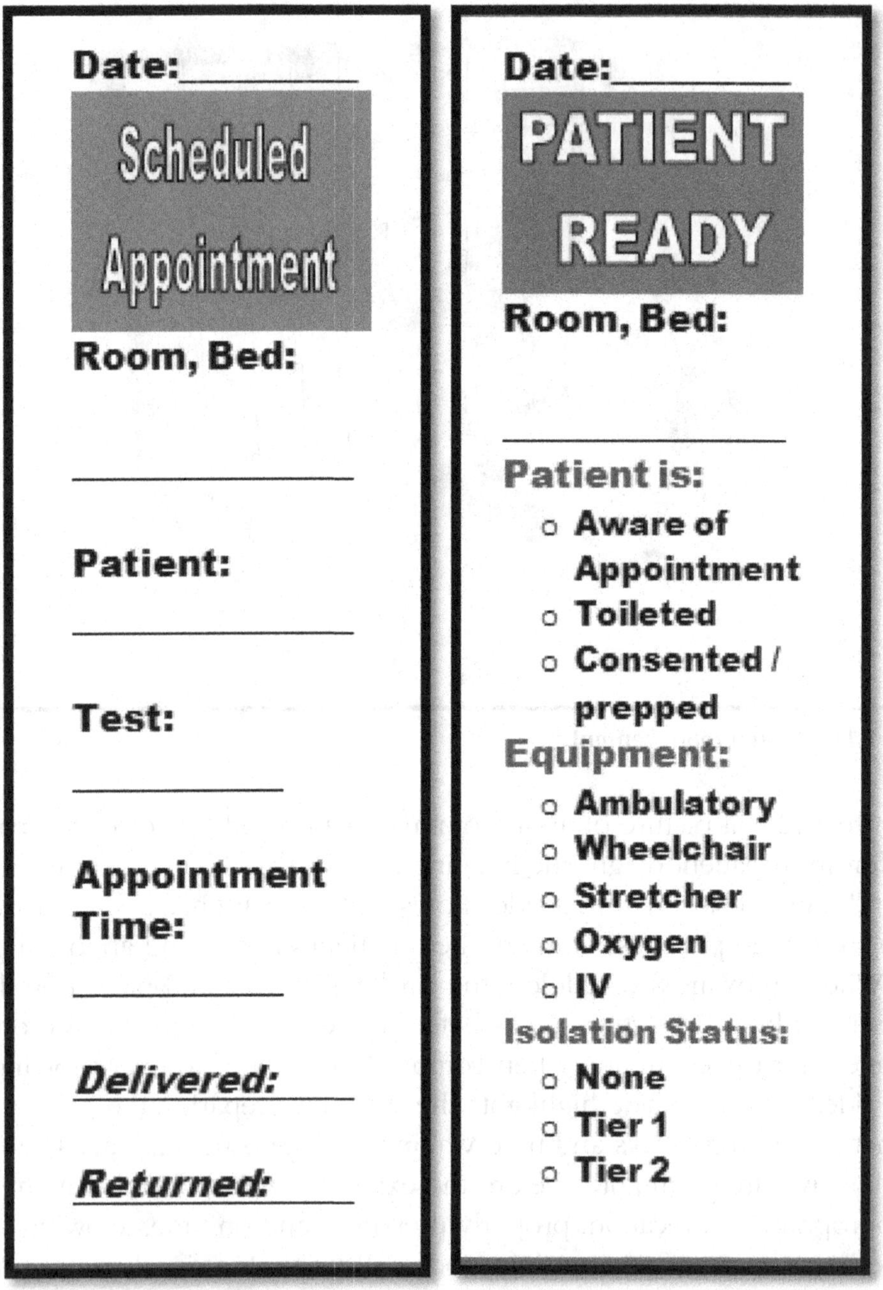

Date:_____	Date:_____
Scheduled Appointment	**PATIENT READY**
Room, Bed:	**Room, Bed:**
_____	_____
Patient:	**Patient is:**
_____	o **Aware of Appointment**
Test:	o **Toileted**
_____	o **Consented / prepped**
Appointment Time:	**Equipment:**
_____	o **Ambulatory**
	o **Wheelchair**
Delivered: _____	o **Stretcher**
	o **Oxygen**
Returned: _____	o **IV**
	Isolation Status:
	o **None**
	o **Tier 1**
	o **Tier 2**

Figure 1.12   Appointment card.

what is the intervention to catch up? If something is not in the correct place, who is going to find the missing item and return it to its home? Many lean visual management systems operate exactly as designed, but the staff and management fail to take action. Action is best taken in real time. Problems rarely get better over time. It doesn't matter how great the lean design was, how great the flow and pull worked, and how many defects were eliminated if the system isn't being managed visually to operate waste free. The culture of your organization will always pull the new system back to the previous status quo without a robust visual management system.

A small list of the key benefits of visual management include:

- Visual management reduces miscommunication by making information consistent and transparent to all. It should eliminate the need for verbal instructions that might be unclear, or outdated.
- It makes information easily understandable. Status of projects, goals, and current performance are visible at a glance.
- Visual management is used to help ensure standards and expectations are followed. Done well, visual management will prevent process deviations, help eliminate errors, and make out-of-place items obvious.
- By making things easier, it prevents mistakes and improves safety for the staff and the patients. Visual management can be used to provide alerts for product and process quality concerns.
- Visual management gives employees the knowledge and motivation to succeed. Staff and Physicians want to do a great job. Providing feedback on process outcomes and patient outcomes gives staff and physicians access to data to which typically only managers and leaders have access. Motivation comes from empowering the team to make changes using lean thinking and getting visual feedback on those efforts.

Sound visual management predicated on discerning normal from abnormal conditions and taking real-time action when an abnormality is discovered is the first key step to sustaining. Great organizations have the ability to see normal from abnormal conditions at a glance and take immediate action when abnormal conditions arise.

Now that we have designed our system to flow, pull, and be defect-free and have a management system that can visualize problems and opportunities in real-time so we can maintain the system, we now need to continue to improve our work processes. This is where kaizen comes into play.

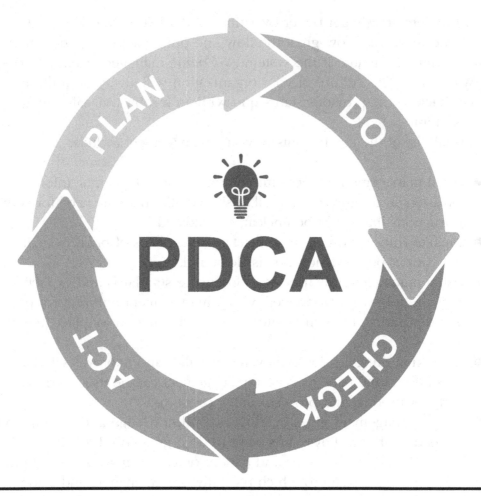

Figure 1.13 Kaizen.

Kaizen (Figure 1.13)

The fifth principle of improvement is known as kaizen. Kaizen is actually two words: The first word "kai" means "change," and the second word "zen" means "for the better." In order to create a culture of improvement, we must build a system that is continuously improving. Great organizations get better every day; employees leave the workplace in better shape than when they arrived. Imagine what that could look like!

To practice kaizen, we want to make small, incremental, continuous changes to our work in order to deliver more value to the customer. This usually shows up in eliminating small amounts of non-value-added activity by creating better standard work, re-locating items to eliminate wasted movement, or mistake proofing something to avoid a defect being made.

Healthcare organizations spend a lot of money and time benchmarking their performance. This process involves hiring high-price benchmarking organizations and submitting mountains of data to compare one organization's performance against another's. Staffing rations, spending values, staffed beds, etc. typically come from the benchmarking exercise followed by a series of cuts to staff and budget. This approach is anti-lean.

In the spirit of practicing kaizen, lean organizations frequently benchmark their performance, but not in the areas you might think. Actually, two types of benchmarking occur simultaneously. The first is benchmarking by comparing your organization against perfection and delivering all value-added activity in continuous flow with no defects. When you compare your current performance against perfection, you will see that you have much to improve upon. This comparison of current performance against perfection is used in lean organizations to create a state of tension spurring further improvement. The second benchmark is to compare their current process against the best in the world. Great organizations compare their processes against industries with world-class performance. How does your performance in infection prevention compare with safe drinking water? How does your quality in medicine administration compare with the safe practices of a nuclear power plant? You can compare your organization to other healthcare organizations, but I am not aware of anywhere in the world that quotes healthcare performance for benchmarks as the best in the world. My suggestion is maybe to consider stopping comparing yourself with your peers and looking outside of healthcare. Industry has many examples that healthcare should aspire to. This suggestion is not meant to put healthcare beneath other industries, but rather, give you a different vision of what is possible. Practice kaizen. Improve every day. You never actually get to a state of being "lean." *Never* be satisfied with your current performance. Challenge the management, staff, and medical staff to do better. One of the ways we show respect for people is to challenge them to improve performance. When you create a mindset of continuous improvement, you are meeting the spirit of kaizen.

Lean Healthcare Defined

Let's return to the discussion at the beginning of the chapter. What is lean healthcare? Envision a system where work is constantly scrutinized to both eliminate waste and deliver more value to your patients. Envision a system where the entire workforce is engaged and inspired to improve daily. A workforce continuously improving the quality and safety of care approaching

Table 1.2 Lean Healthcare

What Lean Healthcare Is	What Lean Healthcare is Not
• Patient focused	• Provider focused • Staff focused • College focused • Organization focused • Insurance focused
• Seamless care	• Care provided in silos
• Collaborative and integrated care	• Profession centric care
• Transparent information	• Hidden and difficult to access information
• Quality and safety first	• Access and cost first
• Inspired and engaged staff and medical staff	• Leadership and management make all the decisions
• Continuously improving	• Spot improvement or firefighting
• Creativity before capital	• Technology, equipment, and adding resources lead the solution set
• Systems thinking	• Program focused
• Problems solved in the workplace (Gemba)	• Problems solved in the conference room
• Focus on the process	• Focus on blaming individuals
• A team of inter-professionals	• Individual contributors and heroes

a defect-free system, reducing wasted time and activity freeing up capacity for other work, decreasing lead times for services, and lowering the cost of the delivery of these services. Envision the delivery of healthcare with accurate and timely information shared seamlessly amongst the care team. A system where the medical staff and staff collaborate to provide patient-focused, evidenced-based care with seamless transitions between specialties and subspecialties. Envision a system where the patients, families, and communities participate in the design of the services leading to healthier communities with preventative strategies driving lower and lower costs. I'm not sure there is enough ink to describe all the attributes of lean healthcare. Table 1.2 provides a brief glimpse into what lean healthcare is and what it is not.

Lean Healthcare is a system of continuous improvement. This system was constructed based on the two lean themes: elimination of waste and respect for all people. Work is designed for the patient, in systems and subsystems that reflect continuous flow processes. Work is pulled through the system, not pushed. Activities are designed and delivered in a defect-free manner. The status of work, results, and process are monitored visually; any abnormalities to the work are identified and fixed in real-time. Every system is continuously being improved by an inspired and engaged staff and medical staff, working side by side with one focus: servicing the patient.

The results of these efforts are reflected in improvement of key measures tied to the strategic desires of the organization, the board, the staff, the medical staff, and the community. These key measures show world-class rates of improvement in quality and patient safety, access, cost, staff morale, and growth. With this vision in mind, we will explore how to provide the leadership to make this healthcare system a reality using Lean.

I can't repeat this enough. Every organization has the ability to perform better, even world-class organizations. Greatness is available to you! What you need is a system, process, and structure to realize this greatness. Lean thinking can guide you on this journey.

Chapter Summary: Key Points from Chapter 1

- Lean Improvement is based on the fundamental concept of value added and non-value added. A value-added (5% of a typical process) activity directly meets the needs of the customer. A non-value-added activity (95% of a typical process) takes up time, space, and/or resources, but does not directly contribute to meeting the needs of the customer.
- The two themes of lean improvement include the elimination of wasted time and activity (continuous improvement) and respect for all people.
- Non-value-added activity is also known as waste; there are seven common forms of operational waste. These include over-production, waiting, over-processing, inventory, motion, defects, and transportation. Two additional wastes that are present within organizations include the waste of unused human capital and the waste of organizational design.
- Waste is eliminated using the five principles of improvement: flow, pull, defect-free, visual management, and kaizen.
- Lean healthcare can be defined as a business system of continuous improvement. This system is operated by an inspired and engaged team to deliver more value to patients. A well-run lean healthcare system will deliver measurable, year-over-year improvement in performance and culture.

Chapter 2

Creating and Deploying a Lean Strategy

Two activities that are key in creating improvement in performance and culture necessary to achieve your organizational vision include tightly linking the improvements in your organization to your strategy and utilizing operational excellence to realize the strategy. The synergies provided by focusing the organization on your strategic goals, linking your improvement focus to these strategies, and utilizing lean tools and techniques to deliver operational excellence will enable you to move your organization toward your vision.

Why is creating alignment in your organization important? It takes resources to improve. I'm not talking about information systems, capital equipment, staff, and brick-and-mortar resources; rather, the hearts and minds of the staff and medical staff are the resources utilized by a lean organization. You might have heard the saying "people" are our most precious commodity. While this statement is true, you also need an improvement system to unleash these precious resources and help you achieve excellence. Improvement in one more key "areas of focus" should link directly to accomplishing your strategy. Table 2.1 discusses the importance of linking strategy to improvement.

There is an additional consideration when linking strategy to improvement: Financial obligations tied to implementing the improvement in a specific area of focus. In order to illustrate the importance of correctly identifying the area of focus, let's walk through some "fuzzy" math on funding improvement. Assume there are eight staff members and one physician on a

DOI: 10.4324/9781003532132-2

Table 2.1   The Importance of Linking Improvement to Strategy

It is very difficult to impossible to improve all areas of an organization simultaneously. Begin improvement in the areas that best enable you to meet your key outcome measures.
Each team requires time from your staff and medical staff. Focus on the high leverage areas to maximize your return on your investment.
The effort to change a process with minimal return is the same as the effort to change a process with a large return. Allow you middle and line management and medical leadership to focus on the areas of highest return.
Change takes time. Do not lose precious days, weeks, and months on areas not directly aligned to your strategy.
All staff and medical staff should be able to immediately see the correlation between improvement and attaining your strategy. This gives the team a sense of purpose and shows them how they fit into the big pig picture.

newly formed improvement team. Assume this team is together for 40 hours. If we take the hourly pay of the staff and add in the physician expense (whether in salary, or loss of salary, or loss of revenue from the physician not seeing patients), we are already at a sizeable investment. Factor in the replacement costs for the staff covering the team while working on improvement. Factor in the investment in training when the new design is complete, and the project expense will be even larger. I estimate a typical team will cost anywhere between US$10,000 and $30,000 for any improvement. With an expense this large, you will want to ensure that you have picked an area that directly aligns with your strategy AND has a return on your investment.

Frequently and regrettably, I have to field the argument that having a "lean" program is too expensive. How can we afford to invest $10,000 to $30,000 per team? Actually, you are likely already making this investment and then some. I find countless teams, committees, and projects working on a variety of topics across most any healthcare organization. Your investment is buried in these teams. The broader question is what is the return for these efforts? And how long does it take you to advance the work in a meaningful way? Lean teams are generally accounted for differently. They end up as an expense on the income statement. This is not a problem if there is a return on investment. Project teams get charged to the department and absorbed as a labor expense. They also meet typically once a week or less frequently for an hour. So, making real change takes months or years or even never. Later we will discuss how to drive results and turn these lean team expenses into a four to one or better return on investment.

Create and Deploy Your Strategy Using Hoshin Kanri (Strategy Deployment)

The word *Hoshin* is composed of two Chinese characters: *Ho* meaning method or form, and *shin* meaning shiny needle or compass. Taken together, the word Hoshin means "methodology for strategic direction setting."[1] Kanri, in Japanese, means management.

No matter how great your strategy is, if you can't execute the strategy, you will not deliver the results you are expecting. Hoshin Kanri provides a step-by-step planning, implementation, and review process for managed change.[2] In a lean organization, Hoshin Kanri is the system used to manage system change of the core business objectives. Hoshin Kanri operates at two levels; first, at the strategic planning level, and second, at the daily management level on the more routine or fundamental aspects of the business operation.* When translated to English, Hoshin Kanri is also known as policy deployment, or strategy deployment. Frequently this process is confused with goal deployment. While goal deployment is part of the Hoshin Kanri process, it is much more than the simple cascading of goals.

There are seven steps to the Hoshin Kanri process broken into three phases: planning, implementing, and review (Figure 2.1).

Step 1. Establish the Organizational Vision

The first step in the policy deployment process is to establish an organizational vision. Organizations should first obtain a thorough understanding of the customer's needs, also known as the "voice of the customer," before establishing their vision. Understanding the voice of the customer helps us with three key activities:

1. Aligning how we measure our organizational performance with how our customer measures performance.
2. Establishing breakthrough targets as set by the customer
3. Developing and deploying objectives that deliver value to the customer

Recall that in healthcare, the customer is the patient and caregiver the majority of the time. When possible, we should use the same measures

---

* Greg Watson and Hoshin Kanri, Policy Deployment for Successful TQM (Portland, OR: Productivity Press, 1991), pg. xxii.

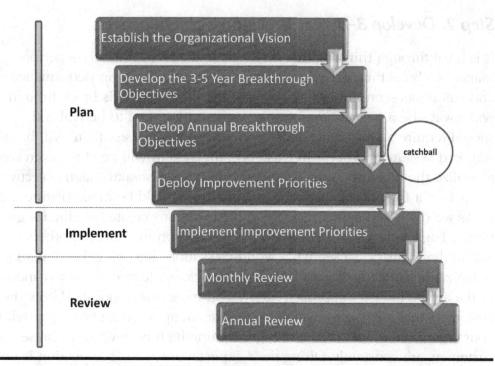

Figure 2.1 Seven Phase policy deployment process.

that our customers would use. In the United States this is harder than it inherently seems. Key stakeholders like insurers often become the source of targets. Insurance payments, value-based care targets, and bundled reimbursement put revenue cycle generation work with its corresponding coding and billing activities require a lot of attention. Great healthcare organizations can tie together patient wellness, medical care, and revenue optimization. While financial viability (or financial stewardship) is a necessity, it need not trump our focus on our customers and our improvement efforts.

From the voice of the customer, we can develop our strategic plan. The strategic plan should answer the two questions, "Where are we going and how do we get there?" Strategic planning is used to develop a shared vision of the future. Using lean principles, this planning should be a pull system, with a vision so compelling that it pulls us into the future.[3] Planning should also follow the scientific method, the method used most frequently in improvement sciences. Planning should include an assessment of the current situation, identify a target condition, and countermeasure the gaps between current and target.

Step 2. Develop 3–5 Year Breakthrough Objectives

It is breakthrough thinking that drives us to achieve world-class performance. A "breakthrough" represents a significant change in performance and culture as seen through the eyes of the customer. This breakthrough will always be a stretch target for the organization, and to be realized, should require a cross-functional approach. In most cases, there will be no standard system or process in existence; the system will need to be created to realize the breakthrough. To understand what a breakthrough objective looks like, a forecast of customer expectations should be made (Figure 2.2).

As we discussed earlier, great lean organizations create benchmark goals targeted against a level of perfection, not based on measures of others within the industry. To see what world-class looks like, view benchmarks of organizations *outside* of your industry. How does the nuclear power industry or the airline industry approach safety? You must first understand how their customers measure performance, determine an appropriate breakthrough for your organization, and then aim high. Aiming high is essential because your customers are constantly raising their expectations, your competition is not standing still, and aiming high will require your organization to constantly change their paradigm about what is possible. The high jumper does not aim for the bar; he instead aims above the bar. Your breakthrough needs

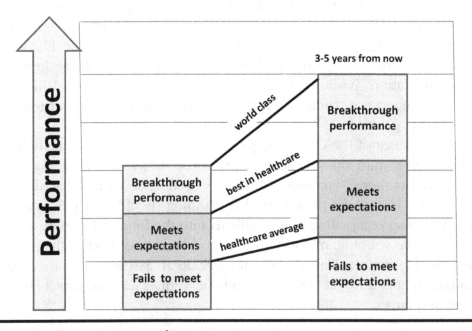

Figure 2.2   Customer expectations.

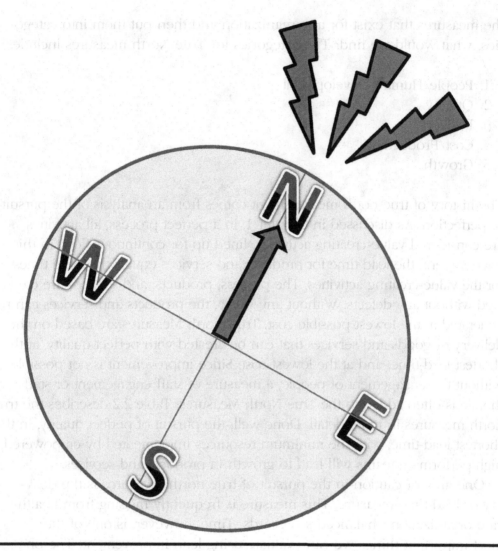

Figure 2.3 True North.

to aim above the bar. A lean organization will measure their breakthrough objectives as true north measures (Figure 2.3).

Establish True North Measures

True North, like a compass, implies direction; this direction is the singular focus of the efforts of an organization. The true north measures of an organization consist of a small suite of operational measures tied directly to your organizational vision. In layman terms these measures would be the equivalent of your board of directors, balanced scorecard. If we could look at all

the measures that exist for an organization and then put them into categories, what would we find? The categories for True North measures include:

1. People/Human Development
2. Quality
3. Delivery
4. Cost/Productivity
5. Growth

The history of true north measurement comes from an analysis of the pursuit
of perfection. As discussed in Chapter 1, in a perfect process, all activities
are considered value-creating activities, lined up for continuous flow. In this
environment, the lead-time for products and services equals the cycle times
for the value-creating activities. The process, products, and services are created without any defects. Without any waste, the products and services can be
generated at the lowest possible cost. True North Measures are based on the
delivery of goods and services that can be created with perfect quality, at the
shortest lead-time, and at the lowest cost. Since improvement is not possible
without the engagement of people, a measure of staff engagement or staff
morale is often added to the True North Measures. Table 2.2 describes the true
north measures in more detail. Done well, the pursuit of perfect quality, in the
shortest lead-time, with the minimum resources implemented by empowered,
high-performing teams will lead to growth in products and services.

One area of caution in the pursuit of true north measures is the delivery or lead-time measure. This measure is frequently missing from healthcare organizations' balanced scorecards. Time, however, is one of the
most important things we can evaluate using lean improvement. The one
universal for waste is that it always shows up in lost time and therefore
besides being really important to the patient, it can also be easily measured. Elimination of waste will result in shorter lead-times for the customer.
Having lead-time as a true north measure is thus extremely important.
Please go back at your convenience and see if lead-time or access or timeliness shows up on your board scorecard. If it is missing and you want to
pursue excellence, I would suggest adding this measure.

To be more specific, we can show an illustration of the True North
Measures for a fictitious hospital known as Pleasant Valley Health. Pleasant
Valley is an urban, teaching hospital with quaternary care services; this orga-
nization supports 800 in-patient beds (Table 2.3).

The requirements for measurements to meet "true north" status are few.
The first requirement is that a true north measure must show a minimum

Table 2.2   True North Measures

True North Category	True North Measure Definition	True North Measure in Healthcare
People	Staff morale or staff engagement	Staff and Medical Staff morale or engagement
Quality	Defects per unit of service or process outcomes related to meeting the customer's requirements	Service Quality – Patient and Family Satisfaction Outcome Quality – Measures of clinical outcomes, and patient safety Process Quality – measures of defects per unit of service
Delivery	Lead time for goods and services from customer need identified to customer need met expressed in time (minutes/hours/days)	Measures of *access* including lead-times for services and wait-times between services
Cost	Hours or $ consumed per unit of service. Typically a measure of productivity	Hours or dollars consumed per unit of service
Growth	Increases in revenues or volumes	Increases in revenues or volumes

of a double-digit improvement, namely, greater than 10%. When waste is reduced, we focus on eliminating or reducing the non-value-added activity. Recall that non-value-added activity comprises 95% of the work in most organizations. With this 95% opportunity, a great lean organization expects 10% plus improvement at a minimum. If we choose a small number, like say 2%, we really do not need to eliminate waste. We can put this process under the microscope, measure it frequently, make it a priority, work a little harder, and will likely get a 2% improvement. How many times do you think we can work a little harder? That card can be played occasionally, but continually working harder is not a sustainable improvement strategy. On the other hand, methods to eliminate waste can be repeated for decades. There is no limit to human creativity. When given the chance, staff and clinicians can develop solutions to continuously eliminate pieces of non-value added indefinitely.

The second requirement for true north measures is that we take a balanced approach to improvement and our corresponding measures of success. We want to balance risk as we embark on our journey of excellence. It may be possible to improve cost by 10% if we sacrifice quality or access. It might be possible to increase volumes by 10% if we sacrifice customer

Table 2.3 Pleasant Valley Health True North Measures

True North Category	*Strategic Direction*	*True North Measure*
People	Create a working environment that inspires our staff and medical staff	Have 100% of our staff and medical staff engaged in verifiable improvement by the end of fiscal year 2029.
Quality	• Eliminate unnecessary mortality and morbidity • Provide patient/family-centered care	• Reduce Hospital Acquired Infections by 80% by December 2029 • Improve patient satisfaction scores by 15% by December 2028
Delivery	Reduce needless patient waiting	Reduce wait times for our five major service lines by 50% by June 2029.
Cost	Become a benchmark, low-cost service provider	Operate in the 98th percentile as a low-cost service provider in all five of our major service lines by the end of the fiscal year in 2029.
Growth	Increase access to all of our service lines	Grow each service line in visits/cases by 10% per year ending December 31, 2028.

service or staff morale. A lean organization wants to have its cake AND eat it too. We do not expect to achieve one measure at the expense of another. When wasted time and activity are eliminated, all five categories of true north (Morale, Quality, Delivery, Cost, and Growth) should improve simultaneously. We want the focus of our staff and medical staff to be on the continuous elimination of non-value-added activity. When this focus occurs in scale, all of the measures should improve simultaneously.

The title of this book is lean leadership. We seek to provide a roadmap to excellence using lean methodology. Our first requirement in providing lean leadership is to be clear on the strategic direction and the true north measures of our organization. This alignment must be supported by all of the senior leadership team, including the medical leadership, and should also be supported by the Board. Any chink in the "support armor" by the senior levels of the organization will have an immediate, negative downstream impact on the management, staff, and medical staff. Do not underestimate the effort it will take to create consensus between the senior leadership team. Nodding heads in agreement is different than a commitment to pursue multiple double-digit improvements. Is the senior leadership prepared to let go of pet projects and shiny objects to support the organizational strategy? You might say, "We are already aligned." If that statement is true, then the following conditions should exist:

1. The number of measures on your highest-level organizational score-card should be between 4 and 7. How many measures does your current board scorecard contain? The most I have seen is over 150 (Can you imagine the effort it takes to simply get the data and report on 150 items and then stratify the data by department, program, etc.), and most healthcare organizations have over 20 measures. Keep in mind that as the measures cascade, 4 to 7 measures at the top of the organization could easily lead to 30 or 40 sub-measures at the unit or department level. When there are many measures, the unit/department often struggles with priorities. Be honest, is this a challenge in your organization? Make this decision simple; we want the focus to be on eliminating wasted time and activity in a few critical areas.
2. The measures should tie *directly* back to each of the five operational dimensions of "true north," namely Staff Morale/Human Development, Quality, Delivery, Cost/Productivity, and Growth.
3. The measures should represent double-digit improvement.

Everyone in the organization should be able to tell how their improvement effort ties back to the true north measures. We will discuss later the management system and how that can show and engage everyone in their connection to improvement and realization of the organizational strategy.

One thing that might not be apparent is the fact that there are only a handful of breakthrough objectives. One of the most important activities within Hoshin Kanri is the process of de-selection. Focusing on the **critical few** breakthroughs related to Quality, Delivery, Cost, and Growth is a key to achieving success. Organizations need to focus on increase the throughput of critical projects. Deselecting breakthrough objectives helps immensely with this focus. I have seen leadership teams really struggle with deselection. Some of this is political. If my project isn't measured it won't get organizational attention, resources, etc. I look at deselection not as hard no, as in "we will never focus on this priority," but rather as a not now. Even the bible states in Ecclesiastes 3:1, "For everything there is a season, and a time for every matter under heaven." Create a season for your critical few!

Twenty key measures and corresponding initiatives at the top can easily translate into more than 100 measures, action plans, teams resourced, and organizational training to drive an enterprise measure by double digits. So, my question to you is if you had 20 or more measures at the strategic level, how many of these measures improved by double digits last year? And how many directly affected your customers, the patients, and their caregivers? Strive to narrow the number of true north measures to 4–7 and keep them focused on the customer!

Step 3. Develop the Annual Breakthrough Objectives and Improvement Priorities

Once the three-to-five-year breakthrough objectives have been identified, they must next be broken down into annual objectives. The annual objective will determine how far toward our longer-range breakthrough objective you will travel in the next fiscal year (Figure 2.4). Assuming that you

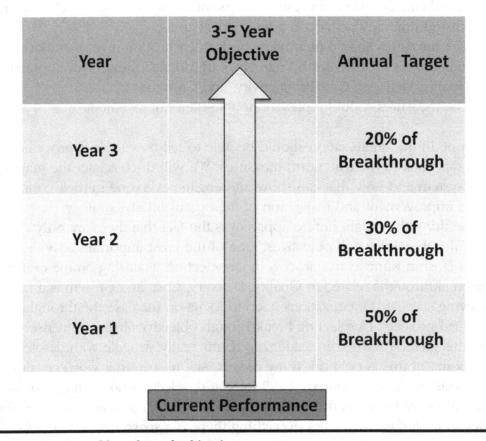

Year	3-5 Year Objective	Annual Target
Year 3		20% of Breakthrough
Year 2		30% of Breakthrough
Year 1		50% of Breakthrough
	Current Performance	

Figure 2.4 Annual breathrough objectives.

have selected a three-year breakthrough objective, it would seem logical to travel one-third of the way toward that target each year. Most organizations that follow that recipe tend to fall short of their three-year goal. I encourage organizations to think about a 50% improvement in the first year. This will accomplish two things: first, a stretch goal will break any paradigms about the status quo immediately, and second, you will want to aim above the bar if you want to get over the bar. Shooting for a 50% target and coming up short will most likely keep you on track to meet the three-year objective.

To identify the annual breakthrough, three steps are necessary (Figure 2.5). First, you must obtain a fact-based understanding of the current situation. Fact-based means that the understanding is based on current, and accurate data. Many healthcare organizations use data that is a quarter behind, or a month behind at best, which makes selecting targets more troublesome. Second, identify how much to improve in the first year in order to meet your three-to-five-year breakthrough objective, as an improvement of 50 percent was merely a suggested guideline. Finally, quantify the gap between the current state and the target area for the first year. When the time comes to cascade the improvements down throughout the organization, it must be clear

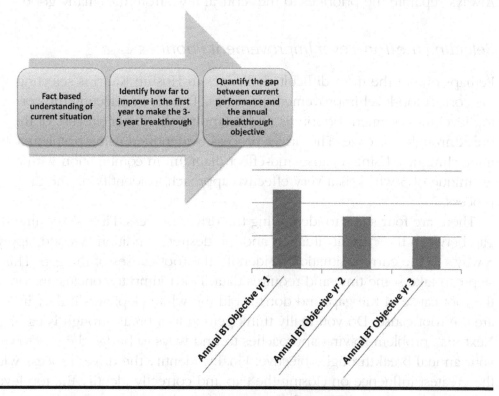

Figure 2.5   Three steps to identify the annual breakthrough.

and obvious what the gap is and what targets need to be met by department, service line, program, etc.

Identify Top-Level Improvement Priorities

Once the annual breakthrough objectives are defined, and the gap between current and target is identified, the second part of step three is to identify the top-level improvement priorities. Selecting the top-level improvement objectives answers the question, "How will we accomplish our annual breakthrough objective?" The top-level improvement priorities are the corporate-wide objectives that will be executed in order to meet the annual objective.

This next paragraph is critical to success. Great top-level improvement priorities should be "process-oriented," meaning that the improvement priority should lead to the creation of a sustainable results-oriented business process. The improvement priority should not be a short-term task. Top-level improvement priorities should also be focused on new or emerging customer needs and should be focused on the critical few, not the many good. Always separate the priorities to the "critical few" from the "many good."

Selecting the Top-Level Improvement Priorities

Perhaps one of the most difficult challenges in Hoshin Kanri is selecting the correct top-level improvement priorities. The art in selecting the correct top-level improvement priority is understanding the driver process of the breakthrough objective. The driver process is identified using problem-solving techniques. Using a cause-and-effect diagram, in combination with the technique of 5 why's, is a very effective approach to identifying the driver process.

There are four steps to identifying the driver process. First, determine the gap between the current situation and the desired condition. Second, apply 5 why's to the current situation to identify the root causes of the gap. This step can take some time and requires data. Don't jump to conclusions on the root cause of the gap, and don't avoid the white elephants if they indeed are the root cause. Do you really think getting to a breakthrough is easy? Next, use problem-solving approaches to find ways to bridge the gap toward your annual breakthrough objective. Finally, identify the driver process with the greatest influence on closing the gap and correctly identify the top-level improvement priority (Figure 2.6).

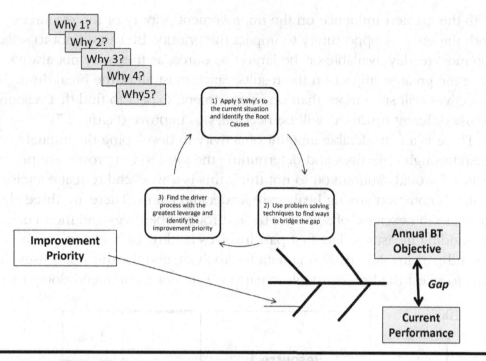

Figure 2.6 Steps to determine the improvement priority.

Once you have selected the improvement priorities, target measures will need to be identified. A target is used to measure the effectiveness of a process and should be used in conjunction with the improvement priorities. The improvement priorities tell "how" and the targets explain "how much." Targets are best expressed in the following format, "from **X** to **Y** by **When**." For example, reduce the cost per case of surgery from $1290 per case to $950 per case by June of 2028.

Now is a good time to check that your improvement priority measures align directly with your true north measures. If they do not, consider selecting a different improvement priority outcome measure. Nothing is more frustrating to both leaders and teams than meeting all the improvement priority outcomes and then coming up short on the true north results. When this phenomenon occurs, it is possible we selected the wrong improvement priority. Great organizations celebrate the success of the priority and use the learning to get better at selecting improvement priorities better aligned to true north in the future. It is also possible the improvement priority did not have enough leverage to move an enterprise number. This is why it takes time and effort to deliver a breakthrough.

Finally, the key resources with accountability for the annual breakthrough objective need to be identified. These resources should be the individuals with the greatest influence on the improvement priority or the resources with the greatest opportunity to impact the priority. Be careful not to select the most readily available or the largest resource, as they may not always have the greatest impact on the results. Since most all of the breakthrough objectives will span more than one department, expect to find that resources across different functions will be necessary to improve (Figure 2.7).

There is a considerable amount of activity in developing the annual breakthrough objectives and determining the top-level improvement priorities. I would caution you to not think this is a weekend retreat exercise which is common among healthcare leadership teams. There are three elements to the exercise of selecting breakthrough objectives and their corresponding measures. The first part involves landing on the strategy, the second part involves gathering data for analysis, and the third part uses the data to select the breakthrough initiatives. I do not recommend doing this in

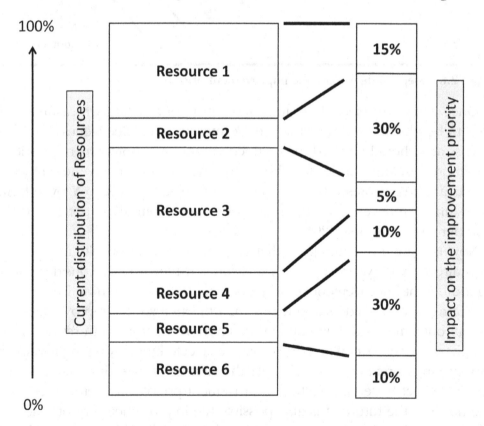

The most available resource will not always have the greatest impact on the improvement priority

Figure 2.7   Identify key resources to deploy priority.

a single session. Use some time between the first and third sessions to carefully mine the appropriate data to deliver the best improvement priorities.

In summary, the annual breakthrough objectives are selected using careful analysis of the current situation, quantifying how far to go in the next year, and quantifying the gap. Once the gap is quantified, problem-solving approaches can be utilized to determine the root cause of the gap, and additional lean tools can be used to determine the potential solutions that will bridge the gap; these solutions become the top-level improvement priorities. Once the priorities are established, then the targets for improvement can be created using a "from x to y by when" statement. The cross-functional resources with the greatest opportunity to impact the target are then identified.

Step 4. Deploy the Improvement Priorities

Now that the annual breakthrough objectives and top-level improvement priorities have been defined, the next step involves deploying the improvement priorities through a process known as *catchball*. As the name describes, the deployment of objectives and priorities requires give and take. This back and forth occurs between both peers, horizontally across the organization, and between managers and subordinates vertically through the management levels. While the priority, along with the target, is defined from the top down, the process to meet the target is not. The purpose of catchball is to link the vision of the company officers and the daily activities of the staff.[4]

Here is an example of catchball in practice. Meadowvale, a 250-bed rehabilitation hospital, has a breakthrough objective to reduce patient safety-related incidents by 90% within a 3-year period. The leadership team, upon a thorough analysis of the voice of the customer and analysis of data selected, identified fall reduction as the top-level improvement priority. This improvement priority, created and led by the senior team and owned by the CEO, is known as level zero. It was decided that the annual target for the upcoming year is to reduce the number of falls by 50% or from 216 annually to 108 by December 31, 2026 (Figure 2.8). Note that this number was determined by looking at the number of falls across the organization. While I recognize that healthcare would normally report falls as a percentage of patient days, it was my intent to measure it differently to keep the example simple.

The target is now deployed to the next management layer of the organization. In the case of Meadowvale, the executive sponsor will be the vice president of patient services. The program that is most influential is the

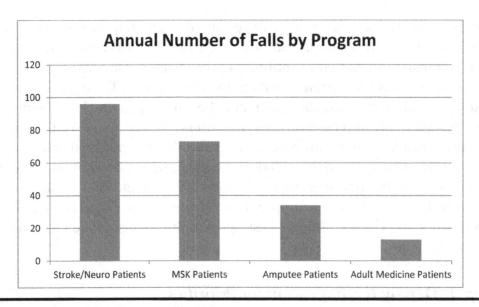

Figure 2.8   Annual falls at Meadowvale.

stroke and neurology rehabilitation program. Using our cascading methodology, and led by a vice president, our strategy deployment framework is identified as Level 1. Catchball will occur between the senior team conduit (the VP of patient services) and the program. The stroke/neuro program will take the top-level improvement "vision" and translate that objective into specific activities that will meet their target. These activities (or hoshins) will then be "tossed" back to the leadership, in essence, to ensure that the approach is correct and will achieve the vision. Leadership will then provide feedback to the program. The "hoshins" might be tossed back and forth several times. In our example, the program will deploy a collaborative care model using "next" practice fall prevention strategies to reduce falls in the stroke neuro program by 75% in the next year. You might say the target is 90% as a system. Why aren't we working on falls in the other programs and why isn't the target 90% as written in the from x to y statement? Our answer is because the 90% target is a 3-year vision. Achieving the 75% target, the stroke/neuro program will realize nearly 70% of the annual target. The balance can be obtained by taking the practices developed in stroke/neuro and "spreading" them to the other programs.

In the early days of practicing strategy deployment, a common occurrence for catchball happens because the receiving area doesn't agree with the target, or perhaps the year one target is perceived to be too high. The catchball will happen several times trying to negotiate an easier target; just keep in mind that a lower target in year one means a higher target for the upcoming years. Lowering a target is not a reason for catchball. Leadership determines the target, and it is not debatable. What is debatable, and the intent of catchball, is the actions needed to meet the target.

The next layer of catchball occurs between the program level and the department or unit level. Again, the cascaded improvement priority, now called the second level improvement priority, is "tossed" to the unit level, where the more specific "Hoshins" are generated. This process of catchball can occur between different levels of the organization, all the way down to the staff level. When action plans can be created in sufficient detail to meet the targets, the cascading can stop. Action plans can be created at any level, but ideally, should be as close to the place where the customer is serviced as possible. Real customer breakthroughs will be seen/realized at this level. Action plans are used to flush out the true root causes of the gaps between current and target.

When starting out, I would encourage your organization to start deploying Hoshin Kanri in the first year as follows:

- Begin with the level 0 planning: developing the 3–5-year vision.
- Create the level 1 plan: the annual breakthrough objectives and top-level improvement priorities.
- Deploy the level 2 plans: develop and deploy the second level improvement priorities to programs and departments.

It takes a solid year to get good at these three levels. Many organizations suffer greatly because of the desire to push strategy deployment organization-wide before the senior team has a thorough understanding of the policy deployment process. It is possible and likely that not every department and program will have a breakthrough objective each year. This is acceptable for two reasons. First, we want to have focus. Improving every area of an organization with a breakthrough is, frankly, impossible. You do not have enough leadership bandwidth and support resource bandwidth to implement this. Secondly, you can still get incremental improvement in all areas with a lean management system that we will be covering later in this book. Not working on a breakthrough does not imply the department gets a pass for seeing and eliminating wasted time and activity. The departments not actively engaged in breakthrough efforts are still expected to deliver continuous improvement from the use of the department level management system.

Our goal in strategy deployment is to create a process that aligns all team members on both the process and results necessary to achieve a breakthrough, mobilizes resources toward the goal, and creates a shared vision of your strategy. One of the big ah-ah's using this planning process is the focus on deployment. Creating clear long-term plans and breaking them down into annual objectives with aligned roles and responsibilities are the benefits of this process. As you move through the catchball process and into the execution of your initiatives, you will need to allocate time to get your data collection systems in alignment with capturing your targets on a timely basis to allow for outcomes to be tracked in near real-time to ensure effectiveness and sustainability of your improvement interventions.

Step 5. Implement the Improvement Priorities

Once the priorities, the means, and the targets are deployed, improvement can begin. Before improving, it is best to have detailed action plans to work from. An example of an action plan for deploying falls reduction improvement is shown in Table 2.4.

Table 2.4 Action Plan for Deploying Improvement Priority

Improvement Priority: Reduce Falls		*Process Owner: Jill Wilson*	*Current Performance: 1 Fall Per Week*	*Target Performance: 75% Reduction*
What	**Who**	**When**	**Expected Impact**	**Status**
Complete Value Stream Analysis	J. Wilson	5–7 May 2012	Detailed plans for improvement	Scheduled
Post daily falls data and deliver updates in a daily huddle	B. Smith	4 April 2012	Gather 3 new ideas for fall prevention per incident	**Complete**
Complete first kaizen event following value stream analysis	J. Wilson	8 June week	Reduce falls 30%	Scheduled

Lean organizations use A-3 thinking as a tool used to implement the scientific method. The scientific method can be used at the strategic planning level via the A3 plan and at the tactical problem-solving level using the problem-solving A3. The A3 reader should be able to understand the content very quickly. Great care should be taken to distill the essential elements of the thinking and activities. In the modern era, digital photographs and charts can be easily inserted to paint the picture graphically. The A3 was designed to tell the entire story on a single sheet of paper. The common paper size for this story is 11-inch x 17-inch paper, which is commonly known (as you might have guessed) as A3 paper. As mentioned above, the A-3 can be used for several different purposes, but the key uses include the following:

- Documentation of Strategy
- Problem-solving/Improvement in the course of work
- Communication of problem-solving/improvement activities (status)
- Approval/justification of resources (business case)

The A3 form template for strategic planning is shown in Figure 2.9. Completion of this form is helpful in getting to a detailed action plan for implementation of improvements. In using the A3 plan to apply the scientific method, we can ensure we understand the gaps in the current processes before generating solutions and plans.

For strategy purposes, I recommend you complete the form in the following order:

1) Document the initiative name, A3 owner, Executive Sponsor, and Team members in the top line.
2) Complete box 1, Reason for Action, with the problem statement, targets, business impact, and in scope and out of scope clearly documented. Take your time on this step. There is a lot of important detail here that gives much of the "why" to the organization.
3) Complete box 2, Current State next. In the current state we want to describe the situation by presenting data and charts. The key in current state is to articulate key issues making it obvious where our attention needs to focus.
4) Complete box 3, Target State. In practice we will likely jump back and forth between the current state and the target state. Each flaw in the current state will lead to an attribute of what we want to realize in the

Strategic Initiative:

Owner: <A3 Owner> Team Members: <Document team members and titles here>

Sponsor: <executive Champion> Attributes, not measures

<Document Initiative here>

1. Reason for Action: *What is the gap between target and actual condition? What impact is it having? What is included in and out of scope?*

3. Target State: *What will success look like when the problem is solved?*

* Define the target state without giving solutions

Problem Statement: <Describe the problem here>

Target for this year: <Define the measurable change desired by when>

Actual for this year: <Document the current performance here>

Impact to business: <Define all the impacts to the business here: consider customers, staff, community, other stakeholders>

In-scope: < Define what departments, areas, processes, measures, populations, etc. are in scope>

Out-of-scope: < Define what departments, areas, processes, measures, populations, etc. are not in scope>

* Think about attributes of the target condition like error free or standardized

* Tie the desired state back to the problem statement

* Measures are not listed here

* Charts and graphs are not generally used here

* Target can is frequently the opposite of current state

2. Current State: *What is currently happening? What issues are occurring and where?*

* Insert charts/graphs/ data sets that describe what is happening
* Consider performance and culture
* What has worked in the past and what hasn't worked
* Where are the key issues occuring and how often

4. Gap Analysis : *What are the top issues we need to address to achieve our goals?*

* Define the issues and cause of the issues here.

* Each current state / target state set of statements will have an issue and scource of the issue

* A fishbone diagram is a good approach to use this section

5. Implementation Plan: *What will it take to put the future situation into play?*

	Action Plans	Owner	Timeline												
			J	F	M	A	M	J	J	A	S	O	N	D
1	<countermeasure to close gap>	action owner												
2	<countermeasure to close gap>	action owner											x	
3	<countermeasure to close gap>	action owner									•		•	
4	<countermeasure to close gap>	action owner										•		
5														
6														
7														
8														
9														
10														
11														
12														

the dot is used for starting or in progress

the x is used to show target completion date

Green shading indicates task on target, Red shading indicates task not on target

6. Measurement: *How will you know this work was successful?*

Measure (update monthly)	Target	Actual	Result
Big dot measure aligned to organizational goal			
pull through or balancing measures (must have at least one)			
pull through or balancing measures			
pull through or balancing measures			

Sponsor Sign Off:

Figure 2.9 A3 plan.

target state. The key point to completing the target state is to define what success will look like when the problem is solved, without prescribing a solution. My suggestion is to use short statements when completing this section.

5) After the current state and the target state are defined, we will move to box 4, Gap Analysis. Our objective in this section is to identify the root cause of the gap between current and target. Two commonly used tools in this section include 5 why's and the fishbone diagram. Both are helpful in identifying the cause of key issues causing our strategic gap.

When the root causes of the gaps are identified, you can now move to create a hypothesis for the solution to close the gaps. From these hypotheses, you can generate tactics (actions) necessary to close the gap. A couple of things I find helpful in action plans include performing experiments to validate the solution close the gap between current and target and then spreading these solutions. This would be two separate steps in your action plan. Additionally, double-check that the timing of actions is spread throughout the year. Many organizations frontload their plans or backload their plans and then are disappointed when the outcomes suffer. An action plan should contain the specific action (the "**w**hat"), **w**ho is responsible, and **w**hen the action will be started and completed. As I was taught 30 years ago, the difference between a plan and a dream is "a what, a who, and a when."

6) Finally, we need to document our measures of success. This is done using a balanced scorecard approach. One of our key measures will be the outcome measure handed down as part of strategy deployment. We will want to look at our initiative to see if there are other outcomes we can experience as a result of completing the work. I prefer to go back to our measures of waste reduction: morale/human development, quality and safety, delivery and access, productivity and cost, and growth. Will any of these dimensions change as a result of our work? It is strongly encouraged to have more than one measure, if for no other reason than to manage the risk of improving the strategic key measure at the expense of a different measure. My final thought is that everyone glosses over productivity. Always review every initiative to see if there is an opportunity to improve team productivity as a result of the solution. Constantly improving this measure is the lifeblood of organizational stability.

An example of a completed A3 plan for nurse retention is shown in Figure 2.10.

Strategic Initiative:	Owner:	Kerry Smith	Team Members: Diane Wislon HR, Bill Owens Nursing Ops, Jill Jackson Nusre manager
	Sponsor:	Marie Hersling	

Encourage retention of current nursing staff. Improve visibility, profile and attractiveness as an employer of choice.

3. Target State: *What will success look like when the problem is solved?* Attributes, not measures

1. Reason for Action: *What is the gap between target and actual condition? What impact is it having? What is included in and out of scope?*

Problem Statement: The percentage of "new" RN hires that voluntarily exit within their first year of employment is higher than the industry benchmark. We need to retain a higher percentage of new hires to stabilize the workforce, reduce reliance on agency nursing (thus improving continuity of care and lowering costs, approx half of those leaving (all new hires) in the first year do so within the first three months (46.8%).

Target for this year: Fiscal 2025/26 target is 12% voluntary exit rate within first year.

Actual for this year: 19.6% for RN for all nursing & allied health exits

Impact to business: Improved/extraordinary patient experience with care team continuity; reduced manager workload (less time recruiting); reduction is costs associated with agency nurses; increased workforce engagement/satisfaction; time and money savings associated with less recruitment activities; ready made talent pool of externs to become nurses.

In-scope: Focus on RN's

Out-of-scope: All other classifications of workers

- Generate savings in time and $$ associated with recruitment
- Vacancy rate reduction and reducing manager's workload on recruitment activities
- Retaining a higher percentage of new hires results in units and departments being closer to "fully staffed", which results in a better/extraordinary patient experience; move towards the elimination of reliance on agency nursing/staffing;
- Improve employee wellbeing which will show a decrease in disability cases and absences
- Employees will be paid competitively which will reduce turnover and improve retention
- New hires/new grads will feel supported and will choose to stay
- Standard recruiting, onboarding, and retention processes to be in place and followed.

2. Current State: *What is currently happening? What issues are occurring and where?*

o Leaders have shared that new nurses are not staying on the units as they don't feel safe as large numbers of those working are newer nurses with less experienced nurses to turn to for help.

o Minimal exit interviews conducted (voluntary) with limited information shared; competitive rates of pay, internally (compression) and externally (market) We now have clinical scholars on some units but it's still a new role so hasn't been evaluated. Their role is to help nurses new to practice or new to that area of practice (e.g. new to ICU)

o 46.87% of those leaving in less then 1 year are actually leaving in the first 3 months.

o 43.5% of those leaving the organization are under the age of 29. Younger staff are making a decision on whether to stay or leave in a short period of time.

Length of Service (years)	Total Count		Age Category (Years)	Total Count
Less than 1 year	392		0 thru 24	124
1	100		25 thru 29	99
2	73		30 thru 34	67
3	23		35 thru 39	53
4	24		40 thru 64	49
>5	100		>45	117

Who's Leaving the Organization (Voluntary Separation)

4. Gap Analysis : *What are the top issues we need to address to achieve our goals?*

Materials
- No regular/formal touchpoints with new hires to address concerns

Method
- No tool or consistent approach to self and flexible scheduling

Externs salaries are not competitive

Machine
- No employee wellbeing strategy to promote a supportive culture
- No exit analysis to understand reasons why

No data currently for 19-29 year olds to understand interests

Measurements

High new hires voluntary separation rate

Limited mentorship/support for new hires/new grads

5. Implementation Plan: *What will it take to put the future situation into play?*

		Owner	J	F	M	A	M	J	J	A	S	O	N	D
1	No exit analysis to understand reasons why RN's leave	MH	•	•	X									
2	RN salaries are not competitive	DW	•	•	•	X								
3	No regular/formal touchpoints with new hires	BO	•	X										
4	No data currently for 19-29 year olds to understand interests	MH					•	X						
5	No employee wellbeing strategy to support supportive culture	DW					•	•	•	•	X			
6	No tool or consistent approach to self & flexible scheduling	BO					•	•	X					
7	Limited mentorship/support for new hires/new grads	KS							•	•	•	•	X	

6. Measurement: *How will you know this work was successful?*

Measure (update monthly)	Target	Actual	Result
Percentage of RN new hires to voluntarily exit within first year	12%	19.60%	
Length of service of those leaving the organization	>1year	<1year	
Who's leaving the organization by age	Broader spread	0-24	
# of 30/60/90 day interviews conducted	100%	12.00%	

	Sponsor Sign Off:	Kerry Smith

Figure 2.10 A3 plan nursing retention.

Use a Value Stream Approach to Improvement

Improvement is best when completed not in isolation, but rather as part of a bigger plan. The lean approach to improvement projects that "see the whole" involves utilizing value mapping and analysis. There are countless opportunities to improve. Where do we begin? Value stream mapping and analysis provides the process and structure to identify knowing what to do. From here, you can begin to improve and do your best.

A value stream, as is contained in its name, consists of the stream of process activities required to deliver value to a customer. Beginning with the customer's definition of value (as defined in Chapter 1), the value stream is all of the tasks done to deliver this value. A value stream typically begins with a customer's need and ends when the customer's need is met. Likely, the work will span many different departments, so a value stream is *not* a department.

For example, if a patient arrives for a pre-admission surgical consultation, this patient will meet with registration, a nurse, and an Anesthesiologist. In addition, there may be a lab test required and a chest x-ray. At the end of the visit, the area is cleaned by environmental services, and supplies are re-stocked by materials management. This work spans at least six departments. The surgical experience is more than the pre-admission consultation which quickly demonstrates how a value stream is bigger than a department's processes.

To make an improvement in isolation, like by only the OR department, would only create marginal improvement. Improvement needs to be made across the entire value stream engaging all departments in delivering value to the patient. In improving the value stream, waste is eliminated from the system, and not simply moved from one department to another. Spot improvements, while holding some promise, rarely add up to revolutionary change.

To complete a value stream mapping and analysis activity, you must first accomplish the following high-level activities:

1. Assemble a team with the cross-functional representation across the value stream.
2. Determine measurable outcomes from the improvement (aligned to your true north measures and top-level improvement priorities).
3. Determine the beginning and ending points of the value stream.
4. Specify Value from the customer's perspective.

5. Process map the current process (the real "as is" process) (Figure 2.11).
6. Capture data on the current process, then add a data box to each process step (Table 2.5).
7. Identify the waste in the current process (Figure 2.12).

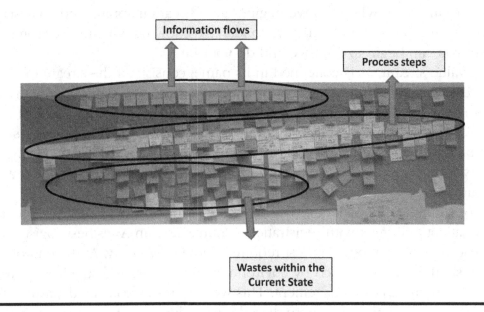

Figure 2.11   Current state map.

Table 2.5   Data Captured for Tasks

Measurement	Definition
Step name	Document the name of the task
Begins with	Document what specifically initiates the activity
Ends with	Document what specifically ends the activity
Task lead-time	The calendar (clock) time from the begins with to the ends with for this specific task
Manual touch time	The actual hands-on time for completing this task (includes walking, writing, talking on the phone, and doing the task)
Items in queue	Document how many identical tasks are sitting in the in-box for this task at this specific time
Process quality %	Document the percentage of the time you can complete this task without having to check, clarify, or repeat the activity

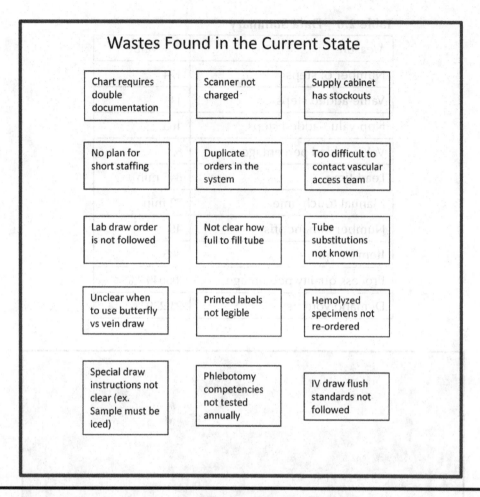

Figure 2.12 Example of wastes identified in the current state.

8. Analyze the current state and summarize performance. This is done by totaling the data from the individual data boxes on each step (Table 2.6).

Can you identify the waste from this data summary example? Why are there so many non-value-added steps? Why does the end-to-end process have more than 40 hand-offs of information? Why is there so much waiting between steps? Why is the reliability of the process so low? However you see your process, the summary of the current state is what your customer actually experiences which makes understanding the current state so valuable.

9. Develop a future state process using the lean improvement principles of Flow, Pull, Defect Free, and Visual Management (Figure 2.13).

Table 2.6 Data Summary

Measure	Value
Number of steps	174
Value-added steps	11
Non-value-added steps	163
Value added percentage	6.3%
Lead-time	845 min
Manual touch time	72 min
Number of handoffs	46
Items in queue	385
Process quality percentage	.000494%
Demand/volume	21,239

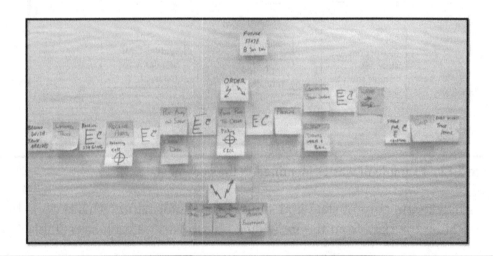

Figure 2.13 Sample of future state map.

10. Perform a gap analysis between the current state and future state to identify the specific projects needed to realize the future state.
11. Prioritize the projects identified in the gap analysis based on an assessment of their impact on goals and effort to implement (Figure 2.14).
12. Sequence the improvements on a timeline (Figure 2.15).
13. Document the improvement plan in detail by completing the reason for improvement, the current conditions, the target conditions, the

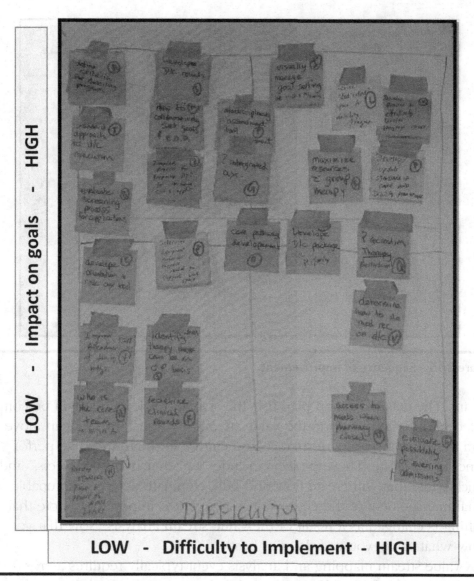

Figure 2.14 Prioritizing the projects.

measures you are trying to move, and the appropriate team to resolve
the problem. This activity can be documented nicely using the A3 plan
we previously discussed.

The three key deliverables from the value stream mapping and analysis
activity include the future state vision, the detailed improvement plan, as
well as the measures of success.

The future state map creates a vision for the team (and the organization) that reveals what the new process will look like across the entire value

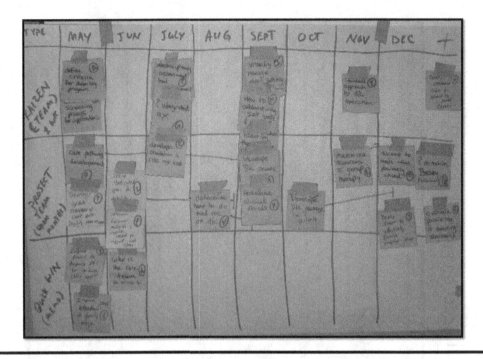

Figure 2.15 Sequence of improvement.

stream. The detailed action plan lists the specific projects that will be completed in order to transform the value stream. By transform, I mean move from the current state performance and culture to the future state performance and culture. These projects include "kaizen activity," "projects," and "quick wins" that will create flow and pull, eliminate defects, and enable visual management of the entire value stream. It is important to note that nothing is changed as a result of the value stream analysis. Now that you know what to do, you can do your best!

A value stream mapping and analysis event typically requires a cross-functional team of 12 to 15 members; it is important that both line staff and management participate in the session. If the focus is clinical, it is mandatory to have physician input as well. The activity can take between two to five **full** days, depending on the scope of the value stream; in healthcare, two and a half to three days is typically what is required. I recommend that you run the session on consecutive days. When the session runs consecutively, the team maintains continuity, which in turn delivers a better end product. Additionally, the activities build on one another, so running the days consecutively improves linkage from one activity to the next, making the process easier for the team.

Lean Tools

Deploying your improvement activities will require lean tools. There are well over 200 discrete lean tools. Some are designed to see waste, some to eliminate waste and some both identify and eliminate waste. A sample of some of the most common tools is shown in the following Table 2.7.

The definitions of these tools are listed in the glossary of terms. Over time, it is expected of the lean leader to have a working knowledge of many of these tools. If you are just getting started, I would recommend that the lean leader focus on the common tools for seeing and eliminating waste, then the tools for visual management, followed by the tools for developing people, and finally the tools for quality improvement.

To excel in the deployment of lean and to meet your targets identified in the true north measures, there are two other approaches worthy of further discussion. The first tool is A-3 thinking using the problem-solving A3 form. Almost all improvement approaches follow what's called the "scientific method" – something you're probably familiar with from ninth grade biology. In healthcare, clinical trials and evidence-based practice are based on the scientific method, which involves developing a hypothesis, testing the hypothesis, and drawing conclusions. Improvement thus becomes an experiment in which new approaches are tested to determine if a measurable impact can be made as a result of the new approach. The problem-sSolving A3 assists in providing a scientific method framework for us to apply lean thinking.

Try not to get hung up on the form. Personally, I *hated* the form when I was first introduced. I thought it was nothing more than another bureaucratic exercise for management. Over time, I came to value the thinking and the clarity the A3 form provided. Now I view it as an indispensable tool in developing strategic plans and in making improvements. When you hear of learn by doing, the application of A3 thinking to a problem is the poster child for this effort. My understanding and appreciation of the A3 form only came from repeated application of A3 thinking to a wide variety of complex problems.

The A3 form and corresponding thinking used for problem-solving look a bit different than the plan A3. An example of the problem-solving A3 form is depicted in Figure 2.16. The problem-solving A3 walks the user through each of the steps in the scientific method. Following A3 thinking steps ensure problems and their root cause(s) are identified before developing solutions.

Table 2.7 Lean Tools

Common Tools to See and Eliminate Waste	Supply Chain Tools	Project Management Tools	New Product/ Process Introduction Tools	Visual Management Tools	Quality Tools	Tools for Developing People
Takt time	Takt time	A3 thinking	Obeya (the big room)	5S	FMEA	5 Why's
Direct (time) observation	Kanban	Vertical Gantt chart	Production Preparation Process (3P)	Performance boards	Fishbone diagram	Leadership standard work
Loading diagram	Supermarkets	Freeze points	Production Preparation (2P)	Production (process) control boards	5 Why's	Gemba walking
Spaghetti mapping	ABC analysis	Toll gate reviews	Vertical Gantt chart	Pull signals	7 quality tools	Skills/ competency matrix
Circle diagram	Standard work	Standard work	Voice of the customer	Skills/ competency matrix	PDCA – Shewart cycle	Kaizen training (Kaizen event)

(Continued)

Table 2.7 (Continued)

Common Tools to See and Eliminate Waste	Supply Chain Tools	Project Management Tools	New Product/Process Introduction Tools	Visual Management Tools	Quality Tools	Tools for Developing People
Flow diagram	Order/due in board	X	Quality function deployment	Heijunka box (leveling system)	Poke-Yoke	Leader standard work
Value-added/non-value-added analysis	Inventory reduction Kaizen	X	Design of experiments	Andon	Andon	X
Standard work	X	X	Process at a glance (7 flows)	X	Variation reduction Kaizen	X
Production (process) control	X	X	X	X	A4 problem-solving	X

A-3 Theme:	Date:		Revision #:
Team Members:			
Reason For Improvement:			

Current Performance and Reflections on Current Performance:	Target Performance:

Dimension	Measure	Current	Target
Morale/HD			
Quality			
Delivery/Access			
Cost/Productivity			

Anticipated Hard savings:

Anticipated Soft Savings

Gap Analysis:	

Waste Theme	Root Cause

Figure 2.16 Problem-solving A3.

Kaizen

The second tool of mention is one designed to deliver real results while simultaneously changing the culture of your organization, and is an approach known as the kaizen event. The kaizen event can also be known as practical kaizen training, kaizen blitz, rapid improvement event, rapid

Countermeasures and Action Plans:

Waste Theme	Root Cause	Countermeasure	Expected Result

Follow Up Plans:

What	Who	When

Measurement Tracking:

Dimension	Measure	Current	Target	Week 1	Week 2	Week 3	Week 4	Week 5	Week 6	Week 7	Week 8
Morale/HD											
Quality											
Delivery/Access											
Cost/Productivity											

Verified Hard Savings:

Verified Soft Savings:

Reflections:

Figure 2.16 (Continued)

process improvement workshop, rapid cycle improvement, or kaizen workshop; all of these are based on the same principles.

A kaizen event follows A-3 thinking to improve part of a value stream, and typically involves six to ten team members. A typical kaizen event takes between three and five days to complete, depending on the scope of the problem you are trying to solve. It doesn't matter how much time it takes;

Table 2.8 Kaizen Event Daily Agenda

Day 1 Define Current Conditions (See Waste)	Day 2 Develop Solutions (Eliminate Waste)	Day 3 Implement/Test Solutions	Day 4 Document New Standard Work
• Team training • Review measures and targets • Use appropriate tools to see waste • Gather time observation data and observe waste • Generate 50 to 100 forms of waste	• Affinitize and Prioritize wastes • Develop countermeasures and action plans to eliminate waste • Use lean principles to design a new workflow • Begin testing of countermeasures	• Implement countermeasures • Train team members on new process • Verify effectiveness of solutions by measuring • Problem solve in real-time	• Finalize Standard work • Finalize visual management systems • Document standard work • Document event Results • Deliver Presentation • Recognize team

what matters is that **all** of the A-3 thinking must be completed with the correct level of detail, discipline, and integrity. The standard agenda for a kaizen event is listed in Table 2.8.

The kaizen event actually begins several weeks prior to the actual improvement week. First, measures and targets are selected by leadership, and then baseline data is collected on these measures. Next, appropriate team members are selected to participate in the improvement team. Finally, support logistics and supplies are prepared to ensure that the team can operate with minimal barriers.

Following the week of the actual kaizen event, there is an intense "sustaining period." During this time period, all of the affected team members are trained in the new standard work. Visual management systems are monitored on an hourly basis to ensure that the new standard is being followed, the correct results are delivered, and that no unintended consequences are uncovered. New problems that arise are solved immediately and communicated to the team.

The key benefits of kaizen include the following:

1. Identification of the correct team members to solve a problem.
2. Selection of focused key improvement measures.

3. Removal of organizational barriers to enable the team to make rapid change.
4. Ability of the team to move quickly through the team cycles of forming, storming, norming, and performing as a result of the kaizen event structure.
5. Compression of the timeline to see results.
6. Transfer of improvement knowledge as team members learn to see and eliminate waste by doing.
7. Improvement is based on the more strategic value stream plan, thus eliminating the spot improvement phenomenon.
8. Consistent application of the scientific method to ensure solid results and build organizational capacity in improvement and problem-solving.

As we conclude this section, I'd like to emphasize the importance of kaizen activity. In all my years of studying lean improvement, I have **never** seen an organization transform without doing kaizen activity. Of course, there are many approaches to improvement, and project-based approaches can and do generate amazing results as well. But if you want to change your culture to become one where everyone has the ability to see and eliminate waste, you must routinely practice kaizen. I have never seen organizations succeed (successfully transform their culture) otherwise.

Step 6. Monthly Review

If your organization is like most organizations, you will not always be hitting your improvement targets. This is particularly true if you are going through your first cycle of Hoshin Kanri. The step within Hoshin Kanri that manages the process of hitting the targets, as well as the results, is the monthly review. This monthly review is a formal process where each Hoshin is reviewed. The difference between a monthly review and an operational review is that the process is viewed as even more important than the result. During the monthly review, each improvement priority is discussed along with the trended measures. The purpose of the review is to determine the degree to which the targets are being met, to verify that the results are sustainable, to understand the sources of both good and bad results, to review the process of achieving the results, and to define if the improvement is adequate (Figure 2.17).

The level one policy deployment review is typically a full-day meeting. A typical agenda for this meeting would include the following topics (Table 2.9):

Monthly Policy Deployment Review Agenda (8 Hour Meeting)

Agenda Item	Percentage of Agenda Time
Review Budget Performance	10%
Review Policy Deployment Actions, Results, and Countermeasures	65%
New Product/ Service/Construction/ Development	10%
People / Organizational Issues	10%
Other	5%

Figure 2.17   Monthly policy deployment review agenda.

Table 2.9   Policy Deployment Process Review

Did I follow the Policy Deployment (PD) Process?	Was the PD process effective?
Are the results sustainable or were they short term?	Did the results become incorporated into daily standard work?
Did the deployment of the targets get cascaded to the appropriate level?	Did the targets get deployed to the action plan level?
Did we appropriately use Lean tools to deliver results	Were the monthly reviews effective?
Did we make the PD process a living and breathing tool or did we glance at it occasionally throughout the year?	Did the customer goal change during the year and did our PD targets change as a result

This review will happen at each of the layers of the improvement priorities. The reviews begin at the department/unit levels, and then cascade up to the program level, concluding with the review of the top-level improvement priorities at the senior team level.

One of the great features of the policy deployment review process is the accountability inherent in the review. For **each** target that is missed, a countermeasure must be developed. A countermeasure is a data-based corrective action to get your plan back on track to meet the target. The countermeasure will follow one of two paths. The first path will involve some quantitative analysis and the critical few corrective actions to get you to the target. Alternatively, the countermeasure will involve changing your action plan since it is not working. **Never** is the target changed due to missing the number. Missing one year's target will require a make-up effort in the outlying years to achieve your strategic plan.

A countermeasure form is prepared for the monthly review meeting whenever a target has not been met. The countermeasure form has four sources of information: historical data showing the trended performance, a frequency chart showing why the target is being missed, a root cause analysis explaining the missed target, and countermeasures (Figure 2.18).

When first starting the Policy Deployment process, many organizations miss their targets frequently. Personally, I gained a lot of experience in completing the countermeasure sheet in the first and second years. A helpful

Countermeasures Sheet

| PD Objective | |
| Date of Review | |

Insert Historical Trend Chart Here -

The trend chart should show past performance the the golal fo the objective

Insert Pareto Chart Here -

The pareto chart is a frequency chart detailing the reasons why the target was missed

Problem Statement:

Countermeasures	Who	When

Figure 2.18   Countermeasure sheet.

hint is that if you wait for electronic data to complete your countermeasure sheet, you will be in serious trouble at the review meeting. Your measurement systems must be capable of capturing relevant process and results data on a daily basis. Otherwise, you cannot implement any countermeasures in the time frame required to show improvement.

Another common problem that many organizations have is that a large portion of leaders simply fail to execute their action plans. In fact, this will be the biggest issue you will encounter when you first launch Hoshin Kanri. To avoid this, make sure everyone is accountable for their plans, the process of improving, and the results. One of the ways to address taking action on the items in your plan is to create a standard agenda that covers actions done during the previous month for the policy deployment portion of the monthly review. The standard agenda for each A3 plan would be as follows:

1. Review the outcome measures for the A3 plan. A trend chart works best here so we can visualize if the trend is positive, negative, or neutral.
2. Review the suite of activities covered in the prior 30 days. Anything in the open window of your action plan chart should be addressed. Let's review the A3 plan on retention again. If we look at the month of March, we see three open actions. Each of these actions should be addressed in the review (Figure 2.19).
3. Discuss the planned activities for the next 30 days. Again, anything in the active window should have activity occurring in the next month. By addressing the actions completed and the actions planned, we shift the monthly review narrative from explaining what happened last month. We don't want to rationalize or explain what happened; we want to dictate what happened, and that only occurs when we take action! If we consistently meet our action plan milestones, but aren't getting results, we need to reassess our action plan. We might not have the right interventions to deliver improvement, or we have the wrong root causes of our problems. We also might not be moving fast enough to deliver results.
4. Discuss any risks to our project. A risk is something that can impede our project but is in the control of the project team. When presenting a risk, we also want to document our risk mitigation strategy, the owner of the strategy, and the due date.
5. Finally present any barriers to process success. A barrier is something that can impact project success that is outside of the team's control. It will require leadership intervention to resolve. Barriers should be

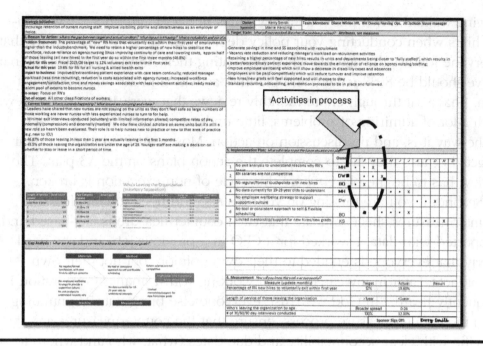

Figure 2.19 Activities in the reporting window.

identified, and problem solved in the review. Barriers are improvement project killers and senior leadership is present to assist in removing barriers. It might be their primary objective in the monthly review.

We should walk away with five things for each A3 plan monthly review:

1. An understanding of how the area of focus is performing on the key outcomes. This shows that our work is generating results.
2. An understanding of the suite of activities completed in the prior 30 days to make the month. This provides confidence that we are completing what we said we are going to do.
3. An understanding of the suite of activities planned for the next 30 days in advancing the work to meet the month. This provides confidence that the planned activities correlate to achieving targets and that the activity will be paced in a way to meet deadlines.
4. An understanding of the risks to making a plan so we have confidence that strategies are in place to mitigate team-controlled risk.
5. An understanding of the barriers to advancing the work and how my portfolio can and will assist in removing the external barriers so we have confidence the barriers will be removed to enable success of the plans.

Having walked down this road a few times before, I can offer a few helpful hints when conducting your policy deployment review. First, ensure that everyone follows the agenda when presenting their A3 plan results. The narrative should be 80% activity and planned activity and 20% data presentation. I have sat through entire monthly reviews that were 100% data reviews with a lot of admiring of problems, little understanding of why the data is the way it is, and no discussion on action. Most teams fail to meet their targets because they fail to complete the action plans on the A3 plan. The review has to be the place where this cycle of non-execution is broken.

Second, if you are missing on your results, and need to complete a countermeasures sheet, validate that each countermeasure is fact-based and supported with data. I worked for a CEO in a previous job, and she used to say that everyone is entitled to their own opinion, but not their own set of facts. Later in my career, when working with Danaher Corporation I frequently heard, "In God we Trust, everyone else bring data." Continuing with the countermeasure process, ensure that the countermeasures are specific with clear accountability and due dates (what, who and when) to get back on track. Follow up in the next review meeting that the due dates were met. Problem-solving tools should be used to develop the root cause of the problem prior to developing a countermeasure; avoid jumping to a solution. Finally, measure the targets frequently enough to provide adequate data for analysis. Daily is preferred and if the existing data structures do not allow for daily measures, find a leading indicator, and use that to ensure your improvement is getting traction. Monthly snapshots of data, including month-end reporting, do **not** meet this requirement.

Step 7. Annual Review

As you execute your A3 plans and complete your monthly reviews and work toward obtaining your target for the current year, at some point, the year will near completion. The final step in the Hoshin Kanri process is the annual review. The annual review consists of *hansei*, deep personal reflection. How did we do? For your areas of focus, document your performance and your team's performance in achieving the targets. This activity is commonly documented as follows (Figure 2.20):

In the annual review process, you will want to evaluate the process of Hoshin Kanri. Most of this evaluation has nothing to do with results, but rather, more with the process. As a starting point, the following areas can be reviewed:

Did I follow the Policy Deployment (PD) Process?	Was the PD process effective?
Are the results sustainable or were they short term?	Did the results become incorporated into daily standard work?
Did the deployment of the targets get cascaded to the appropriate level?	Did the targets get deployed to the action plan level?
Did we appropriately use Lean tools to deliver results	Were the monthly reviews effective?
Did we make the PD process a living and breathing tool or did we glance at it occasionally throughout the year?	Did the customer goal change during the year and did our PD targets change as a result

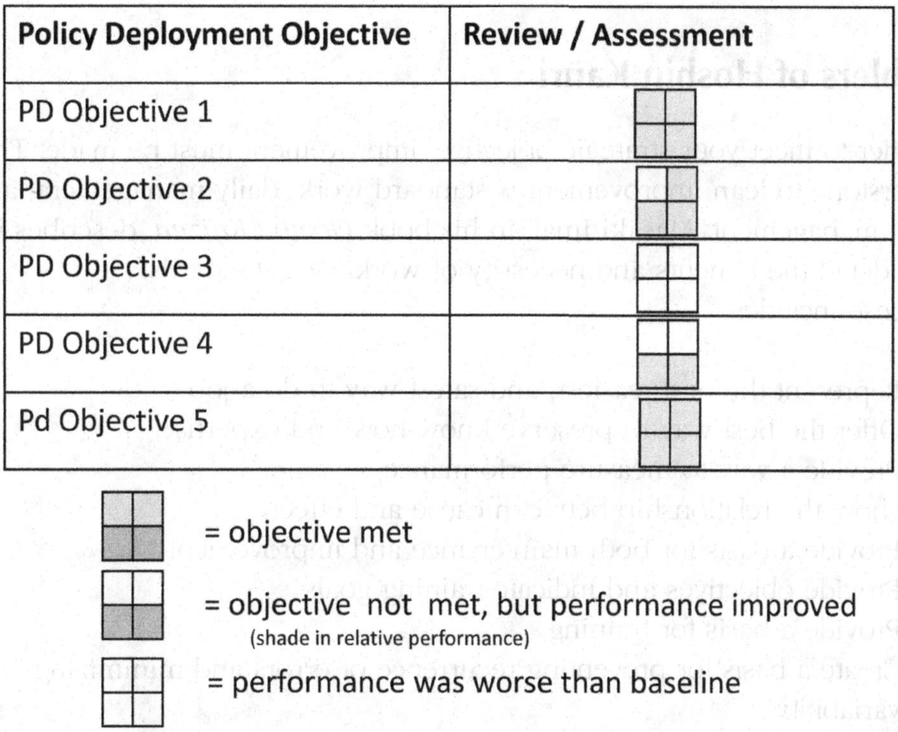

Policy Deployment Objective	Review / Assessment
PD Objective 1	
PD Objective 2	
PD Objective 3	
PD Objective 4	
Pd Objective 5	

= objective met

= objective not met, but performance improved
(shade in relative performance)

= performance was worse than baseline

Figure 2.20   Policy deployment review.

Along with your annual review, you will be repeating steps 3–5 in the Hoshin Kanri planning process to prepare for the next year on your path to meeting your strategic objectives. Steps three through five encompass developing or refining the next year's breakthrough objectives and top-level improvement priorities, deploying the improvement priorities using catch-ball, creating detailed action plans using the A3 plan, and implementing the improvement priorities using A3 thinking and value stream management.

Organizations new to Hoshin Kanri frequently want to change the targets when they realize that the targets are going to be very difficult to reach. As a guideline, you should **not** change your policy deployment targets during the year. However, there are some circumstances in which you might be well served to change your improvement activities and their corresponding targets. Circumstances might include completing a top-level improvement initiative(s) mid-year, or a significant shift in the market caused by regulation, competition, or market conditions. If your top-level improvement priorities are completely ineffective, you might also change the priority mid-year, but not the target.

Enablers of Hoshin Kanri

In order to meet your strategic objective, improvement must be made. The cornerstone to lean improvement is standard work, daily management, and visual management. Masaki Imai, in his book *Gemba Kaizen*, describes in great detail the benefits and necessity of workplace standards.[5].

These include:

1. Represent the best, easiest, and safest way to do a job
2. Offer the best way to preserve know-how and expertise
3. Provide a way to measure performance
4. Show the relationship between cause and effect
5. Provide a basis for both maintenance and improvement
6. Provide objectives and indicate training goals
7. Provide a basis for training
8. Create a basis for preventing recurrence of errors and minimizing variability

Standard work is like a recipe. If we follow the recipe, then we create the ability to provide a consistent outcome. Let's use baking pies as an example.

If we mix the right ingredients in the right order and in the right amounts and then bake at the correct temperature for the correct amount of time, we end up with pies that consistently look and taste great. In healthcare, the recipe is different, but the expectations are the same. If we follow the correct recipe for administering medication – following the correct order, for the correct dosage, for the right medicine, at the right time, delivered to the right patient – then we end up with favorable outcomes. The first favorable outcome is that the patient is safe, and the second is that the treatment will do what it is intended to do.

Now consider an alternative method for delivering medicine; assume we do not have a consistent recipe for medicine administration. Different physicians and different nurses use different approaches to ensure that they're following the most current order. The safety systems in place to ensure that the right medicine is delivered to the right patient at the right time vary slightly. Some people may double-check their steps, while others may take information at face value. Is it unrealistic to think that we will get different outcomes? Perhaps a dose is missed, or the dose is wrong since the orders were updated but have not yet cycled through the system. In severe cases, we may even see an adverse drug event. Standard work ensures a consistent and repeatable outcome. This is the first step in creating improvement. As a broader benefit, this is also a key step in becoming a high reliability organization.

In any work environment, we can define our recipe as the easiest, safest, and best-known method of performing a task. In healthcare, many sources of evidence-based care are documented. There are many research organizations whose existence is based on developing standards for care. Some of the recipes are well known, such as how to administer CPR for example, or how to perform proper hand hygiene. But thousands of standards do not exist in many organizations. What is the standard method for cleaning a patient's room? What is the standard work for O.R. turnover? And most importantly, if there is a standard, is it consistently followed? There are many ways to document standard work, but a common healthcare form is the standard work activity sheet. An example of standard work is shown in Figure 2.21.

Standard work enables daily management systems to flourish. Effective daily management systems need to be in place as a prerequisite for strategy deployment. An effective daily management system governs routine, day-to-day activities. These activities have known and followed standards in place.

	Standard Work Activity Sheet	Author(s): Laurie Jameson, Jeff Kodiak, Julie Moscow		Rev Date: 03/16/2024
	Purpose: Standard for Routine Discharge Room Clean	Value Stream: In Patient Medicine		

Seq. No	Task Description:	Key Point / Image / Measure (what good looks like)	Who	Cycle Time mm:ss
1	EVS Housekeeper has AM conversation with US for potential discharges after 10:30	US provides list of potential discharges. Consider the time of discharge to potentially avoid a double room clean	US EVS	10 sec
2	Nurse/Care Partner informs Unit Secretary of D/C	This will occur when the Nurse Care Partner transports the patient past the nurse's station. If the Unit Secretary is unavailable, let the charge nurse know that the patient has discharged.	Nurse Care Partner	10 sec
3	Acute Care US calls EVS House Phone to inform EVS that the room needs to be cleaned	Call must occur within 5 minutes of patient departure	US	10 sec
4	Room stripped for cleaning by clinical staff	This should be done as part of the discharge process	Clinical Staff	1 min
5	EVS Housekeeper travels to the room for cleaning	Response time should be within 15 minutes of notification. If the room is not stripped per standard, then immediately notify the charge nurse	EVS	5 – 15 minutes Walk time dependent
6	EVS Standard process conducted to clean the room. 1. Empty Waste Can/Trash Clean the room Clockwise or Counterclockwise at the housekeeper's discretion: 2. High Dust 3. Sanitize 4. Spot clean Walls 5. Clean Bathroom 6. Dust Mop 7. Inspect your work. 8. Damp Mop	Change gloves each time you go in and out of the room. Place the trash bag in the hallway until the room is finished clean, then take the trash to the soiled utility. The standard time for a room clean is 30 minutes from the start time. If the room had a COVID patient, the room needs to remain empty for 2 hours prior to starting. The standard for a terminal clean is 45 minutes	EVS	30 minutes standard time 45 minutes for a terminal clean
7	Ensure the room is set up according to the model configuration	Refer to the picture on your cleaning cart	EVS	Included in cleaning time
8	Place trash in the soiled utility and go to next room or return to cleaning schedule.		EVS	5 minutes

Figure 2.21   Standard work activity sheet standard for room clean.

Daily management systems usually, but not always, have limited cross-functional activity. Improvement within the daily management systems is typically incremental, and process and outcome measures are monitored. Key process indicators are monitored and managed by exception. Small levels of improvement can and should be obtained. Action is taken against these measures when an abnormal condition or a gap between expected and observed performance arises.

The major improvement work resulting from the top-level improvement priority deployment must be moved to daily management, thus ensuring the results are sustained (Figure 2.22).

The process used to monitor the daily management systems is known as visual management. This visual management system is the same one discussed in Chapter 1. There are many "things" a lean organization will manage visually, but at this point I want to discuss two key elements of visual management: management of process and results. An example of visual management used to monitor results is shown in Figure 2.23. These four charts are an example of a closed loop system that allows "seeing normal from abnormal," in this case x-ray production. The first chart illustrates the monthly targets for productivity. The second chart breaks the monthly target down into daily targets. The third chart captures sources of variation. When the targets are missed, the reason is documented in real-time. The fourth chart shows the corrective action to be taken to allow the team to meet the target.

One visual management tool that feeds the data for the performance system is the process control board. Process control is used to manage process;

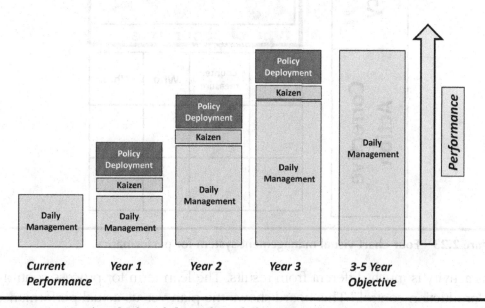

Figure 2.22   Moving the breakthrough to daily management.

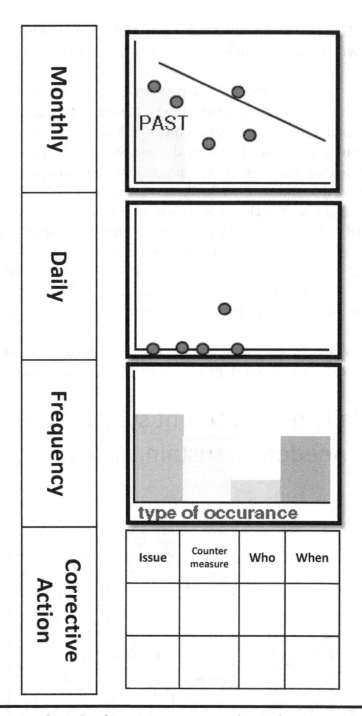

	Issue	Counter measure	Who	When

Figure 2.23 Four chart visual management system for performance.

this activity is much different from results. The lean term for process control is "production control." This board shows the plan versus actual performance for the daily schedule captured on an hour-by-hour or patient-by-patient basis. Sources of variation are documented in the comments section (Figure 2.24).

X-Ray Process Control Board			Date: January 26, 2011
Hour	Plan	Actual	Comments
0700-0800	5	5	no issues
0800-0900	5	4	outpatient failed to show
0900-1000	5	5	no issues
1000-1100	5	3	couldn't find O/P req, and isolation clean held up room
1100-1200	5		
1200-1300	5		
1300-1400	5		
1400-1500	5		
1500-1600	5		
1600-1700	5		
1700-1800	5		
1800-1900	5		
1900-2000	5		
2000-2100	5		
2100-2200	5		
2200-2300	5		

Figure 2.24   Process control board for X-ray.

When the documented comments detailing sources of variation from expected are placed into a histogram, or even better, a Pareto diagram, a great source of information is now provided. Since our goal is to create a culture of improvement, this data provides the prioritized information necessary for the next layer of improvement. In the example shown in Figure 2.25 the largest source of variation is patients failing to show up to their

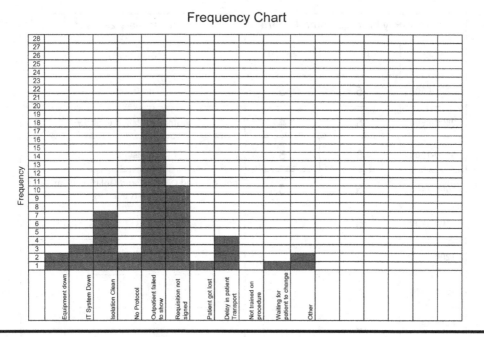

Figure 2.25   Sources of variation.

appointment. This opportunity can now be studied to develop the root cause(s) of this problem and then to develop countermeasures to resolve the cause(s). Verifying the effectiveness of the solutions should be easy to determine as well. The data from the histogram chart provides the baseline, and the future performance will show the impact of the solutions.

An organization that has developed a lean strategy and then deployed this strategy through the organization using Hoshin Kanri will see results when the improvements have made their way into daily management. Results will be managed visually through the performance board, and the process will be managed visually through the process control board.

World-Class Targets for Improvement

When I first was introduced to lean, there were no fancy PowerPoint presentations. Training was delivered through handouts, or if you were lucky, through overhead slides viewed on an overhead projector. In my very first indoctrination to lean, I was shown a slide about what world-class performance looked like, as depicted in Figure 2.26:

I learned two things from this slide. First, benchmarking against competitors or your industry is not a tremendously useful activity if you want to get

Benchmarks for World Class

❖ 1-2% per month productivity improvement

❖ 2-4% per month improvement in inventory turns

❖ 25-50% year over year reduction in cost of quality

❖ 99%+ fill rate to true customer demand

❖ Lead-time in hours/days versus weeks and months

Source: J.D. McCormick Associates, Inc

Figure 2.26 World-class rates of improvement.

to excellent. You are performing how you are performing. Said differently, your jump-off point is where you are right now, regardless of how everyone else is performing. Secondly, what I needed to be interested in is the world-class rates of improvement. I was told by my Sensei that if you try and improve faster than the world-class rates of improvement, then you will have a hard time sustaining your improvements. This was clearly great news! No need to worry about a stretch target that couldn't be obtained! The journey on cloud nine lasted about 15 seconds, as I was exposed to the world-class rates of improvement as outlined below.

■ Productivity – improve output divided by input (labor hours per unit of service) by 2% per month
■ Lead-time – reduce by 50% per year for the first six years
■ Quality – reduce defects by 50% per year
■ Inventory turnover – improve inventory turnover by 2–4% per month or 50% annually

I was used to getting a 2–3% productivity improvement a year. World-class organizations improve productivity by 25% year over year! Would this rate of improvement help with cost control and slow your need for additional resources? Imagine your cash flow if you can get improved inventory turns from your pharmaceutical, therapeutical, and operating supplies. Envision your organization with wait-times and access to services slashed in half or better. Imagine the high quality of care provided when measurable quality and safety performance improves by 50% to 60% year over year.

Now is the point where you might be thinking, I can never get my organization, program, or unit to that level of performance!" There are too many barriers, both internal and external, to my area of responsibility. And you might be right. But you also might be missing the point. What if you could get to 25% of the rate of improvement of a world-class organization? What if you could get to 10% of that pace? I can assure you that even at the 10% year-over-year improvement rate, you would be thrilled with the quality, access, and cost performance of your organization. Table 2.10 shows the sample of the results delivered by some lean organizations.

Table 2.10 Sample of Results from Lean Improvement

Medicine patient flow	• Reduced Acute Length of Stay by 15% across all programs • Reduced discharge-planning resources by 17% by creating a new patient navigator role which combined discharge planning, clinical coordination, and resource utilization functions (reduction of 5 FTE)
Emergency services patient flow	• Reduced average emergency department length-of-stay from 3.1 hours to 2.1 hours per patient for lower acuity patients with 9% higher patient volumes (32% reduction) • Reduced average emergency department length-of-stay from 5.1 hours to 3.3 hours for non-admitted medium acuity patients (35% reduction) • Reduced the left-without-being-seen percentage from 6.1% to 0.78% (allowing ~2000 more patients to be seen each year)
Outpatient rehabilitation services	• Increase in number of clients seen per clinician per day from 8 to 12 (50% increase) • Increase in patient satisfaction (overall rating of care) from 90 to 96 (7% improvement) • Reduction in time from approval to initial visit from 12.3 days to 4 (67% reduction)

(Continued)

Table 2.10 (Continued)

Physician lead clinic flow	• Lead-time reduced for medical record preparation from two weeks to 2–3 days (75% reduction) • Patient total visit time reduced from 80–90 minutes to 40 minutes (50% reduction) • Provider capacity increased by 3 patients per day • Provider work day decreased from an 11-hour day to an 8-hour day with transcription, e-mail, and voice mails completed by the end of each day (27% reduction)
Diagnostic imaging	• Reduced MRI Pt LOS by 24% while reducing staff MCT by 42% • Increased a 2 x-ray unit capacity by over 100% negating the need for 2 techs and an additional machine • Value stream improvement in MRI resulted in an 18% increase in daily throughput with 25% less technologist manpower yielding annualized savings of $100K • Optimized Imaging schedule utilization with a net result of additional 15% capacity
Mental health services outpatient referral processing	• Rejected referrals received per month reduced from 47 per month to 23 per month (50% reduction) • Reduced the referral processing time from 30 days to 6 days (80% reduction) • Reduced the cost of travel in support of referral process by $800/month (20% reduction)
Peri-operative services	• Reduced the cost per case from $1290 to $1150 over nine months during value stream improvement (10.8% reduction). • Reduced overall budget variance by a favorable 14%. • Increased same day surgical volume by 10%.

The bar to get to world class is very high. Even the examples above, with their double-digit gain in performance, did not always get to world-class rates of improvement. Not everyone achieves world-class status, otherwise it wouldn't be world class, but every organization that gets the focus and attention from senior management, uses lean thinking aligned to strategic objectives, and engages team members in process and quality improvement has seen dramatic increases in performance and culture.

Chapter 2 is the longest chapter, and we covered a lot of content. We could have easily separated out the management system as its own chapter. What might be valuable in understanding is that lean has many different tools and approaches inside its improvement approach. An arbitrary but sometimes useful way to differentiate between the tools and approaches is to separate the breakthrough improvement thinking from the day-to-day management systems. Both approaches are necessary to create a culture of improvement, but it is easier to learn them independently.

One frequent question I get asked is where to begin. If your team and culture have the patience, I would begin with the management system. This is the sustainability framework and where most of the leadership development will occur. If you have a group of skeptics, you might consider starting with the improvement system to demonstrate the ability to deliver breakthrough change. Without the management system you will not likely sustain your breakthrough improvement, and without your improvement (operating) system you won't likely see breakthrough gains. Figure 2.27 shows the different tools and approaches inside the management system and the operating system.

If you have been at lean improvement for a while, you might see something on this list you haven't yet been exposed to. I think we should all constantly be learning. There are wonderful resources out there on the approaches, tools, and applications of most of the activities within this list. Start with an internet search and see if there is something in there to help

Management System

- ☐ Strategy, Governance and Systems
  - ○ Enterprise Steering Committee make-up and standard work
  - ○ Value Steam Steering Committee make-up and standard work
  - ○ Strategy deployment / Hoshin
  - ○ Transformation A3
  - ○ Enterprise strategy wall (Transformation Control Center) templates and standard work
  - ○ VS strategy wall templates and standard work
- ☐ Daily Management
  - ○ Process Control templates, instruction, and standard work
  - ○ Daily Stat Sheets templates and standard work
  - ○ Tiered MDI huddles with templates, standard work, and data gathering standard work
  - ○ Suggestion System templates and standard work
  - ○ Kamishibai templates and instruction
  - ○ Leader standard work templates and instruction
    - ▪ VP sample
    - ▪ Director sample
    - ▪ Manager sample
    - ▪ Team Leader sample
  - ○ 5S

Operating System

- ☐ A3 template and instruction and samples for both A3 plan and Problem solving A3
- ☐ Visioning prep standard work
- ☐ Visioning facilitation standard work
  - ○ Flip chart templates
- ☐ Visioning report out template and sample
- ☐ Value stream prep standard work
- ☐ Value stream facilitation
  - ○ Flip chart templates
- ☐ Value Stream report out template and sample
- ☐ Kaizen prep standard work
- ☐ Kaizen facilitation standard work
  - ○ Flip chart templates
- ☐ Kaizen report out standard work and template

Figure 2.27   Realizing and sustaining breakthrough improvement

get you to the next level. But don't chase tools! Applying tools for the sake of learning without a business need is costly and can be quite wasteful.

Another important consideration as a leader is that while we are paid to create the strategy, priorities within the strategy, the deployment and execution approaches to realizing the strategy, and the allocation of resources to make improvement happen, we are also concerned about culture. The Hoshin Kanri framework and the management system are used to create focus, develop detailed plans, create a mechanism to action those plans, and sustain the corresponding improvements. Executing this process repeatedly will result in a high-performing culture.

Companies and organizations, at the end of the day, are a collection of people. Lean organizations understand this and develop systems and processes designed to get the most out of their people, while simultaneously building capacity and developing people at all levels. Everyone can participate and contribute to improvement. Whether it be through the implementation of strategic priority, or through the incremental improvement from the management system. A force of hundreds or thousands of staff and clinicians all focused on improvement creates momentum for positive, measurable change for the benefit of patients and caregivers, staff, clinical staff, and your community. It is through repeated application of seeing and eliminating wasted time activity, at all levels of the organization, that we can influence the culture for the better. Organizations with great culture perform better, have better engagement and retention of employees, and make your organization a magnet to create future talent.

Chapter Summary: Key Points from Chapter 2

- To make improvement meaningful, it must be linked to your organizational strategy.
- Creating a culture of improvement involves developing and deploying a lean strategy. This process consists of two main steps:
  - Effectively using a "strategy" deployment process
  - Sustaining the improvements with standard work and effective daily management systems managed visually
- Hoshin Kanri is a system used to manage enterprise change of the core business objectives. This approach provides a roadmap for planning, implementing, and reviewing managed, intentional change.

- There are seven steps to Hoshin Kanri:
  - establish the organizational vision
  - develop the 3–5-year breakthrough objectives
  - develop the annual breakthrough objectives and top-level improvement priorities
  - deploy the improvement priorities
  - implement the improvement priorities
  - conduct a monthly review of the results and process to get the results
  - conduct an annual review of the process
- Implement your strategy using value stream improvement plans, lean techniques, and A3 thinking.
- Effective daily management systems used to maximize the effectiveness of standard work are a pre-requisite of Hoshin Kanri.
- Daily management systems are managed visually.
- Try to get your organization to focus on world-class rates of improvement. This focus will help eliminate complacency when you are leading your peer group in performance.

Notes

1. Pascal Dennis, Lean Production Simplified (New York, NY: Productivity Press, 2007), pg. 123.
2. Greg Watson and Hoshin Kanri, Policy Deployment for Successful TQM (Portland, OR: Productivity Press, 1991), pg. xxi.
3. Pascal Dennis, Lean Production Simplified (New York, NY: Productivity Press, 2007), pg. 123.
4. Pascal Dennis, Lean Production Simplified (New York, NY: Productivity Press, 2007), pg. 130.
5. Masaaki Imai, *Gemba Kaizen* (New York NY: McGraw–Hill, 1997), pages 54–56.

Chapter 3

Leading Change – The Transformation Roadmap and Phase 1: Getting Ready to Transform

The content covered in Chapter 2, developing and deploying your lean strategy, might seem a bit ambitious, or even overwhelming, depending on where you are in your improvement journey. For those of you who are just starting out on your road to transformation, great lessons can be learned from the organizations that have gone before you. Keep in mind that the road to lean transformation is now over 75 years old. Organizations large and small, public and private, and union and non-union have "left a trail" to follow.

Beginning the Journey

A word of caution as you begin this journey; the road to enterprise-wide transformation is *very* long and can take up to 20 years to complete for a large organization. Transformation is not a three-year plan. It is not a project, nor is it a toolkit. Transformation is a process where the culture slowly changes, one team at a time, one unit at a time, one program at a time, and one system at a time. There is no "easy button" to success. In my nearly 38 years of experience working in either operations or consulting, I have never

DOI: 10.4324/9781003532132-3

once met a management team that would be honest about this fact. Most organizations set out to "transform" in two years, with three years at the high end of their timeline. This is simply not a realistic target, and you will do well to not make bold claims of "transformation" to the staff or to the board in this narrow period of time.

Implying that transformation is a long process, however, does not imply that you should have to wait a long time for results. And getting results sooner will support you on your longer-term transformation journey. A properly trained team with the right measures and the right improvement process can generate local improvements in a week. Recall the discussions on the world-class rates of improvement; drastic changes in performance and culture are what are possible, but not with your current improvement infrastructure, organizational structure, improvement focus, improvement process, and management practices. Each of these will change over time. Fortunately, you will not need to change all of these at once.

The Three Phases of Transformation

There are three phases to transformation as shown in Figure 3.1. The first phase is the "get ready" phase. In this phase, you will need to establish the infrastructure to begin improvement. While you do not need a massive infrastructure to begin creating a culture of improvement, you also cannot start with nothing. I will explain the roles in the improvement process that need to be filled, as well as define a few tasks that will help you to prepare your organization for change and manage the issues that will arise as you begin your improvement journey.

The second phase is the "accelerate" phase. In this phase, you will identify where to begin your improvements, deliver on your operational improvements, sustain those improvements, and then spread those improvements across your organization. It would be helpful to refer back to Chapter

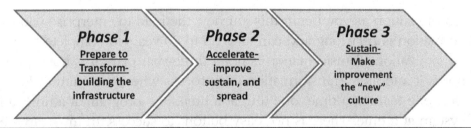

Figure 3.1 The three phases of transformations.

2 where it was discussed in detail how to link your improvement initiatives to your strategy. For those of you that are just getting started, I will offer an approach that utilizes a blend of objective and subjective tools to identify a few key "value streams" to help you get started. An explanation of delivering, sustaining, and spreading improvement will follow; a special emphasis will be placed on sustainability, as this is where many organizations struggle, and some even fail.

The third phase is the "sustain" phase. Perhaps the "endure" phase is a better term. In this phase, I will discuss how to anchor the changes into the organizational culture. Through these activities, you will establish and cement your "new" culture. The focus will initially be on capacity building and using this capacity effectively. Explanations of taking your improvement approaches to support areas, business systems, and even outside your four walls will follow.

Phase 1 – Getting Ready to Transform

I am often asked how I know if an organization is ready to take on a performance and cultural transformation. Is there some type of readiness assessment that can be taken to determine if a performance and cultural transformation is right for the organization? I can answer this in the simplest of terms; when the pain of change is less than the pain of staying the same, your organization is ready for a transformation. It is that simple. No one organization is better prepared than another to take on change. The factor that makes the difference between success and failure is the will not to fail. Notice, I specifically did not say the will to succeed. Lou Holtz, a retired hall of fame college football coach, once gave a motivational speech. He was talking about the difference between winning and losing in college athletics. There is a famous saying that "the team that wants to win 'more' finds a way to win the game." Lou Holtz said that this statement is dead wrong. Everyone wants to win. The difference is winning teams hate to lose and do all the little things it takes not to lose. This includes game planning, preparing, practicing the right way, conditioning, etc. The team that wins the game is the team that refuses to lose. A successful transformation is the same in that it requires the will not to fail, and more importantly the will not to give up.

My readiness assessment consists of having the senior leadership team answer a single question, "Are you prepared to do what it takes *not* to fail in your transformational efforts?" If you can answer yes to this single question, then your organization is ready. It will not matter about your size, infra-structure, funding model, level of capitalization, public or private, union or non-union, etc. Having the will not to fail is the single readiness assessment question you will ever need to answer.

The second question I often get is when should we start? This question is answered with another question? "When is the best time to plant a tree?" The answer to that question is 25 years ago. Thus, the best time to transform is now! Your competitive advantage and results will scale over the years as more of the staff are engaged in seeing and eliminating wasted time and activity. Starting soon gives your results the soonest.

Once you have firmly decided to move ahead, there are some steps you can take to prepare your organization for success. These steps include iden-tifying your champion, finding a coach, preparing your infrastructure, decid-ing on a governance model, and training your team. While this list might not be exhaustive, the steps taken to prepare your organization to transform include:

1. Find your change agent
2. Get informed
3. Get help
4. Establish a steering committee
5. Train your internal experts
6. Develop and deploy a communication campaign

Let us review each of these steps in more detail.

Finding Your Change Agent

Of all the steps in preparing your organization for change, perhaps none may be more important than selecting the right change agent. The change agent is the person, internal to your organization, who will lead the transfor-mational efforts. This person will orchestrate and guide the transformational efforts of your organization. Not just anyone can do this work; there is a special skill set required to lead a major performance and cultural transfor-mation. The four requirements of a successful change agent include:

1. Commanding the respect of the organization.
2. Ability to navigate around and through cultural and organizational barriers.

3. Ability to manage a room.
4. Skilled at local, department level, and organizational communication.

The change agent will need to energize large groups of diverse people with different interests, talents, and goals toward a common vision. This is not likely delegated to a junior person or a new hire within the organization. The best change agent is a senior, executive-level position with a proven track record of results. This person will need to be trusted, as your organization will be going to a place it has never been. As you make change, all answers will not be known, the risks will not be identified, and the outcomes are not guaranteed.

The change agent also needs the political clout or savvy to navigate around or through organizational barriers. In many cases, this means seriously challenging the status quo and dismantling the bureaucracy that prevents real change. Do not underestimate this step. Many times, the change agent helped create the existing policy and bureaucracy leading to the current performance. As a famous saying goes, "every organization, including yours, is perfectly designed to achieve the results it delivers." So, if you want to change your results, you will need to change your organization. Waiting three weeks for a purchase order to be placed, a maintenance work order sitting in the queue for two weeks to be processed, completing a four-page document for an IT change request, and waiting six months to get a form through your forms committee are all symptoms of a bureaucracy, not an organization that will enable rapid change of performance and culture. The change agent must navigate these wickets to enable the team to make changes using A3 thinking and lean principles. Over time, being able to make changes in real time is a signature of great lean organizations.

Are you going to make some people "angry" while you jump the bureaucracy queue, expediting the change processes needed to transform your organization? **Count on it!** This is why I encourage organizations to have a senior executive in the change agent role. In the majority of the organizations delivering world-class rates of improvement, the change agent was the CEO. In none of these cases was the change agent a project manager, a continuous improvement director, or a mid-level manager. Not that these roles are not important, or that these change agents were not skilled individuals and incredibly valuable in the change process, but these roles simply do not carry enough organizational horsepower to bust through the barriers.

Improvement in performance and change in culture comes from breaking down the functional silos of the organization and enabling process, information, and value to be delivered seamlessly across the organization. Turf protecting behaviors that discourage or prevent collaboration at the expense of certain leader preferences, a departmental budget, an organizational policy, or foster a "that's the way we do it here" mentality have got to be eliminated.

Support departments play a key role in enabling performance and culture transformation. Questions that you must begin to ask yourself at the outset of transforming your organization include: Do the human resource policies support a rapidly changing organization? Are the payroll and scheduling systems enabling change and reducing waste in the system, or are these processes squelching creativity and sapping time from the manager that could be spent on improvement? Do the fiscal policies and activities provide meaningful managerial data and analysis needed for improvement, or are you stuck in the 1950s spending all of your time providing financial reports that satisfy the financial reporting requirements but deliver little valuable data to improve the business?

Improvement also comes from changing the way an organization responds to change. One "real-life" example I have encountered on more than one occasion is the change cycle associated with updating a clinical form/template. Let us assume one of the improvement teams has developed a new way to document the initial nurse assessment. This new approach requires half the effort, yields better clinical results, and takes half the time. I have seen this great idea languish for six months or more waiting to get approved by the forms committee/IT change committee. The change agent needs to be prepared to take on this challenge and likely several others. Processes that can stifle change include small capital approval requests, small expense requests that take a week or more to get through purchasing, and small IT changes that demand a requirements document that takes longer to complete and get approved than the actual programming change.

I am not advocating that we eliminate all the controls that are in place to manage risk and help prioritize the organizational needs, but the teams need to be supported with a "fast track" approach that usually is driven by the senior level change agent. Especially in the critical areas that drive strategic improvement. The change agent has to be prepared to take on all the "sacred cows," or "white elephants," or any other name you choose to call these barriers, to enable improvement of performance and culture. This might be the single, most important requirement of the change agent.

The third and fourth requirements of being a successful change agent is the ability to carry a room and to be an excellent communicator. What do I mean by the ability to carry a room? This is the skill of inspiring and engaging others in a team setting. Great change agents exude confidence and charisma. They are skilled in public speaking and great communicators. You will be taking your organization on a new journey, one that no one, likely, has been on before. It will require a high level of targeted communication to inspire people to follow you through this change and let them know that the "other side" will be better for the patients, their families, the staff, the organization, the board, and the surrounding community.

I have personally witnessed some change agents that were very well respected in the organization and had the ability to navigate the organizational barriers but lacked the group communication skills needed to inspire the team to put in the effort to change. In the end, the change agent was unable to create the mass momentum necessary to transform the organization. This is why the "ability to carry a room" and to be an excellent communicator across all levels of the organization has been added to the list of requirements desired in a change agent.

Get Informed

Once you have selected your change agent, you need to get informed about lean and process improvement. In other words, you need to have your leadership team gain some knowledge about lean, lean in healthcare, and enterprise-wide lean transformation. At this stage in your improvement journey, you are not required to be an expert on lean tools, applications, and techniques, but you do need to understand at a minimum what is required to transform your organization, what resources are required, and what behaviors are needed from the senior leadership team to enable your cultural transformation to be successful.

There are many ways to get informed on lean healthcare. Table 3.1 lists a few of these approaches and the advantages and disadvantages of these approaches.

If you are just getting started, my recommendation on where to go to get informed would be to pursue all of these options, preferably in the same sequence as I listed the alternatives. Begin with some reading. You can research a specific area, like peri-operative services, or you can choose enterprise-wide transformation. There are hundreds of thousands of web pages and blogs that support lean healthcare and hundreds of books. A simple web search will yield a wide variety of information on lean healthcare both free and for purchase.

Table 3.1   Getting Informed

Approach	Advantages	Disadvantages
Read internet articles	• Lowest cost • Can be targeted to your area of concern • Instantaneous access	• No ability to ask questions/ not interactive
Read books/ white papers	• Lower cost than remaining alternatives • Many reviews available to assist in your selection • More comprehensive than internet articles • E-book options are now available	• No ability to ask questions/not interactive • Multiple copies might be needed
Attend a lean conference or lean training	• Many options are available with various lengths, pricing, and topics • Ability to interact with presenters and attendees • Conferences are available in regional, national, and international forums • Training topics can be held on-site or off-site • Topics can be tailored to directly meet your organization's needs	• May require travel • Conference fees can be pricey • Cannot always validate the content of the presentations or the break-out activities • Lean Healthcare conferences are improving, but the best lean conferences currently are not exclusive to healthcare and provide lean examples from a wide variety of industries • Training will likely require some type of fee payment
Visit another lean organization	• Ability to see what a lean organization looks like • Ability to ask questions and get real-time feedback • Can target specific areas or choose an organization that is undergoing organizational-wide transformation • Allows you to see visual management systems in action	• Some organizations charge a fee for this service • Likely will require travel and living expenses • Numbers of people you can send might be limited • May not get to see the specific area you are interested in seeing

(Continued)

Table 3.1 (Continued)

Approach	Advantages	Disadvantages
Participate in another organization's improvement team	• Provides the opportunity to learn lean with hands-on approaches • Ability to interact with others and ask questions and receive feedback • Limits distractions since you will likely be off-site • Limits risk since you will be working on someone else's project	• Requires a time investment of 3–5 days depending on the improvement activity • Likely will require travel and living expenses • might not be able to participate on a team with the same focus as your organization

Read a common article or book as a team and hold a group review. What did you learn? What are the keys to success? What are the common mistakes organizations make? How did other's get started, accelerate their change, and then sustain? Reflecting on such questions as these will help to build lean knowledge.

Next, I would encourage the leadership team to attend a few lean conferences. There are many to pick from and they all have something to offer. I personally prefer the conferences with break-out sessions since you can get detailed information on the topics of your choosing. At the time of this writing, I can recommend the following annual, international conferences for their lean expertise and knowledge sharing:

■ The Shingo Prize International Conference
■ AME Excellence Inside Conference
■ ASQ World Conference on Quality and Improvement
■ IHI Annual National Forum on Quality Improvement in Health Care
■ LEI Lean Healthcare Transformation Summit

There are dozens of other national, regional, and local conferences and training workshops held each year. Conferences are a great way to network and speak with others pursuing excellence. Remember, you are not the first organization to pursue enterprise-wide transformation, and you can learn a lot from other's experiences. I find attending these conferences with like-minded individuals also energizes you to stay engaged. You are not alone in this journey.

Training workshops are another way to get informed. There are a wide variety of public workshops held regionally and nationally each year. If you want to get the best experience, however, I encourage you to bring some training into your own organization. Holding the training onsite leverages your training dollars since you can have many people attend simultaneously with no travel expenses. Host a one-day lean leadership workshop and have the following questions answered:

1. What is lean?
2. How do you see waste?
3. How do you eliminate waste?
4. How do you get started in deploying a culture of continuous improvement?
5. What are the leadership behaviors necessary to drive change?
6. What are the key risks and how do you mitigate these risks?

If you can get a simulation to help, see and eliminate waste included in this one-day workshop, it would be even better. There is no better way to learn improvement than attending "dirty hands" university. Remember, we learn best by doing. Getting these questions answered will enable your organization to answer the readiness question, "Are we prepared not fail?"

Following some research and education through reading, conferences, and training, visiting another lean organization would be a great next step. There are hundreds of organizations deploying lean improvement both within healthcare and outside of healthcare, although not all organizations are as successful as others with their efforts. The greatest lean organizations in the world are not in healthcare, but rather in the manufacturing sector. But that does not mean you cannot learn a whole lot from a "manufacturer." I would encourage you to conduct a little research on who has won the Shingo Prize, an award given to those organizations that deliver lean excellence. A tour of one of these organizations will show you what the pursuit of excellence in performance and culture looks like although the winner will not likely be a healthcare organization.

The final recommendation on getting informed would be to participate in another organization's improvement team. In the spirit of scholarship, most lean healthcare organizations are happy to support outside team members. There are many things to be learned from being on an improvement team. Some of the key takeaways would include:

- How did the team get organized?
- How were the targets selected?
- How was rapid change enabled in support of the team?
- What was leadership's role in the change?
- What tools were used? How were they chosen?
- How did the specific project get identified?
- How did the team embrace change? How did the affected area embrace change?
- What was the sustainability plan?
- Were the targets met?
- How were the physicians engaged?
- Who attended the final presentation? How excited was the team?
- How long would an identical change take within our organization?

Any organization seeking to get informed would benefit greatly by having each and every member of the executive team participate in another organization's improvement team prior to getting started. It is through these experiences that you build an understanding of how to create the will to not fail.

Get Help

If we were entering the healthcare industry and we wanted to get an expert opinion on our heart, we would likely visit a cardiologist. If we needed expertise on diabetes, we would visit an endocrinologist. I do not know too many people that try to become experts on cardiology and endocrinology by simply reading a few internet articles and attending a few conferences. Yet, it is not uncommon for organizations to take an individual or two, send them to some basic lean training, and embark on a culture of continuous improvement.

Just as you would find an expert in cardiology or endocrinology, you also need to seek out an expert in lean enterprise transformation. In "lean" circles, this person would be known as a Sensei. Loosely translated, a Sensei is a master or teacher. The more accurate translation is one who has traveled the road before, i.e., has been through one or more lean transformations. The Sensei has many important roles to fill in a transformation including:

- Teaching your organization the lean tools and concepts
- Coaching your leadership team
- Helping to select the right areas of focus

■ Assisting in developing the right measures
■ Coaching on the development of your infrastructure

Bringing in some outside expertise to help with training, leadership development, infrastructure development, and team improvement is a wise investment for many organizations. External lean expertise comes in many forms, from a lean expert with expertise in one field to a lean sensei that has expertise in many business areas.

A good external resource will shorten your lead-time for results, accelerate the breadth and depth of your improvement, minimize your organizational risk, and assist in your development of management and leadership. Additionally, an outside resource is not tied to your political structure and organizational structure. This is a tremendous asset when it comes to the impartial ability to focus on process, rather than designing an improvement system based on personalities. I have one piece of advice, should you wish to go outside for expertise. Pay attention to the experts who have practical experience in management development and prior senior leadership experience. The lean tools, while potentially overwhelming at first, are the easiest part of improving. The most difficult aspect is changing the way management thinks, acts, and behaves. You will see a wide variation in lean expert capability when you move beyond tools and into management/leadership development.

To close this section on getting help, I will refer to "Lean Thinking," one of the early, well-recognized books on the application of lean. In Chapter 11, authors Jim Womack and Dan Jones provide a step-by-step transformation process. Step 1, as we have discussed, is to identify a change agent. Step 2 is finding a sensei.[1] I am not aware of any organization that truly transformed into a lean enterprise, inside or outside of healthcare, without a sensei. It is simply that important.

Establish a Steering Committee

When your organization begins to take on a large change initiative, there are two areas of infrastructure that need to be developed from the outset. One is the governance structure to manage and monitor the change, and the second is creating your internal improvement expertise. Both are equally important, but I would like to begin by first discussing the governance process.

When you begin to see results from your first value stream, you will start getting requests from many areas of the organization to come and help them improve. As you should! After all, everyone has a need to improve quality, improve access, and lower costs, while simultaneously creating an inspired staff. Your organization may also be asking about speed, scope, and results. How fast you should be improving? How many resources are needed? Are you getting a return on your investment? These questions are best answered by establishing a guiding coalition or a lean steering committee.

The lean steering committee has several key responsibilities in guiding your organization through the change process. The committee will:

- Establish the measurement systems and targets for monitoring success
- Ensure that the results are being captured
- Select the areas of focus (value streams) for the organization
- Provide oversight that staff, medical staff, and management are being developed. (They should be developing their skills through training and hands-on activity.)
- Remove the organizational barriers. (These may be organizational structures, systems, people, policies and procedures, compensation programs, promotion policies, etc.)
- Monitor the pace of change. If you move too slow, you will lose momentum, and if you move too fast, the sustainability of the program will suffer.
- Ensure you get a solid return on your investment. It is expected in lean transformations to generate a 2 to 1 return on investment in the first year and 4 to 1 from that point forward. The lower return in year one is due to the investment in infrastructure creation and training needed to build capacity.

Many organizations do not want to set up yet another steering committee; perhaps they feel that there are too many committees across healthcare organizations already. They prefer instead to add the lean activity to the strategy council, operations committee, or quality council. I do **not** recommend this practice. In lean improvement, there will be enough activity going on to warrant a dedicated committee's full attention. Remember that lean is *not* a project; it is a management system of continuous improvement that results in a transformation of your organizational culture. The enterprise steering committee meets monthly, and the length of the meeting is approximately 90 minutes to 2 hours. The committee is made up of 8 to 12 people. My recommendation is shown in Table 3.2:

Standard meeting rules are used. A timekeeper is established. Someone is assigned to take the meeting minutes. Minutes from the previous meeting are approved. A standard agenda should be followed. An example of this agenda is shown in Table 3.3.

During the meeting, action items are assigned, and the team members are expected to complete their assignments before the next meeting. Accountability for completing assignments is a prerequisite for effective meetings. This group will provide oversight and governance for the overall lean improvement journey for your organization. Establishing the governance structure for your organization is an important task in creating a successful infrastructure for improvement.

Table 3.2 Lean Steering Committee Makeup

Position	Committee Role	Core Responsibility
CEO/President	Committee Chair	Leads lean steering committee
Operations Executive for the Organization	Committee Co-Chair	Co-leads lean steering committee
Chief of Medical Staff	Team Member	Drives the physician engagement strategy
Chief Financial Officer	Team Member	Drives the measurement Capture and reporting from lean savings
Representative from Human Resources	Team Member	Leads the re-deployment policy discussions and actions
Leader of the Lean Program/Department	Team Member	Leads discussion on improvement standard work and lean improvement calendar
Corporate Leader for Quality, Patient Safety, and Risk Management	Team Member	Ensures lean improvements are directly aligned with quality and safety goals for the enterprise
Representative from Marketing/ Communications	Team Member	Leads the communication strategy for lean enterprise transformation
Various	Team Members	Assist in lean transformation governance

Table 3.3   Sample of the Lean Steering Committee Agenda

Agenda Topic Leader	Activity	Length
Chair	• Check-in and review and approve previous meeting minutes	5 minutes
Value Stream Leader #1 (Guest)	• Value stream results – YTD • Countermeasures to address gaps • Action plans for the next 90 days • Upcoming improvement calendar	15 minutes
Value Stream Leader #2 (Guest)	• Value stream results – YTD • Countermeasures to address gaps • Action plans for the next 90 days • Upcoming improvement calendar	15 minutes
Value Stream Leader #3 (Guest)	• Value stream results – YTD • Countermeasures to address gaps • Action plans for the next 90 days • Upcoming improvement calendar	15 minutes
CFO/Lean Leader	• Corporate roll-up of lean results	10 minutes
Lean Leader	• Review and approve integrated lean improvement calendar for the next 90 days	10 minutes
Lean Leader/ CMO or CMS	• Developing capacity • Review participation engagement statistics	10 minutes
Chair/ Co-Chair	• Discussion of organizational barriers that need to be addressed • Updates from other team members	10 minutes
All	• Tour one area that had recent lean improvement	30 minutes

Train Your Internal Experts

The next step in developing your infrastructure for improvement and in completing the activities necessary for the preparation phase of your transformation includes developing your internal experts. Most organizations underestimate how many resources it takes to improve. The preparation activities, the actual improvement team activities, and the sustaining activities all require skilled facilitation – which requires some full-time resources in order to be done well. My rule of thumb is that you need one full-time person for each value stream you are improving. This person can be a dedicated resource or a seconded resource – but either way, he or she should be full time.

The responsibilities of the internal expert are summarized in Table 3.4.

Table 3.4   Internal Expert Core Responsibilities

Role	Purpose
Become the internal expert for lean improvement	Organizational leader for lean tools, approached, methods, and techniques
Leads improvement preparation activities	Uses standard work to ensure the team has the right team make-up, the right area of focus, the right measures/targets, and effectively uses organizational resources
Assist in the sustaining activities	Helps process owner to ensure standard work is in place and followed, and visual management systems and controls are used effectively
Teach visual management to the organization	Helps the organization understand the principle of managing visually: being able to see normal from abnormal conditions that an intervention can be taken in real-time
Coordinate the logistics for improvement	Ensures that everything is in place to allow the teams to be effective and use their time wisely
Develop additional team leaders	Builds improvement capacity for the organization
Assists in managing the improvement plan both at the value stream and corporate levels	Helps provide data for decision-making that the improvement calendar is known, communicated, and followed
Train staff and medical personnel on lean principles, practices, and process	Builds improvement capacity for the organization
Facilitate the improvement activities	Helps the team to deliver improvement using A3 thinking. build organizational capacity in the team members

(Continued)

Table 3.4 (Continued)

Develop line management	Teaches line management the skills of lean improvement to include A3 thinking, leadership standard work, and visual management
Assist in managing the breadth and depth of improvement	Provides feedback on the proper timing for introducing new lean tools, and to spread improvement across the organization
Assist in capture and population of the improvement scorecard	Teaches the process owner and assists finance in capturing and reporting the hard and soft savings associated with lean improvement.
Assist in the development of visual management systems	Leverages the principle of visual management to create systems that help the staff, medical staff, and management monitor and improve both process and results

The data collection activities and the suite of sustaining activities require extensive amounts of time. Part-time resources generally are ineffective in completing these two specific activities well. Ineffective data collection leads to less-than-optimal results. Ineffective sustaining activities can lead to slow results or even project failure. It is often asked, why can't the manager, supervisor, or team leader perform these preparation and sustaining activities? The reality is they can. In a mature lean organization this is often the case. But until you transition your management and leadership from daily firefighting to a system of standards managed visually, this collection of individuals will simply not have the time to complete the required amount of work. Completing this work off the side of your desk is one of the bigger failure modes of transformation. Additionally, as was stated above, the work requires skilled facilitation. It will take a few years of skill building and practice for this group to be able to work on improvement independently. Now that we understand how many full-time resources we need and what they will be doing, let us review what type of training is needed to get through the preparing to transform phase.

Over time, this group of experts will need to become skilled at both the science of improvement and the management skills needed to be successful, but in the preparation phase we are mostly interested in improvement skill building. The visual management expertise, the management skills required for change, and the sustaining skills will be built in the acceleration phase. We do not want to wait too long to start developing these additional skills, but they are not necessary to get started.

In the start-up phase, we simply desire for your organization's internal experts to become skilled in the application of the scientific method. This starts with a thorough understanding of A3 thinking and completing the A3 form. To use A3 thinking effectively, an understanding of some improvement tools is necessary. At a minimum, I suggest the following training for your internal experts.

1. A3 thinking and completing the A3 form.
2. Understanding the operational seven wastes and the waste of unevenness and overburden to be able to effectively see waste.
3. Understanding the five principles of lean improvement to effectively eliminate waste.
4. A working knowledge of the common tools to see and eliminate waste. There are nine of these tools.
   a. Takt time
   b. Direct observation
   c. The loading diagram
   d. The spaghetti map
   e. The communication circle
   f. Process mapping
   g. Value-added and non-value-added analysis
   h. Standard work
   i. Process control
5. How to prepare for and run a value stream analysis.
6. How to prepare for, run, and sustain a standard work kaizen event.
7. Basic facilitation skills.

The skills utilized by the internal experts will be constantly growing and evolving. This initial training will get everyone on the same page and establish a common language for everyone to use. I would encourage as many executives and leaders as possible to also participate in this initial training. Over time, every executive will be expected to become skilled in the topics listed above.

Develop and Deploy a Communication Campaign

The final step needed to get through the preparation phase is to develop and launch your communication campaign. One of the important pieces of change management is to communicate to the entire organization the reason why change is necessary. And not just change, but transformational change. Communication campaigns help organizations communicate goals, and the underlying importance of achieving those goals. As a lean thinking organization, we can communicate the why in terms of the benefits to the patient and their caregivers, the staff and clinical staff, and the organization.

Besides communicating the "why do we need to change" message, we also need to communicate the "how are we going to change" message. Having everyone understand the burning platform for change is an essential step in energizing the team toward change. Defining your burning platform for change answers the "why change" question. In healthcare, the burning platform should not be difficult to develop and communicate; there are several factors coming together that are creating a perfect storm for healthcare transformation. These include an aging population that creates additional demand on our systems, rapidly advancing technologies and therapeutics, an aging workforce leading to staff and physician shortfalls, lower revenues coming into our healthcare systems, and several chronic quality problems leading to patient harm. Each organization needs to create its own burning platform, but making the business case for change needs to be made early and often. The staff and medical staff need to be clear on the reason for change and the immediacy of this need. Without a sense of urgency, your transformational efforts will never get off the ground.

The second big question that needs to be communicated is how the organization is going to change. The communication here needs to cover several key topics. First, you will want to answer why lean was chosen as the preferred approach to change. There are several improvement approaches in practice today; why specifically was lean chosen in your organization? Next, you will want to answer what parts of the organization will be affected and when. Answering this question will depend on your pace of change. Are you beginning organizational-wide or are you only starting in a few value streams? How were the value streams chosen? Why were other value streams not selected? When will change begin to affect the areas selected? What about the other parts of the organization?

Next, in answering the "how" question, you will want to cover who specifically will be affected by the upcoming change (which programs, which functions, which teams, which physicians, which support groups, etc.). For each of these team members, you will need to answer the "What's in it for me" question (WIIFM). To create lasting change, you will need to discuss how all three stakeholder groups are affected as shown in Figure 3.2.

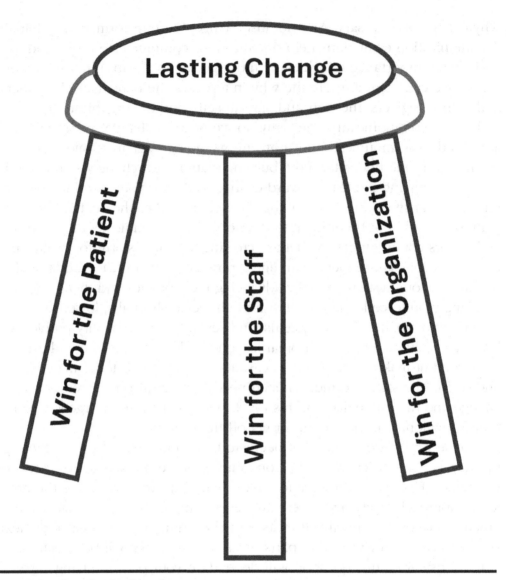

Figure 3.2 Creating lasting change.

Each stakeholder groupcan impact the change process favorably and unfavorably, so in your communications, you will want to ensure that you have covered the WIIFM for each of the three groups.

While answering the "how" question, you will also need to cover what will happen for those staff, medical staff, and management that do not wish to be part of the change. There will be a portion of the organization that does not wish to participate and having an answer for how the organization will deal with this group needs to be answered before beginning. I recommend that you have a plan for those that step forward upfront (and provide this group a soft landing) and have a separate plan for those that do not step forward upfront (and provide this group a less soft landing).

At a later time, you will expand on your communication strategy. You will want to highlight team results and the benefits of those changes to the patients, the staff and medical staff, and the organization. At this point, I do not recommend speaking about anticipated results; hold off on the success stories and over-selling the change initiative until you have some tangible results. Holding off on the pre-sell is very difficult for most organizations. The saying goes, "do not over sell and under deliver, but rather under sell and over deliver." The why and the "how" should be sufficient in the preparation phase of your transformation.

You will also need to decide on your communication forum(s). I encourage you to use any and all vehicles to communicate and to continue with this approach as results begin to be realized. The forums used by many healthcare organizations include:

- Face to Face – Town hall meetings
- Department level staff meetings, program level staff meetings, and physician meetings
- Newsletters or e-Newsletters
- Bulletin boards, posters, information posted on elevators
- Social media

I recommend you use as many forums as you can afford and keep current. Please do not underestimate the importance of the launch communication, as it is one of the reasons why some organizations fail to transform.

Your communication campaign begins with a communication strategy answering the questions of why change is needed now, how the change will be realized, who will be affected, when the process will begin, and what the options are for those who chose not to participate. The strategy is deployed when the messaging is delivered to the organization through a wide array of forums.

Having now completed the key tasks of selecting your top-level change agent, getting informed on lean and lean transformation, getting help from a qualified sensei, establishing governance through the creation of a steering committee, training your internal experts, and developing and deploying your communication strategy you should find yourself well prepared to launch and then accelerate your lean transformation.

Chapter Summary: Key Points from Chapter 3

- An enterprise-wide lean transformation will take one to two decades; transformation is not a two-to-three-year project.
- There are three phases to the transformation journey:
    1. The *get ready* phase establishes the knowledge, infrastructure, and change management necessary to get off on the right foot.
    2. The *accelerate* phase begins improvement in a part of your organization and strategically spreads improvement across the organization by simultaneously building capacity and generating results.
    3. The *sustain* phase makes change part of the new culture by institutionalizing the systems and processes to allow change to continue forever.
- There are six key steps in the get ready phase to prepare your organization for change in performance and culture.
    1. Find a senior level change agent
    2. Get knowledge in lean and lean transformation
    3. Get help through an experienced sensei
    4. Create the governance structure for change by establishing a lean steering committee
    5. Train your internal experts in the fundamental tools and concepts of lean improvement
    6. Develop and deploy an effective communication campaign to let everyone know why change is needed now and who is affected
- Completing the six steps of the *get ready* phase will have your organization well-positioned to deliver meaningful change in both performance and culture, hallmarks of a lean transformation.

Note

1. James Womack and Dan Jones, *Lean Thinking* (New York NY: Free Press, 1996), pg. 249.

Chapter 4

The Transformation Roadmap – Phase 2: The Acceleration Phase (Improve, Sustain, and Spread)

Delivering on Your Preparation Efforts

At this point, your organization has covered a lot of territory. You have spent several months getting ready to transform your organization. A change agent has been identified; a respected individual with an inclination toward change, the ability to challenge the status quo, and the charisma to lead a room and communicate effectively to the organization. Knowledge has been sought on lean improvement and what is involved with an enterprise-wide transformation by you and the senior leadership team. You have found an experienced sensei; someone who has traveled the road you are now on. A governance process to manage the pace of change has been established through your lean steering committee and this team will ensure barriers to change are dealt with quickly. Your internal experts have been trained in lean thinking with a base understanding of A3 thinking, the seven wastes, the five improvement principles, and a working knowledge of the lean techniques of value stream mapping and analysis and kaizen improvement. You have launched your communication campaign to let everyone know why change is needed and who is affected.

DOI: 10.4324/9781003532132-4

The time has come to deliver on these efforts. Your organization now needs to show some double-digit gains in an area of high visibility to establish some momentum. Nothing gets people more excited than tangible results; you will want to get some early wins to quiet the skeptics. Early wins will not shoo the skeptics away, but it will keep them quiet long enough to give the transformation some wiggle room.

This improvement will come from the repeated application of A3 thinking within the value streams that you identified during strategy deployment. For each area that has been selected, a value stream mapping and analysis activity will be held. Recall from Chapter 2, that the deliverables from the value stream mapping and analysis include a future state vision and a detailed, monthly action plan for improvement. The action plan will include quick wins, kaizen events, and projects that will be completed along a timeline using the scientific method guided and documented using A3 thinking and the A3 form.

Direct linkage should occur between the improve project measurable outcomes, the value stream key measures, and the true north measures of the organization. This ensures no activity occurs that is not directly aligned to your strategy. If you cannot directly see the correlation between the project outcomes and the true north measures, change the outcome measures or move on to a different project within the value stream plans. Time is too valuable to waste on activities that do not deliver breakthrough improvement and strategic change.

Once you have made the change and have realized some positive, measurable results, the focus of the management will need to quickly shift from making change to sustaining change. This shift happens by shifting the focus of management results to process *and* results; this shift will not be intuitive, and it will not be easy. Most organizations happy with the improvement want more improvement in other areas and forget about sustaining and hard-wiring the changes to ensure the results stick. You have likely heard the saying it is easy to start a project, it is harder to close one. Seeing initial results is a fantastic start! And we want to celebrate those successes. But your organizational culture will begin to dig in and fight back to keep things the way they are.

A thorough understanding of the principles of visual management and standard work is necessary in this making the transition to sustained improvement. But be warned, this is not Management 101. It will take courage, persistence, and tenaciousness at all levels of management to make this transition.

When a good understanding of sustaining improvement is developed, then your organization can discuss spreading the improvements to other parts of the organization. When I discuss spread, I am referring to spreading the thinking, not spreading a solution or an artifact. Spreading solutions or spreading artifacts is one of the most common mistakes organizations make. The desire to spread allows management to feel that rapid progress is underway. In a culture change, we want to change the way people think, act, and behave. This shift is not helped dramatically by spreading solutions and artifacts. Spreading solutions creates the illusion of progress without changing the thinking of the organization.

The keys to success in accelerating your transformation involve several key tasks, including:

1. Ensure you have selected the right value streams on which to focus. This creates the linkage from strategy to execution.
2. Establish value stream governance and set up your value stream performance system. This task provides a framework to prioritize, plan, govern, and adjust your improvement work.
3. Utilize A3 thinking to realize improvement. This task utilizes the core of lean thinking to be sure we see and eliminate wasted time and activity.
4. Sustain the improvements and manage visually. This task is the hardest and most valuable. It assures you your improvements will last and that you see the organizational benefits in both performance and culture. It also will deliver incremental improvement into perpetuity.
5. Capture the savings and celebrate successes. This step is critical to ensure you have a return on investment from your efforts and funds the additional improvement work in the future.
6. Support your change with ongoing training and coaching.
7. Spread lean thinking across the organization. This step involves taking your improvement approaches and migrating them to other departments and approaches.

Most organizations underestimate the effort it takes to make and sustain meaningful change. The result of underestimating is that the organization will be in too many value streams initially, launch too many A3 improvements, and attempt to spread solutions across the organization far earlier than the results warrant. At the end of the day, without sustaining change, there is no improvement. After a period of time, the leadership team will pull back and slow down the pace of change. To avoid this pull back, consider starting in only 1 or 2 key value streams. Once your organization understands the discipline, effort, and activity necessary to support world-class rate of improvement, you can move on to other value streams. This leads to the first key task, ensuring you have selected the right value stream(s) on which to focus your improvements.

Ensure You Have Selected the Right Value Streams on Which to Focus

Not every organization leads with strategy deployment. If your organization is committed to lean quality improvement to deliver enterprise transformation leading to world-class rates of improvement in performance and culture, then I would recommend you launch your initiative with strategy deployment. However, not every organization is ready to bet the farm on lean as their approach to greatness. Many organizations want to dip their big toe in the lean waters and ensure the water is not too cold; this is understandable. And if this is where your organization currently sits, then a different approach to selecting the key value streams can be taken. Simply follow the first three steps in strategy deployment to identify the key value stream(s) within your organization. Begin by establishing the organizational vision and developing the 3–5-year breakthrough objectives. Next, develop the annual breakthrough objectives and the top-level improvement priorities. From the top-level improvement priorities, you can select the 1 to 2 value streams that best leverage meeting your breakthrough objectives.

Let us assume that one of the top-level improvement priorities is to significantly improve the patient experience as measured by patient satisfaction scores. In trying to improve the patient experience, we should go to an area of the organization where the patient satisfaction scores are low. Patient satisfaction would fall under the true north dimension of service quality. If we are trying to increase the true north dimension of delivery, or access to services, we should focus on the areas with the longest wait times. One of the ways to analyze your organization is to use a histogram with data prioritized from highest to lowest (more commonly known as a Pareto diagram) to help make sense of your comparison data. An example of a Pareto diagram is shown in Figure 4.1. In this case, we are sorting staff and medical staff satisfaction by program.

As you review this data, keep a few points in mind. The definition of a value stream is all of the activities, both good and bad, that make up the way we deliver value to a customer. A value stream is not a department, a

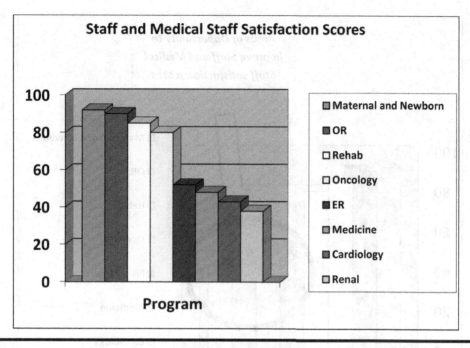

Figure 4.1   Pareto analysis of staff and medcial staff satisfaction by program.

program, or a unit. Analyzing our data by individual program makes sense because it is easy to understand geography, resource requirements, and budgets. In application, when we map a value stream, we see that the customer's experience actually crosses over several departments. For example, one patient's trip to the emergency department can impact the emergency department staff, patient registration, laboratory, pharmacy, diagnostic imaging, and environmental services in a single visit. I want to re-emphasize that a department or program is *not* a value stream.

Secondly, as we return to our discussion of identifying the key value streams, we ask how this data can be interpreted. In terms of improvement potential, clearly the leverage lies within the four areas circled in Figure 4.2.

With good data and an objective eye, identifying the first couple of value streams is not too difficult. There are a few other considerations when selecting the place to begin your lean improvement. First, make sure that you have solid leadership in place for both the staff and the medical staff. Any weaknesses in management or medical management will be glaringly obvious when improvement begins. This weakness will be enough to derail your entire improvement effort. And this is not a good thing to happen if we are running a pilot. Solid management also implies that the

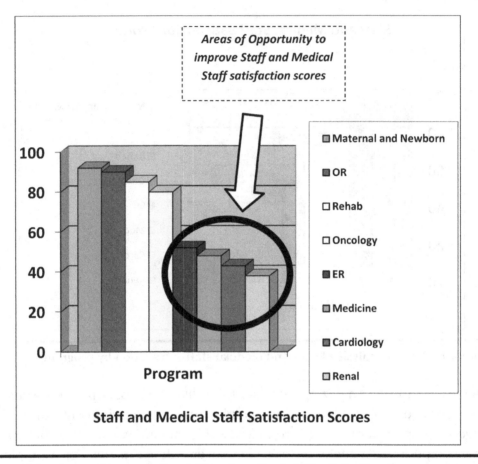

Figure 4.2 Areas of leverage for staff and medical staff satisfaction by program.

key management positions are filled. I would not recommend beginning in an area with a vacant management position or a leadership position that is retiring, being promoted, transferring jobs, etc. You will also want to verify that no major disruptive organizational changes are scheduled in the near term. These disruptive changes can include launching a new IT change, a major facility redevelopment, or a location move. If these activities are far enough out, you can influence them significantly with lean thinking and build the planning and improvement work into the value stream analysis. If the planning is 80% complete and the work cannot be influenced by lean thinking, then hold off the launch until these activities have been completed. Assuming that the leadership positions of staff and medical staff are filled with strong leaders, and the disruptive technology will not be a factor in the near term, you can map your value stream and begin delivering improvement.

Establish Value Stream Governance and Set Up Your Value Stream Performance System

Having selected your initial one to two value streams, you will need a process to manage and govern the changes at the value stream level. Recall that in the get ready phase, we established a lean enterprise steering committee. A similar committee will need to be established at the value stream level, but with a different focus. The value stream steering committee will focus on the value stream performance and deal with all the local issues that need to be addressed to enable change in both performance and culture. The value stream steering committee has a smaller make-up than the corporate steering committee. Typically, the value stream steering committee will have co-leaders, an administrative leader, and a physician leader. The value stream administrative leader is frequently a director level person, and the physician champion is typically the medical director or the program chief. The value stream steering committee will also have the process owners (department managers) as members and the internal lean expert. The executive champion, typically a vice president or c-suite member, who presides over the value stream is encouraged to attend but is not a required member of the value stream steering committee. This committee will meet weekly and will manage the pace of the change which consists of the improvement plans from the value stream analysis, manage the follow-up plans and results from both the improvement A3's and the value stream A3, resolve any sustainability issues, ensure standard work is being followed at the staff and medical staff level, and manage the visual management systems of both process and results. Additionally, the value stream steering committee is responsible for dealing with all the elements of change management for the staff and medical staff. Keep in mind a value stream is not a department, it is a collection of processes that deliver value to a patient/customer. This group will also need to pull in other department leaders as necessary to ensure results and change is happening in those areas as well. Depending on where the organization is on their improvement action plan, different department leaders will be added and subtracted to the steering committee as needed. The list of responsibilities for the value stream steering committee is long and important in achieving transformational success.

It is asked if the team can meet less frequently than weekly. I do not encourage that for a couple of reasons. First, the amount of change that will occur through "kaizen" is massive. Not having a process to manage the changes, deal with issues that arise, handle any accountability issues, etc. will impede progress on your efforts. Secondly, the value stream action plan is based on a monthly rhythm of improvement. Being late on critical preparation and sustaining activities, completing action items on time, and escalating or helping early when issues arise will keep your improvement plans on track. We have seen in practice that weekly meetings help ensure deadlines are not missed.

One final thought on value stream steering. Most organizations already have a weekly program meeting, quality council meeting, etc. My recommendation is you use or re-purpose this time to cover the value stream issues in addition to the normal book of business. In this way you do not add another meeting to busy leader's calendars. One caution though, you will not be able to get through all the items on the weekly agenda with any quality in 15 minutes. This meeting generally runs between 30 minutes and an hour depending on the issues that arise. I find that many organizations do not allocate enough time for either the enterprise steering committee meeting or the value stream steering committee (Table 4.1).

The value stream steering committee meeting should be held in front of the value stream performance wall. *"Using the wall"* is a term for managing the value stream performance system. This system uses all of our wisdom from visual management to make improvement a living and breathing tool for the chosen value stream. Figure 4.3 shows an example of the value stream performance system. For the meeting to be effective and to meet the agenda timelines, it is vital that the information in the performance system be kept current. That responsibility generally falls on the lean internal expert supporting the value stream with support from the value stream leaders.

Table 4.1   Value Stream Steering Committee Meeting Agenda

Activity	Lead	Length
Review value stream True north measures	Administrative and physician Leaders	5 minutes
Review open A3's • measures • follow-up plans • issues to be resolved	Process owners	10 minutes each (30 minutes total)
Review preparation for next A3	Internal lean expert	15 minutes
Other business	All	10 minutes
	Total time	60 minutes

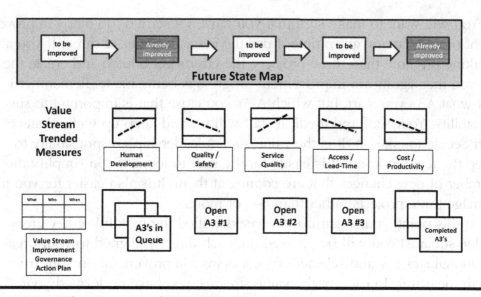

Figure 4.3   Value stream performance system.

The system contains the following elements: the future state value stream map, the value stream true north measures, the rapid improvement plan, and the status of open A3's. As a result, the entire status of value stream performance is known at a glance. The future state map highlights what areas have been improved and which ones have not. The value stream true north measures are trended so we can see the planned performance and the actual performance. The rapid improvement plan shows completed activities as well as the upcoming activities and the timing of those activities. The open A3's show the three latest improvement efforts and detail the status of those efforts using the eight steps of the scientific method. Since the COVID response in the early 2020s, some organizations have moved away from a "wall" and paper charts and moved to an electronic value stream performance center. There are advantages to doing this. The information is easier to update electronically, and forms do not need to be printed and placed on a wall. Should you choose to go this route, I would still advise you to have a face-to-meeting when you run through the standard agenda. Eighty percent of communication is non-verbal and body language plays a keep part in assessing buy-in and acceptance of change. The disadvantages include lost time scrolling between charts and not being able to see the entire performance of the value stream at a glance.

You will want to make sure that you have not started too many improvement projects at any given time; I use the magic number of three. If you are working on more than three projects, the efforts get diluted and create the illusion that significant improvement progress is being made. Remember it is not what A3's you start, but which A-3's you close that is important to sustainability. Your staff and medical staff will try and keep up with whatever you decide to take on. It is the value stream leadership's responsibility to keep the team focused. It is easier for the staff to focus if you simplify the number of new changes that are coming at them. It is also easier for you to manage three projects rather than 5–7 or more.

At this point, your organization has identified the handful of key areas (value streams) you will be focused on, each directly aligned to your organizational strategy and selected to best deliver improvement on your true north measures. In each of the value streams, you have performed your value stream mapping and analysis and created a rapid improvement plan. Each value stream has established a governance structure and created the value stream performance system to visually manage the improvements by tracking the value stream measures, detailing the improvement plan, and showing the open A3's where the lean principles of flow, pull defect free, visual management, and kaizen are being utilized. From here you will want to follow the scientific method and A3 thinking to continue to execute your improvement plans.

Utilize A3 Thinking to Realize Improvement

As we discussed in Chapter 2, the third step in the accelerate phase is to ensure all of the improvement projects continue to follow A3 thinking. Lean organizations use A3 thinking to create a community of scientists, focused on conducting small experiments in the spirit of improvement. Why would I mention A3 thinking again as part of the accelerate phase? When your organization deploys your improvement strategy, you will likely uncover several different approaches to improvement with your organization. Parts of the organization might be using the Plan-Do-Study-Act (PDSA) improvement science, others may be using project management approaches, IT might be using Agile, and yet another area may be using the Define-Measure-Analyze-Improve and Control (DMAIC) process which is cornerstone to the six-sigma methodology. If you believe that lean improvement is a toolkit, then continuing the use of multiple sciences makes sense. And I am confident saying if you view lean as a toolkit, then you are not interested in transforming your organization. If you believe that lean is a comprehensive transformational management system engaging all staff and medical staff in continuous process improvement based on the themes of continuous elimination of waste and respect for all people, then you will quickly want to settle on a single science.

The greatest lean organizations utilize A3 thinking documented on the A3 form. It takes a lifetime to learn one science, let alone four or five. Additionally, as we expect for staff and medical staff, we want to follow standard work for improvement. Standard work implies that you identify and select the known best way to accomplish the task. If the task is improvement, recognize that the greatest lean organizations all use A3 thinking as their standard.

A3 thinking has an additional benefit beyond creating a standard for improvement. Following the steps in the A3 *prevents* improvement teams from jumping to a solution. The non-lean approach to problem-solving follows the following steps:

1. Discuss the opportunity/problem with data, and sometimes without data.
2. Identify solutions based on experience or personal preference.
3. Implement solutions which may include adding resources, changing the electronic health record, or some type of capital investment.
4. Repeat steps 1–3 when the problem returns.

A lean organization will follow the steps in the A3, where problem-solving approach would look more like the following:

1. Identify the reason for action
2. Define the problem statement by capturing the current conditions
3. Define the target conditions using data
4. Quantify the gap between current conditions and the target state by understanding the waste and the root cause of the waste causing the problem
5. Generate solutions based on this information

Following A3 thinking would then lead to countermeasures and action plans to test the solutions to see if these solutions do indeed close the gap between current and target. A non-lean thinking organization goes directly from step 1 to step 5. A lean organization gets to the root cause of a problem *before* generating solutions. A3 thinking supplies a constant reminder not to go from step 1 to step 5 without completing steps two, three, and four. As the organization gets more comfortable with A3 thinking, the quality of the improvement projects will increase. Creating the improvement standard for your organization will shorten the learning curve for everyone. Through the hard work of the teams, guided by A3 thinking, your organization will now be delivering improvement to portions of the value stream. The key activity now is to sustain the improvements.

Sustain the Improvements and Manage Visually

Step 4 in the acceleration phase is to sustain the improvements and manage the process and results visually. It is generally accepted by lean practitioners that this step is the hardest in creating a culture of improvement. I tell organizations that all of the items we have discussed thus far; the strategy deployment process of improvement, selection of key value streams, establishing governance, and delivering improvement through A3 thinking, the communication campaign, etc. constitute 20% of the work; 80% of the work comes in sustaining the improvements. In order to manage visually, visual controls need to be established. At a minimum, visual controls are needed for both process and results, which is a shift in traditional thinking. Recall that visual management requires the ability to *see* normal from abnormal conditions at a glance so that problems can be resolved in real time.

Every organization has some type of performance measurement system. This system of ratios, graphs, performance statistics, budgets, and scorecards is used to evaluate the effectiveness of the organization over a prior period of performance. The flaws in this type of reporting are twofold. First, the data is typically retrospective. Frequently, the data is usually 30 days old, the result of the prior month's efforts. This is magnified even more if clinical charting is not timely, and notes are closed out long past dates of service. Even worse, sometimes data, such as patient satisfaction survey results, lags a full fiscal quarter. It is difficult indeed to make adjustments to systems and processes based on data that is 30 to 90 days old. The second flaw is that the data is not very transparent. Typically, the reports are generated in an electronic spreadsheet or on rarer occasions, on a series of hard copy reports. While useful to the manager or leader who has access to the information, the data is invisible to the staff and medical staff. In creating a culture of improvement, measurement is used to motivate and make staff knowledge-able. This only happens if we give the staff access to the information.

To make information useful and to use it effectively, it should be provided in a timely manner. This enables decisions to be made in a window that allows for a change in performance within today's time horizon. It is not motivating to make a change that requires 30 days to see if any change for the better (or worse) was made. What does timely mean? For results, world-class organizations provide meaningful data on a daily basis. For process, world-class organizations provide data on a patient-by-patient or hour-by-hour basis. The best data shows the expected and the actual results. In this way we can repeatedly see gaps in performance which can be acted upon.

Results do not merely happen, they are produced. Each process has a recipe or a formula that is followed to produce the results it achieves. So, if you want to change the results, you need to change the process. A lean organization pays attention to both processes and results. This is a significant shift in managerial culture over a traditional organization that waits for electronic reports to be generated showing how the department, program, and/or organization is performing. In contrast, a lean organization goes hunting for data. Within the workplace, process data is generated constantly. The process data is monitored frequently to ensure the "recipe" is being followed. If there is a deviation in the process, then necessary interventions are taken to get the process back on track.

5S: A Beginning Place for Visual Management

Visual management of process has several different forms. In the physical workplace, visual management is guided by the principles of 5S. 5S is a management system for creating a high-performing workplace. Table 4.2 illustrates the five principles of a 5S system.

Beginning improvement with a 5S system can be valuable in several ways. First, 5S improves productivity and safety by ensuring that everything has a place, and everything is in its place. As an example, one of the cornerstones of a great code blue system is a fully stocked, consistently organized cart to deal with code blue emergencies. Staff and medical staff do not waste valuable time running around looking for supplies and medicines during a code blue. This would create a great loss in effectiveness and negatively impact the ability to provide safe, emergency, time critical care. Seconds matter in these circumstances. In most organizations, the code carts are identical floor to

Table 4.2 5S Definitions

Japanese Word	Principle	Very Loose English Translation
Seiri	Remove un-needed and unnecessary items from the workplace	Sort
Seiton	Organize the remaining items in a way that promotes standard workflow and enables standardized work	Set in Order
Seiso	Return the workplace to like new conditions	Shine/Scrub
Seiketsu	Create standardized consistent work practices	Standardize
Shitsuke	Personal discipline to maintain the previous 4S's	Sustain

floor and unit to unit. Why not provide this level of service and performance with all of your supplies and equipment? This is what 5S seeks to create. A high-performing work area where time is not lost hunting and gathering supplies, material, and equipment. Additionally, the supplies, materials, and equipment can be organized in a manner that promotes standard work. This organization can help make sure that the proper process is followed by organizing the items in a manner that encourages following the "recipe."

Let us review a real-life example within a primary care clinic. Most physicians agree it is a good idea to track basic vital signs and capture weight and height of patients each visit. Surprisingly, compliance with this data collection is not as high as you might think. Specific to capturing the patient weight, in one clinic, I will call them clinic Z, the compliance rate was only running 60% in adults. A team from clinic Z decided to figure out why the capture rate was so low. After auditing nearly one hundred charts without the weight recorded, the data for the reasons in which staff failed to capture weights broke down into the following:

- **Fifty-five percent – patient refused to get on scale**
- **Thirty percent – medical assistant forgot to capture the weight**
- **Fifteen percent – other**

After some problem-solving, the root cause for patients refusing to get on the scale came as a result of the scale being located in the exam room hallway, in potential plain sight of other patients and staff. Said differently, the patients were embarrassed to have their weight displayed near the public eye. The countermeasure was simply to put a scale in each exam away from the public eye. The second problem was the medical assistant forgot to capture the patient's weight. By locating the scale in the exam room, it became pretty difficult to forget to capture the weight of each patient. Moving the scale to an area that promotes standard work meets the spirit of the second S, set in order. This simple change increased the compliance of capturing patient weights to nearly 100%.

The pictures below follow some improvements made in a dermatology clinic using 5S principles. A quick audit of the area quickly showed that the primary drawer in each of the exam rooms was stocked differently, or not at all as shown in Figure 4.4. This leads to wasted time hunting and searching for supplies.

Following the sorting of unneeded and over-supply of items, the drawer was then standardized to optimize not only the inventory levels but also the standard work of the clinical staff. This led to improved performance of the clinic, better use of cash, and improved staff satisfaction. The before and after picture of this work is shown in Figure 4.5.

The final and most important benefit of 5S is that it instills discipline in the staff. While it seems relatively simple to put things back when you are finished with them and clean up the workspaces, especially the common workspaces, these activities are difficult to sustain over the long haul. Common workspaces are the most difficult to maintain because since everyone has the responsibility to keep the area clean and organized, no one has

Same Drawer, Different Room

Figure 4.4   Primary drawer variation in clinic room.

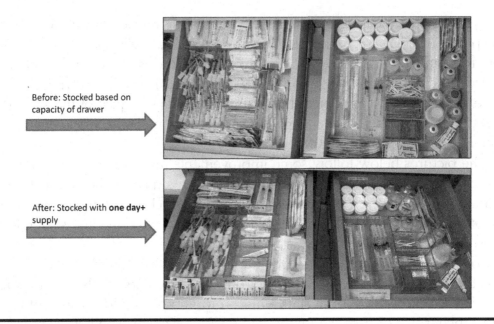

Before: Stocked based on capacity of drawer

After: Stocked with **one day+** supply

Figure 4.5   Before and after 5S.

the responsibility to keep the area clean and organized. Maintaining a neat and organized workspace is a fundamental building block for what is to come later, namely following standard work. I was taught very early in my personal (industrial-based) lean journey that if a staff associate cannot put a broom back when they are finished with it, our organization would have no chance of consistently following standard work on a complex, multi-step process. For reference, aren't many procedures and tasks in the healthcare environment complex, multi-step processes? Taking a short cut in how to maintain the discipline of the work environment leads to taking shortcuts in essential tasks required to produce high-quality work in a cost-effective manner.

So, let us translate this thinking to the healthcare realm. If a staff member cannot put an IV pump back to where it goes when finished, or return the vital sign machine to its home space when vitals are recorded, what chance do you think there is that the staff will follow a complex, clinical pathway? A pathway is healthcare's standard work for the delivery of care. Compliance with pathways in the best organizations is difficult to achieve, let alone in an organization that lacks discipline. 5S builds the discipline that is essential for what comes next, *standard work.*

Tying 5S back to step 4 in the acceleration phase, 5S allows an organization to manage visually. The system visually differentiates normal from abnormal conditions related to the location of material, supplies, and equipment and allows problems (missing or excess material, supplies, and equipment) to be spotted at a glance. The abnormal condition can be corrected immediately. 5S is visual management of process; it highlights workplace conditions necessary to operate an effective work environment. We need a high-performing work area to assess, diagnose, and treat patients with less waste.

Using Visual Management for Process Control

Another example of visual management of process is the process control board. Process control aims to manage process, which leads to the correct outcomes and results. Results capture can be automated and analyzed after the fact. But the process *must* be managed in real time. Process control allows for the entire team to manage the process on an hour-by-hour or patient-by-patient basis. An example of an hour-by-hour process control board is shown in Figure 4.6.

To qualify as an hour-by-hour process control board, several conditions must be satisfied. The output of a process is based on takt time. First, we need to understand takt time. The process control board documents the completed units (in this specific case, patients are the output), but the units per hour are based on the takt time. If we need to "process" three patients per hour, then what is the takt time? In this example the takt time is calculated as 60 minutes divided by three patients, or 20 minutes. The plan column is always the units per hour to be completed based on takt time. The actual column records the true number of patients completed within that hour. The takt time can change on an hour-by-hour basis, based on patient demand. The plan should change accordingly, to reflect the change in takt time.

A process control board requires real-time capturing of actual output. The actual column should be completed by the people who do the work each hour, based on the actual output. We are trying to see the difference between normal and abnormal. By capturing the plan versus the actual output, we can see abnormal at a glance. Seeing abnormal is important because it makes the waste visible; once the waste is visible, we can intervene and get the work back on plan. It is important to note that seeing the waste is only valuable if someone does something about it.

The next item required on a process control board is the capture of the sources of variation. Each time we have a deviation from standard, good or bad, we want to capture the source of the variation. These sources of variation are critical in performing future improvement, and they must be

CTProcess Control Board			Date: November 3, 2024
Hour	Plan	Actual	Comments
0700-0800	3	3	no issues
0800-0900	3	2	contrast not given prior to arrival
0900-1000	3	3	no issues
1000-1100	3	2	no patient to scan
1100-1200	3		
1200-1300	3		
1300-1400	3		
1400-1500	3		
1500-1600	3		
1600-1700	3		
1700-1800	3		

Figure 4.6 Process control board for CT.

captured at the time they occur, by the people who do the work. We can create a histogram of sources of variation, which is useful since the leading causes of variation are typically candidates for future problems.

Let us review a common scenario. We were supposed to complete primary care visits for 24 patients yesterday. At the end of the day, we worked an hour of overtime and only completed 19 exams. So, we missed the standard ending time by an hour, and we missed the target of seeing 24 patients by 5 patients – or nearly 20%. Can anyone explain what happened yesterday to lead to these results? If we are lucky and the same staff happens to be scheduled, we might capture part of the data. But more likely, we will just absorb the variance and vow to try better today. Using a process control board, we can determine hour by hour what is happening. Maybe we can do something to prevent the hour of overtime if, by noon, we already know we are three patients behind. We definitely can capture the sources of variation to deliver valuable data in future problem-solving. The key principle to visual management is to see normal and abnormal (also known as expected versus actual) at a glance so we can take immediate action.

Continuing with our primary care visit example, after a week of variance reporting, the staff generates the data shown in Figure 4.7:

Which problem should we tackle first? Clearly the largest source of variation is that the patients are not showing up for their appointment. This detail becomes a golden nugget that we can mine for further improvement.

Process control cannot be re-created after the fact, it must be managed in real time. Sources of variation must be captured in real time as well. And yes staff, including physicians, do have time to complete the process control board. Completing the process control board should not take more than five seconds, and we should be able to determine variance from standard in five seconds or less. If filling out the board takes longer, we know that its design is too complicated, or that it is not easy to understand visually.

The process control board data capture can sometimes be automated in an electronic health system, but I do not recommend you start with automation. In capturing the data, we aim to refresh adherence to standard work and to capture sources of variation, and these activities are difficult to automate. Also, your board and corresponding data are likely to change over time, so before you automate, take the time to become very clear about what you want. Lean experts have found that staff will happily complete the board if management pays attention to the process and does something

Frequency	Patient failed to show	Physician late to clinic	Clinic canceled visit	Patient was late	Patient got lost	Searching for supplies
	X					
	X					
	X					
	X					
	X					
	X					
	X			X		
	X			X		
	X			X		
	X	X		X	X	X
	X	X	X	X	X	X
	X	X	X	X	X	X

Figure 4.7 Variance histogram – primary care patient visits.

meaningful with the data. It is important to use the sources of variation (the data captured) for further improvement. Having staff generate data that is not used is not only wasteful but also disrespectful. And recall respect for all people is a fundamental tenant of a lean organization.

How does process control help sustain? First, the process control system makes all the data necessary to monitor the process on an hour-by-hour basis transparent. If we want staff and medical staff to help us in meeting our plan, the first step is to provide them with access to the information. In this case the information is the expected and the actual values of the measure defined by the organization. Secondly, sources of variation are captured in real-time so, if possible, an immediate intervention can be taken. If it is not possible to resolve the issue in real-time, the sources of variation can be summarized into a histogram so that the leading sources of variation can be addressed. Figure 4.8 takes the data from the frequency chart and presents the data in a Pareto chart format. Recall a Pareto chart is a histogram prioritized from high to low. Let us review some data from CT scan output. The chart shows the reasons why the planned number of CT scans were missed.

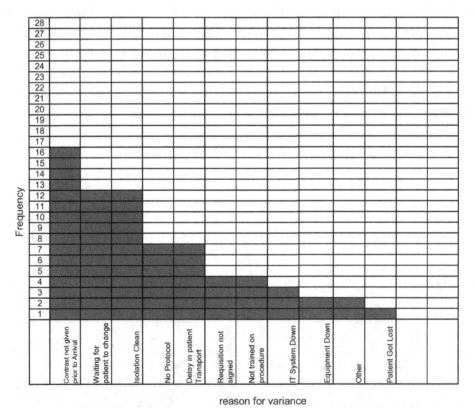

Figure 4.8   Pareto diagram.

The Pareto principle holds that 80% of the problems are caused by 20% of the issues. With this data, the CT team, staff, radiologists, and management, can now address the critical issues to improve safety, quality, access, and productivity. From this example, the key issues would be addressing timely giving of contrast, ensuring the patients are changed and ready for their exam, and improving the turnaround time for an isolation clean.

Process control can also be used to monitor a process on a patient-by-patient basis. This is helpful in the case of an in-patient visit because work progresses over days not hours. An example of a patient-by-patient process control board for an in-patient visit is shown below in Figure 4.9. In this specific case, the process is patient discharges to plan. For an admitted patient, the goal is to safely discharge the patient with the highest quality service, with a great and safe outcome, in the least amount of time and with the minimum necessary resources. That is a lot to ask of any process, let alone a process with a complex medical patient.

In this example, visual management is used to create total transparency of the discharge plan, where the expected date of discharge is shown and all the relevant information leading to this discharge. The expected discharge date is the plan. On the dry-erase board, or an electronic process control board, any barrier to discharge is identified and documented with the person responsible and the due date for barrier resolution for each patient. This way we can ensure nothing is missed and ensure that the inter-professional team can meet the plan. When the patient is discharged, the actual discharge date is captured so that the variance between the planned date and the actual date can be analyzed. These variances can be reported and captured on

Patient initials	Primary Diagnosis	Target Length of Stay(days)	Actual Length of Stay	Variance from Target	Comments
F.W.	COPD	5	5	0	no issues
E.S	CHF	5	6	+1	No one to D/C on weekend
B.O.	Pneumonia	4	5	+1	lost a day waiting on specialist consult

Figure 4.9   Patient by patient process control.

a frequency chart. The top reasons for missing the plan can be prioritized with a Pareto analysis and improved. Calculating conservable days, weeks, or months after the patient discharge is not helpful data, as it is not possible to reconstruct where the conservable day came from. Knowing in real-time what the barriers are and resolving them is necessary to effectively manage the process for success. I have seen organizations using this visual management system for discharge planning reduce the average length of stay for patients by as much as 30% and reduce conservable days by as much as 75%.

Some of the leading healthcare organizations are starting to use artificial intelligence to predict discharge dates. This is helpful in space and capacity planning but will only be helpful in improvement if the organization is also working on reducing lead-times for services (tests, consults, and interventions). You will still need to actively measure variances between the predictions and actual results to determine where your improvement efforts need to go next. Being accurate to prediction is not improvement. If the lead-time to purchase a new car from a dealer in the dealership is 4.5 hours plus or minus a minute is that a good thing? It certainly is a highly accurate prediction. What if I said the lead-time to buy a car is 2 hours plus or minus 30 minutes? Which experience would you rather have?

The management of process is one of the fundamental differences between a lean organization and a traditional organization. Managing the process is the key to getting fantastic results. In a lean organization, the entire staff is in tune with what is happening on a moment-by-moment basis. Slight changes to process are made repeatedly during the day to maintain flow. Changes are possible because the visual management system makes it obvious to everyone, at a glance, that something abnormal is occurring. Standard interventions are in place to deal with abnormalities until a permanent solution can be found. Done well, the process (recipe) should deliver the correct results.

Using Visual Management for Improving Results – Managing for Daily Improvement

Every organization is concerned with results. Results are how we measure success and frequently; compensation and promotions are based on the ability to deliver consistent, reliable performance. In a lean organization, results are the outcome of following good processes based on standard work and visual management. All managers get monthly reports, budget summaries, and statistics that try to make sense of the prior period's activities, but correlating cause and effect is quite frequently difficult. We strive to follow our standard work, which is based on our best-known way of doing something. Standard work is our recipe, which when followed is the easiest, safest, fastest, and best way to do our work. We measure results to evaluate the effectiveness of our standard work. Our work is also visually managed so we can solve problems in real-time to be sure we are achieving our results.

Earlier in the book we discussed the value stream performance system. This performance system is visual management in action. From this system, everyone can see at a glance the key measures for the value stream with target and actual performance, the improvement plan, and the key improvement initiatives (A3's). Great lean organizations take the visual management of performance to the unit level, and since merely tracking performance is insufficient, the goal is to improve performance. A lean organization uses the measurement of performance to get better every day! That was not a typo. A lean leader will always leave the workplace in a better place than when the lean leader walked through the door that morning. Remember that when you walk through the door at work today. Our goal is not to firefight, maintain, and survive. Our goal is to improve, and great organizations improve every single day.

The system used to get better every day is known as *m*anaging for *d*aily *i*mprovement, or MDI. For reference, some organizations also refer to this system as the daily management system (DMS). The MDI system tracks the key measures of the department, identifies, and prioritizes variances from plan, and develops and implements plans for improvement. This work is done daily by the entire staff. While management has the responsibility for the MDI system, everyone is expected to contribute toward the daily improvements. Imagine, your organization for a moment. If you are a medium-sized healthcare organization, you might have two thousand staff. What could your organization look like if each of these staff members were engaged in improving your core processes on a daily basis? Would this daily engagement help change your culture? Two thousand staff marching toward a shared vision can make a significant amount of change in a short period of time. Now compound this daily change over 90 days, six months, a year, five years. I think everyone can envision the end-state.

MDI begins with a thorough understanding of the true north measures of the organization. These are the same true north measures, we discussed earlier, that were developed through strategy deployment. The true north measures are cascaded down to the value stream level, and next to the department level. An example of the cascading of measures is shown in Table 4.3.

It is important that the unit based, daily measures are aligned to the organizational true north measures. Our role as a leader is to establish the vision, allocate the resources to accomplish the vision, and inspire people to take action toward this vision. Be sure you have aligned the staff against a common goal. Managing for daily improvement establishes the local level vision, creates the infrastructure to accomplish the vision at the unit level, and inspires the staff to meet the vision. What a great system!

The tools used for MDI include a performance board, a daily huddle, and a project management system for managing the improvements. An example of the performance board is shown in Figure 4.10.

Each dimension of improvement has a set of four charts. The first chart in the column is the year-to-date performance updated monthly with targets and actual performance. The second chart is month-to-date performance, updated daily, with targets and actual performance. The third chart is the

Table 4.3 Cascading True North Measures

Dimension	Organizational True North Measure	Value Stream Measure	Unit Level Measure
Morale/human development	Implemented suggestions for the enterprise	Implemented suggestions for the program	Implemented suggestions for the unit
Quality/safety	Reduce falls by 50% across the enterprise	Reduce falls by 75% across the program	Reduce falls by 80% on the unit
Service quality	Compliments received for the enterprise	Compliments received for the program	Compliments received for the unit
Access	Reduce conservable days by 50% for the enterprise	Reduce conservable days by 50% for the program	Reduce conservable days by 75% for the unit
Cost	Reduce the staff hours per patient visit by 10% across the enterprise	Reduce the staff hours per visit by 20% across the program	Reduce the staff hours per visit by 20% across the unit

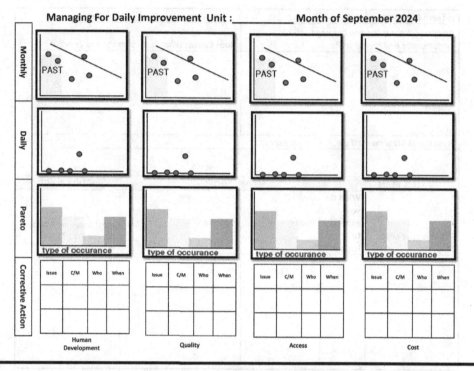

Figure 4.10 Managing for daily improvement performance board.

sources of variation between the month-to-date plan and actual performance, and the fourth chart is the improvement plan. Some organizations call the improvement plan the kaizen newspaper because it summarizes the kaizen (continuous improvement) activity needed to meet the daily target. Some organizations have a fifth form below the improvement plan. This form can be a Plan-Do-Study-Act Form (PDSA) or an A3 form. An example of a PDSA form is shown in Figure 4.11.

These forms, when used as part of MDI, are used to run experiments on our interventions or to do more formal improvement work using A3 thinking.

The board is located in a central hallway where the entire staff can easily see the content. I actually prefer that patients and families can see the data as well, as it encourages questions from your customers. For those of you concerned about the transparency of the data, what is so top secret that it needs to be hidden from the public? It is becoming more common for the MDI board to be electronic. I do not recommend this for a unit-based MDI huddle. The forms are designed to be rapidly completed using a pencil and I prefer the full-time transparency of the board. Obviously, if a host of staff is

Team Members:		Date:	

Problem: *What is the gap between actual performance and the target?*	**Root Cause:** *What is causing the gap to occur?*

Hypothesis Statement: *If we .... then we expect....*

PLAN			DO	STUDY & ACT
What is your next step?	What do you expect to happen?	Who?	By When?	What happened? What did you learn? What action will you take?

Figure 4.11 Plan-do-study-act (PDSA) card.

working remotely, like in the revenue cycle for example, then an electronic MDI board is necessary.

The data is updated *daily*. I prefer to have a staff member update the data, as they are able to engage in the process and it encourages them to understand the measurement system and the supporting data. The assignment for who updates the performance boards changes weekly. Once a shift, the *entire* staff huddles in front of the board for a 6–10-minute meeting. The meeting will be held to 6–10 minutes if the agenda is scripted. The typical agenda is as follows:

- Morale measurement results, variance, and action plans – 1 minute discussion
- Safety/quality measurement results, variance, and action plans – 1 minute discussion
- Service quality measurement results, variance, and action plans – 1 minute discussion

- Access measurement results, variance, and action plans – 1 minute discussion
- Cost/productivity measurement results and action plans – 1 minute discussion
- Unit level communication update – 1–5 minute discussion

After 15 seconds of daily review for each of the different measurement dimensions, ideas for improvement should be solicited and documented in the improvement plan. Results of improvement projects from earlier assignments should be briefly discussed as well as the idea that work should be incorporated into standard work and used by everyone. The improvements can be as simple as a suggestion that can be tested, to a more formal PSCA (plan-do-study-act) plan, all the way through a project documented on an A3. The key is to be continuously engaging staff in improvement around the key measures of the unit aligned to the true north measures. Total transparency gives everyone an opportunity to be informed and to participate. It is through engagement and participation that the culture is changed. The meeting can be held at shift hand-over to ensure consistency in messaging and communication. This may differ depending on if the unit is a 24 × 7 unit or a single shift unit.

The huddle process is designed to occur at three distinct levels within the organization. The first huddle occurs with the staff and the staff line leadership. Line leadership can be the charge nurse or a unit team leader along with the supervisor/manager. This huddle would take on the day-to-day challenges and generate local improvement through quick wins and small PDSA cycles of improvement. The second huddle would occur between the line leader/supervisor/manager and the administrative director, and medical leadership. This layer of the organization would take on problems that can be influenced at the value stream level. Solutions at this level may involve A3 thinking and potentially kaizen events which when generated can be spread to the entire program. The third level of huddles happens between the value stream leadership and the executive team. This layer of leadership resolves barriers between value streams or barriers that need to be addressed by corporate policy. The cascading huddles change the focus of the organization from monitoring results to managing for action and improvement. The cascading huddles occur best daily and should only take a few minutes. Resolving the open issues may take much longer than a day, but the key is trying to get better every single day!

Many organizations are embracing high reliability concepts to improve staff and patient safety. High Reliability Organizations (HROs) are entities that operate in complex and high-risk environments while consistently delivering impeccable results and avoiding accidents that would cause harm. These organizations prioritize safety, resilience, and error reduction as core values[1].

The five key principles that define high reliability organizations:

1. **Sensitivity to Operations**: HROs maintain constant awareness of the state of systems and processes that affect their operations. Leaders and staff actively monitor risks and take preventive measures to avoid failures.
2. **Reluctance to Simplify**: While simple processes are beneficial, HROs avoid overly simplistic explanations for why things work or fail. They recognize that work is inherently complex and can fail unexpectedly.
3. **Preoccupation with Failure**: HROs view near misses as opportunities for improvement rather than proof of success. Any deviation from expected results is addressed immediately and completely.
4. **Deference to Expertise**: HROs value insights from staff with pertinent safety knowledge over those with greater seniority. Expertise is respected, and decisions are informed by the best available information.
5. **Practicing Resilience**: HROs prioritize emergency training for unlikely but possible system failures. They build resilience to handle unexpected challenges effectively.

By embracing these principles, organizations can enhance their reliability, minimize risks, and consistently achieve outstanding results.

We are interested in high reliability organizations because they also use tiered huddles to anticipate and mitigate risk, and rapidly communicate daily safety concerns (actual or potential) to improve the delivery of safe care. If your organization uses HRO principles and practices, I strongly encourage you to combine your safety huddle with your managing for daily improvement huddle. In the spirit of lean, and eliminating wasted time and activity, it is possible to combine both agendas into a single meeting. Many organizations do this successfully today, and both the audiences who listen to the messages and the people involved with solving both operational and patient safety issues are the same. Adding the HRO requirements to the operational huddle only adds one to two minutes to the huddle so the time constraint is also not excessive.

Control Systems for Visual Management

Visual management is only effective with frequent audits of the visual tools. The 5S system needs to be audited to ensure that abnormal conditions are being identified and corrected. It also needs to be audited to ensure that new items that enter the workplace, or a change in existing supplies, material, and equipment, are addressed in a timely manner. 5S systems need to be updated when changes in process and workflow occur. The process control systems need to be religiously audited to make sure variances from the plan are identified and interventions are taken. Failure at this stage will result in waste creeping back into your systems and performance targets not being sustained. Similarly, the managing of daily improvement systems needs to be audited to ensure that opportunities are being captured and addressed. Actions need to be assigned to the staff and medical staff for resolution. Broader issues need to be escalated up the chain of command for action.

A great lean healthcare organization never accepts that things are always running as designed. Time and efforts at all levels are management are spent "satisfying their curiosity that things are running as designed." Is this auditing because we do not trust the staff to do the right thing? Far from it. The auditing is used intentionally to identify and fix the barriers that prevent the staff from delivering compelling value in the least waste way. The vigilance to focus on process is assisted by two techniques in a lean improvement system: leadership standard work and peer task audits. Leadership standard work is the technique used by great organizations to ensure the focus of management and leadership is placed on continuous process improvement. Standard work is the step-by-step recipe followed to ensure a good outcome in the right amount of time. Leadership standard work is the routine and structure followed by management to shift the focus from process to results.[2]

There are a few key features of leadership standard work. First, the structure and routine given to a manager is process dependent and not person dependent.[3] A new manager can quickly come up to speed in their new role since their work is scripted to create the right focus. Secondly, observing who will and will not follow leader standard work makes it obvious which managers are not willing to make the transition to the new culture.[4] Knowing this is important because the line management role is essential in successfully creating a culture of improvement. You will want to deal quickly with those people who are "not on the bus." Finally, leadership standard work allows poor and marginal managers to quickly improve performance. Masaaki Imai, in his book *Gemba Kaizen*, said that supervisors (supervisor in this context is another name for the line manager) do not know exactly their responsibilities.[5] In this excellent book on lean management, Imai further states, "This situation arises when management does not clearly explain how to manage in *gemba* and has not given a precise description of supervisors roles and accountability."[6] Leadership standard work makes the responsibilities and accountabilities of the manager clear.

Leadership Standard work is a recipe for where to spend time during the workday. Think of this like a daily schedule of important tasks associated with running the day-to-day AND working on improvement. With the availability of electronic calendars and smart phone alarms, creating this daily calendar seems pretty easy to accomplish. The concept is not difficult to understand but requires tremendous discipline to accomplish consistently. Time is budgeted each day and specific tasks are designed to accomplish two things: focus on the process and spend time on improvement. If we are honest, we must admit that most of our days are spent on firefighting. The schedule needs to be adjusted to accommodate situations such as a staff member calling off, a patient complaint that needs to be handled immediately, the budget getting out of whack, etc. Getting this type of work done might feel rewarding. Heck, look at all the stuff I got completed today! But it did not help the organization improve. You did not leave the workplace in better shape than you found it.

Key tasks in leadership standard work might include the following:

- Review the performance and process control boards and make interventions as necessary
- 5S audits
- Review the task card (kamishibai) audit results (this will be discussed next)
- Review A-3's in progress
- Review the suggestion system status for open projects
- Audit staff standard work
- Hold/attend the daily huddle at the performance board
- Take a Gemba Walk
- Audit safe work and patient safety standard work processes
- Work on improvement tasks
- Root cause a new problem
- Work on any open follow-up plans on your A3 improvement projects

Actually, the list can continue on for quite a while; the key is to spend dedicated time **daily** on improvement. If you do not budget your time to focus on improvement, the day-to-day firefighting will consume all of your time, treasures, and talents, and an opportunity will be lost.

How much time should be spent on improvement? After all, there are administrative tasks that need to be accomplished, important things like payroll, attendance management, scheduling, and budgeting. Table 4.4 lists the preferred time allocations to be governed by standard work by position in the organization.

It might be extremely difficult to "jump off" and begin with this amount of time per day at the different management levels of the organization. I would encourage you to start with some allocation of time, say an hour each day, and then build to these percentages gradually over time. What are you going to have to give up or let go of in order to start spending time on improvement?

The following document is one of the better examples of leadership standard work. This specific example is for a nurse manager. The daily tasks are broken down by key time buckets during the day, and weekly tasks are documented separately. A mixture of tasks oriented toward both improvement and unit level administration are documented. Reasons why tasks are not met are captured, which allows for improvement of the standard at the end of each week. The leadership standard work should be discussed with the manager's superior on a weekly basis. Barriers to accomplishing standard work should be removed (Figure 4.12).

How does this standard work compare with yours? Usually, the first substantial difference is that in a lean organization, the entire day is not spent bouncing from meeting to meeting. In a lean organization, the management and leadership, and physician leadership are not pinned down in their offices or in meetings all day. The management team will be seen in the

Table 4.4   Time Allocated for Daily Standard Work

Position	Daily Percentage of Time Dedicated to Standard Work
Staff/physicians	100%
Staff lead or charge nurse	75%
Line manager	50%
Middle manager	33%
Executive level	20–25%

Time of Day	Standard Work	Deliverable
0730 -0830	General Unit Administration	respond to e-mail and voice mail requests, payroll, scheduling, etc.
0830 -0930	Managing for daily improvement huddle Walk the Gemba and review visual controls	team engagement, problem solving, and real-time intervention
0930 -1030	Attend bed meeting work on preparation or sustaining issues from past or upcoming kaizen activity	alleviate bed flow pressures as required, and prepare or sustain for improvement as required
1030-1130	Attend managers meeting or work on assigned committee work	increase awareness and support organization as required
1130-1230	Walk unit and monitor visual controls Lunch	team engagement, problem solving, and real-time intervention
1230- 1330	General Unit Administration	respond to e-mail and voice mail requests, payroll, scheduling, etc.
1330 -1430	Walk unit and monitor visual controls	team engagement, problem solving, and real-time intervention
1430 - 1530	Meet with charge nurse to resolve open issues, plan for night shift, and review action plans from performance system	planning, problem solving, and work time to improve
1530 -1630	Walk unit and monitor visual controls Prepare for the next day General Unit Adminsitration	team engagement, problem solving, and real-time intervention

Figure 4.12   Nurse manager daily leadership standard work example.

workplace, problem-solving and removing barriers to delivering the highest quality, in the shortest time, and least cost. Leadership standard work will get you out of the conference room and into the workplace!

Peer Task Audits (Kamishibai)

A control point for the visual management systems and standard work that leverages staff engagement is a system known as Kamishibai. This daily audit system is used as a peer-to-peer feedback mechanism to reinforce the maintenance of operational standards. Kamishibai loosely translates to "paper theatre" and is part of a long tradition of picture storytelling, beginning as early as the 9th or 10th centuries when priests used illustrated (cartoon) scrolls combined with narration to convey Buddhist doctrine to lay audiences.[7] The Buddhist monks used the kamishibai scrolls to allow the audience a self-reflection to determine if they were living the correct Buddhist lifestyle. This system is wildly popular in Japan today with children and the cartoon-based stories are used to teach behaviors such as sharing and punctuality.

In a lean organization, the kamishibai system is used to reinforce to the auditor that he/she is living a "lean lifestyle." An example of a visually managed kamishibai system is shown in Figure 4.13:

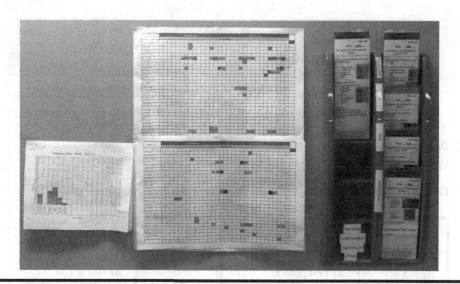

Figure 4.13   Kamishibai system.

First, audits are created. On any unit, or in any department, many different types of audit cards can be created. For example, standards already exist for IV sight markings, hand hygiene, narcotic counts, fall prevention, and preventing ventilator-attributed pneumonia. Ideally, the audits are pictures that represent the key standards for the organization. An example of a Kamishibai card is shown in Figure 4.14.

Every staff member then conducts a single 3–5-minute audit using one of the cards created from one of the department standards. If the audit is passed, the green side of the card is slotted in the board. If the audit fails, the red side of the card is slotted. A red audit is dealt with in real-time and the auditor discusses the result with the person being audited. Real-time feedback, both positive and negative, is the best way to change behavior. In addition to re-enforcing the standard for the person being audited, the value created is for the auditor. While completing the audit, the auditor gets a chance to reflect on the standard and evaluate if he/she is following the standard.

Both passed and failed audits can be dcumented as shown in Figure 4.15. The frequency of the failures can be summarized in a Pareto diagram for further action as shown in Figure 4.16. The type and number of cards in the system are dynamic. Cards can be added and subtracted based on what is being found in the audits. For audits that fail frequently, more cards can be added to the system so these standard adherence shortfalls can be reviewed more often. In the same light, for audits that pass consistently, cards of this type of audit can be removed, thus they are audited less frequently.

Card: # 2 Hand Hygiene	Card: # 2 Hand Hygiene
Area: EXPRESS ADMISSION UNIT This audit can be completed by anyone.	**Area: EXPRESS ADMISSION UNIT** This audit can be completed by anyone.
Please observe 4 hand hygiene opportunities. Check **ANY** of the following: Hand hygiene **BEFORE** patient/ environment contact. Hand hygiene **AFTER** patient/ environment contact Hand hygiene **BEFORE** aseptic procedure Hand hygiene **AFTER** body fluid exposure Pass Criteria: Hand hygiene performed correctly at any of the 4 opportunities.	Please observe 4 hand hygiene opportunities. Check **ANY** of the following: Hand hygiene **BEFORE** patient/ environment contact. Hand hygiene **AFTER** patient/ environment contact Hand hygiene **BEFORE** aseptic procedure Hand hygiene **AFTER** body fluid exposure Fail Criteria: Hand hygiene NOT performed at any of the 4 opportunities. Corrective Action: Inform the person of the missed hand hygiene opportunity.
↑ **Green Side of the Card**	↑ **Red Side of the Card**

Figure 4.14 Sample task audit card.

The key point of Kamishibai is that while completing the audit, the auditor is re-enforcing their own understanding of the importance of following standards. It is through this self-reflection that the staff assesses if they are following a lean lifestyle. A lean lifestyle is one where everyone follows standards until a better standard can be created.

Two common issues that every organization faces when implementing a culture of continuous improvement include getting every to follow standard work and creating the capacity to audit all of the standards which typically

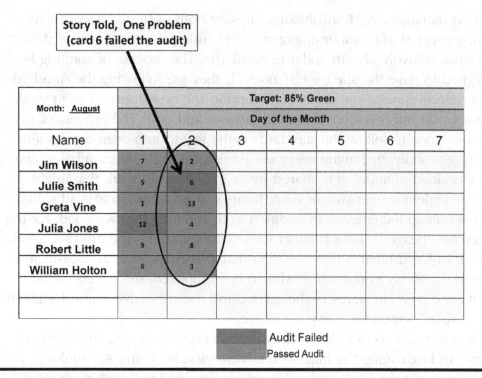

Figure 4.15   Story told–one problem.

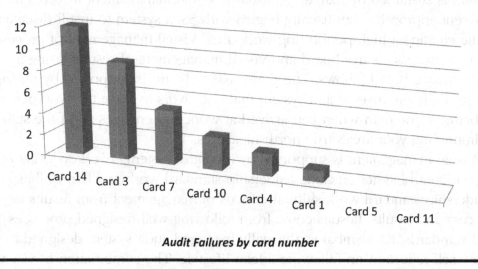

Figure 4.16   Pareto chart on failed audits.

falls on management; Kamishibai addresses both of these concerns. By having every staff member engaged in the audit process, everyone doing the work is involved with auditing standards. The process of auditing is designed to have the auditor self-assess if they are following the standards. This reflection helps the entire staff support the new approaches to work that support improvement in quality, access, and cost. The process of getting everyone to follow the standards is the key to improvement sustainability. Secondly, by having everyone participate in the kamishibai system, the workload of auditing is shared by everyone. Audit work that might take a single manager two or more hours can be spread across all shifts in 3–5-minute increments. In addition to distributing the workload, having everyone engaged allows broader coverage of all the standards. Yet another benefit of kamishibai is that like the other management systems, the audit system is entirely visual. The audits to be completed, the results of the audits, the pass-fail status of the audits, and the corrective action for failed audit are all posted for everyone to see.

Step 4 in the acceleration phase encompasses sustaining the improvements and managing the improved system visually. Using A3 thinking, your improvement teams will be implementing flow and pull within your key processes. These teams will also be implementing zero-defect systems to reduce errors; the new processes will be supported by standard work. The system is sustained by managing visually. Visual management involves many different approaches but usually begins with 5S, a system to instill discipline while creating a high-performing work area. Visual management of process, using a process control board and visual management of results, using a performance board follows. The performance board is supported by managing for daily improvement, a system that endeavors to leave the workplace in better shape than when you arrived at work and engages all of the staff in improving your area's true north measures.

Visual management is supported by a control system. Two key levers of a great control system include leadership standard work and kamishibai. Leadership standard work shifts the focus of management from results to process and results. Results come from following well-designed processes and standards. Kamishibai is a visually managed audit system designed to allow self-reflection on following a lean lifestyle. The combination of visual management and the supporting control system is how lean organizations not only sustain but also improve on their systems every day. The collection of these approaches supports creating a culture of improvement.

Capture the Savings

When visual management systems are brought to life and improvements are sustained, you can expect double-digit improvement in your key measures. By double digit, I am implying 10% plus improvements. Results will start to be realized beyond anything you will have experienced in the past. Having a system that captures these results will be important for the long-term viability of your lean efforts. Without a detailed understanding of the results, the improvement efforts will be viewed more as an expense than a benefit. It takes resources to support the kaizen teams, and the labor hours add up in a hurry. If you follow Step 4 diligently, your results will be at hand. The trick is to quantify these results.

Measurable results will come from two key areas: hard savings and soft savings. Hard savings are those items that will show up on your income statement and balance sheet. Said differently, these are bottom-line and top-line benefits that make their way to the financial reports. Soft savings are items that reflect the elimination of wasted time and activity but do not flow through to budget line items. While not exclusive, some examples of hard savings found in healthcare include:

- increase in top-line revenue
- reduction in supplies and materials
- reduction in therapies and pharmaceuticals
- reduction in labor
  - less full-time equivalent employees
  - reduction in agency costs
  - reduction in overtime
- decrease in utilities and energy consumption
- reduction in facilities repair and maintenance expenses
- reduction in inventory

These items result in benefits that can be incorporated into the budget in future years. Savings from this category result in lower costs per unit of service, increased operating margin, and also improved working capital and increased cash flow. Some examples of soft savings include:

- reduction in steps traveled
- reduction in hand-offs of information
- reduction in approvals or signatures
- reduction in square footage utilized

There is a third category of savings that can turn into either hard or soft savings depending on what happens with these results; this category is called cost avoidance. Examples of cost avoidance include:

- capital avoidance (equipment, facility square footage)
- improvement in quality and safety indicators (infection rates, complications, etc.)
- canceled requisitions for open positions

Savings should be captured by the finance department for two reasons. First, nothing is going to flow through to the income statement and balance sheet without finance's blessing. Secondly, finance needs to be engaged in the improvement process and is the area most capable of understanding and extracting the value derived from improved staff more/engagement, quality, delivery/access, and cost. If finance is not capable of extracting the hard dollar value, then capture the successes as soft savings. Great organizations work collaboratively to convert soft savings to hard savings.

The process used to capture savings does not begin after the change is made, but rather when the first three sections of the A3 document are developed in preparation for an improvement. Finance should be a partner in developing the reason for improvement, the current conditions, and the target conditions. Most importantly, finance should be a partner in developing the key measures for the improvements. Such questions that may be asked during this process include: Which key measures can be converted into hard savings? How will these measures be captured? Who will capture the baseline and target measures?

Transactional activities and financial report development is not the main focus of the finance department in a lean healthcare organization. Finance is a partner in the improvement process and consults with the areas of focus to develop meaningful measures and assists in the analysis and financial calculations that deliver the bottom-line results every organization craves. Thirty days following the implementation of the new standard work and the visual management systems used to sustain the improvements, finance can provide their initial snapshot of the savings. This savings audit is initially completed at the 60-day point, with the final savings audit being completed at the 90-day point. After confirming the savings, the results should be incorporated into the budget to institutionalize the new process and hardwire the savings. A summary of all of the savings should be rolled up. A sample of the scorecard of this summary is provided in Figure 4.17.

Lean Improvement Savings Capture

$'s in 000's	Hard Savings (Annual)								Soft Savings (Annual)					Capital Avoidance (Annual)		
	net FTE's	Overtime	Agency Cost Reduction	Increase in volumes	Increase in Visits	Supplies	Drugs and gases	Diagnostic and Therapeutic	Hours free-up for other services	Hand-offs reduced	reduction in patient steps traveled	reduction in staff steps traveled	Increase in patient satisfaction	construction/expand footage reduction	Cancelled capital $	Improvement in quality/safety
Value Stream: Peri-Operative Services																
A3 #1	$75	$175	$32								14,000					
A3 #2				$300												
A3 #3				$37							24,000					X
A3 #4						$42						26,000				
A3 #5													+10 pts			
A3 #6				$67							47,000				$300	
Value Stream Totals	$75	$175	$32	$404	$0	$42	$0	$0	0	0	71000	26000	N/A	$0	$300	
Value Stream: Emergency Services																
A3 #1		$36	$22						22,000		75,000	1,12,000				
A3 #2											1,10,000	2,10,000		$250		
A3 #3					$1,100											X
A3 #4							$13			14,000						
Value Stream Totals	$0	$36	$22	$0	$1,100	$0	$13	$0	22000	14000	1,85,000	3,22,000		$250	$300	
Value Stream: Recruiting Cycle																
A3 #1	$55								1400							
A3 #2		$475	$300													
A3 #3										47,000						
Value Stream Totals	$55	$475	$300	$0	$0	$0	$0	$0	1400	47000	0	0		$0	$0	
Enterprise Totals	$130	$686	$354	$404	$1,100	$42	$13	$0	23400	61000	256000	348000		$250	$600	

Total Hard Savings = $27,29,000
Total Capital Avoidance = $850,000

Figure 4.17   Savings capture spreadsheet.

Hard and soft savings can be captured at three levels. First, capture the savings on an A3-by-A3 basis. Secondly, roll of the savings within each value stream. Finally, roll up the value stream results into an enterprise total.

What level of return on investment (ROI) should you expect? The general rule of thumb is that the return on investment in the first year should be at a minimum of the breakeven point. Personally, I like to see the first year positive, but there are some investments in the first year that do not provide a hard return. These investments include setting up the infrastructure, establishing your true north measures, training your internal experts, contracting your Sensei, and buying supplies to operate the performance system and strategy wall. Your first few value stream analysis sessions do not return any hard savings, either. These are planning sessions designed to create a shared vision of the future and develop an improvement plan. These one-time expenses should quickly give way to meaningful results in quality, access, and cost that should reach the bottom line. None-the-less a 2 to 1 return on investment in the first year is typically realized. In years two and beyond, the general rule of thumb is a return on investment of 3 or 4 to 1 for every dollar invested into lean improvement. How much money would you invest in the stock market if you got a 3 to 1 return on your investment? How many of your organizational projects of capital and IT infrastructure return 3 to 1?

There are some common causes why organizations do not receive a great return on investment for their lean efforts. The most common causes for failure to deliver a return include:

- Failure to sustain improvements (standard work not followed, visual management systems not utilized, management control systems not utilized)

- Finance is not involved with measurement development, leading to measures without hard savings potential or the inability to convert the measures to hard savings
- No system in place to capture results
- Focusing on the wrong measures
- Measures with low expectations (not double-digit improvement)
- Line management fails to implement/execute the changes

It will take great leadership to steer the organization through all of the issues to create, realize, and capture bottom-line results. Sustaining the improvements, engaging finance, and learning how to convert soft savings to hard savings are great places to begin.

An important point when capturing savings, as you realize measurable success, be sure and celebrate your successes. You should expect a variety of measures that trend favorably and we have discussed these previously; better engagement of staff, improved quality and safety outcomes, better access and lead-times for products and services, improved productivity and cost positions, and increased growth of healthcare services. Share these results with the organization and celebrate these organizational wins!

Support Your Change with Ongoing Training and Coaching

The more the world learns about lean improvement, the more we understand what we do not know, and there is a *whole* lot we do not know. As you remove waste from your operations, new wastes will emerge that you did not even know you had. These wastes will be more difficult to remove and may require more sophisticated tools. Consequently, great lean organizations constantly augment their improvements with ongoing training and coaching.

Lean Coaching

If you were going to undertake flying a plane, would you read a few articles online, attend a few seminars, play an online flight simulator, and go fly? Not likely. You would probably begin by finding an expert and asking many questions. You might find some other pilots with flying experience and pick their brains as well. If you are still interested, you would sign up for a ground school, complete the course work, make some instructor-assisted flights, and eventually fly solo. After approximately 80 hours of training, frequently spanning weeks, or months, you might be ready to pass the skills exam and receive your pilot's license. Even then you would be a novice pilot and would benefit from some further instruction and coaching.

If you want to be great at improvement, you might consider a similar track. I would find an expert, talk to others who have walked the road before you, and then seek out extensive coaching. Finding a Sensei was covered briefly in chapter three, and the role of a Sensei in providing coaching will be expanded upon here. There are lean Sensei available who have mastered lean improvement and who are capable of guiding you and your organization through the improvement processes. Having a lean Sensei teach your organization improvement tools and approaches, train your infrastructure, minimize your risk, coach the senior leadership, assist you with your change management, and keep you focused on your journey is a step I would not recommend you skip. To find a lean Sensei, find another lean practicing organization (either within or outside healthcare) and find out who they use as their Sensei. The question you want to ask, to differentiate between a lean expert and a Sensei, is: "in how many industries have you provided lean expertise?" Virtually every world-class organization has used a Sensei for many years (often twenty years or more). Their goal is not to go on their own, but rather use the experience of an expert to strengthen their journey and continually challenge their approaches to improvement. The coaching aspects of lean are multi-faceted; there are dozens of areas of specialization for lean coaching and several in particular that are used in getting started. The key areas that will require coaching in the first year of your transformational effort are listed in Table 4.5

Other coaching areas needed as part of the infrastructure creation can include:

- Project planning and improvement sequencing
- Physician engagement strategy
- Communication strategy
- Board engagement strategy

As your journey continues, you will begin to identify new and exciting opportunities to see and eliminate waste. The improvement concepts of flow, pull, defect-free, and visual management offer hundreds of tools and

Table 4.5 Sample of Year One Lean Coaching Topics

Coaching activity	Description
Infrastructure coaching	Helps in defining your resources for improvement: including internal facilitators, improvement governance, and deployment planning and execution
Gemba walking	Model to learn based on a master/apprentice approach. Gemba Walking involves walking the work area to review the visual management system and management actions to support improvement
Management coaching	Supports line, middle and senior management in learning how to manage in a constantly improving environment
Managing for daily improvement (MDI)	MDI coaching teaches an operation to stabilize the Four M's (manpower, methods, mother nature/environment, and materials) for daily improvement.
Problem-solving	Using a blend of cause-and-effect diagrams and 5 Why's, real-time problem-solving approaches are learned.
Visual management	Coaching on the management of 5S, process control, and results management. Can cascade to include program-level improvement and enterprise-wide improvement.
Kamishibai	This system uses a series of cascading audits to teach your organization how to live a lean culture.
Management development	Coaching on the fundamentals of management to include setting/maintaining standards, improving standards, and developing people
Kaizen standard work	Coaching preparation, execution, and follow-up activities and improvement of standard work
Measurement capture and reporting	Establishing the infrastructure of capture and report hard, and soft savings
Cascading leadership standard work	Learning the lean approach to developing, executing, and improving leadership standard work to create a culture of improvement
Dealing with difficult staff and antibodies	Group or individual coaching on engaging and inspiring the staff

improvement techniques you can use. The good news is that because many organizations have been using lean for decades, the advanced tools we need already exist. The unwelcome news is, there are hundreds of tools to choose from, and knowing which one to use, how to use them, and when to use them can take a while to learn.

As your organization gets better with the fundamental tools of improvement, you will soon be ready for some more advanced approaches to eliminating waste. Some of the more advanced tools are shown in Table 4.6.

In addition to expanding knowledge in new tools and approaches, the staff and medical leadership at your hospital will need ongoing training to understand lean and the corresponding behaviors needed to transform performance and culture. Everyone will need to be grounded in the five principles of improvement, the seven wastes, and A-3 thinking. Over time, we expect everyone to become competent in the common tools for seeing and eliminating waste and in the team-based improvement techniques of value stream mapping and analysis and kaizen improvement.

While learning by doing is encouraged, training of this breadth and depth will eventually require a more formal plan. World-class organizations begin by educating the senior leadership and then having this team train the organization. Since it is exceedingly difficult to master all of the tools, expertise is usually divided across the leadership team. For example, one leader will become the expert on flow, another on pull. One person will become the internal expert on 5S and another on visual management. Over time, the responsibilities can be rotated so each member of the team can continue their own personal development and develop expertise in multiple areas. A great lean improvement system will provide support for ongoing coaching and training. Continuous improvement takes a lifetime to learn, so in the acceleration phase, you will want to have both a training and coaching plan in place.

Spread Lean Thinking across the Organization

If you have made and sustained improvement in one or more value streams, have captured the savings, and are now augmenting your improvement with the needed coaching and training to further develop your improvement skills, you are ready to "spread" some of your improvements; that is, extend your improvements into additional areas. All organizations want to go faster in their rates of improvement, but you can only go as fast as you can sustain. Taking improvement across the organization should follow a calculated approach.

Table 4.6 Sample of Advanced Lean Tools

Tool	Description
Vertical value stream	Lean approach to world-class project management. Used for construction, IT deployment, and spread of lean improvement, or anywhere else a project plan is needed and used.
Quality function deployment (also known as the voice of the customer)	A structured process to develop the voice of both the customer and internal stakeholders when developing a new product or service. QFD is sued to determine which features provide the greatest leverage in a new concept and also helps identify project risk and trade-offs that might need to occur during the development phase.
3P	Production Process Preparation – new product/process development technique that invents new capability
2P	Process Preparation – new product or process development technique that delivers new capability using existing technology
Heijunka	Involves leveling volume or mix of work to prevent batching and enable single item flow
Hoshin Kanri	Technique used to deploy a strategic plan. Powerful senior leadership approach to aligning the strategy horizontally and vertically across the organization to deliver sustainable results. Monitors process and outcomes of the strategy to deliver world-class rates of improvement.
Problem-solving and corrective action	A process to understand a difficult problem and use a series of quality tools to get to the root cause of the problem, develop a series of countermeasures, test the countermeasures, and hard wire a solution. Frequently uses A4 thinking captured on the A4 form
Statistical process control	Statistical tools used eliminate variability from a process. These will need to be introduced when defect rates approach defects per million
Kanban	Lean supply chain management system

The pace of improvement should be based on meeting criteria (goals or milestones), and *not* on meeting time targets in a plan. When we talk about spread (sharing our improvements), there are two distinct types. In one type of spread, we take artifacts, products, or solutions developed in one area, and move them to another area. For example, maybe we have developed a great way to manage glucose testing on an in-patient unit. It is such an effective solution that other departments want to replicate this new "best practice."

However, another type of spread means increasing the breadth of value streams that are being improved by the organization. In this form of spread, new areas of the organization are introduced to lean improvement for the first time. As an example, let us assume we began our improvement in two areas of our organization, the laboratory and in a specialty endocrinology clinic. These two areas have completed their value stream mapping and analysis sessions and have begun to deliver measurable improvement, sustained through standard work managed visually. The results have been quantified and the organization now wants to add additional value streams for improvement. Perhaps we want to now venture into the cardiac catheterization lab and emergency services, starting as always with value stream mapping and analysis sessions and continuing the improvement process accordingly. Spreading solutions and adding value streams require different implementation strategies. Before we talk about the strategies, we should differentiate between the two approaches. Table 4.7 evaluates the two alternatives.

As we deploy lean across our enterprise, we are not faced with choosing one approach or the other, because both approaches will be utilized to spread the improvements. Let us review both approaches in detail.

Replication of Artifacts, Products, Solutions, and Process

This approach is used when we want to adopt a solution from one area to another in its exact form (or in a form very close to the original). Perhaps you have piloted a new standard process for cleaning a room on one unit and now want to take that process hospital-wide. To successfully achieve this replication, you will want to use a project management-based technique. Lean organizations use a tool known as a vertical value stream to manage projects; a vertical value stream is like a vertical Gantt chart. Using such a system, the project moves through several distinct phases and passes clearly defined "tollgates" before moving to the next phase. An example of a vertical value stream is shown in Figure 4.18.

Listed below is a simple overview of how you can use vertical value stream mapping to spread your solutions.

1. Identify a representative sample of the key stakeholders affected by the change.
2. Thoroughly review the known solutions so the entire team has an understanding of the process, tools, and visual management systems.

Table 4.7　Spread Approaches

Spread approach	Advantages	Considerations
Introducing additional value streams	• Buy-in from the start as current conditions, future conditions and action plans are generated • Engages many more team members in improvement • New innovation with each opportunity • Tailored improvement plans for each value stream	• May be more resource intensive than replication approach • Can take longer than a replication approach • Requires more infrastructure (skilled facilitators) within your organization
Replication of tools, process and artifacts	• Leverages tested solutions • Training key points are defined • Solutions are based on lean principles • More rapid approach • Design resources are not consumed	• Usually we are replicating a product and not the thinking • Less buy-in to someone else's solutions • Limits new ideas and innovation • Difficult in "not invented here" environments • Project management resources are needed to manage the change

3. Assign an end date for the project.
4. Develop and document the phases of the tollgates that must be completed to complete the project.
5. Develop the criteria for passing each tollgate. Criteria are measurable outcomes of process and or results that must be met before moving to the next phase of the project. Table 4.8 shows an example of two milestones and their input criteria.
6. Determine the tasks needed to pass the tollgate.
7. Assign accountability for the tasks to meet tollgate criteria.
8. Execute the tasks needed to meet the tollgate.
9. Hold a review to confirm that the tollgate criteria have been met before beginning the next phase of the project plan.
10. Capture lessons learned from the tollgate reviews to improve the organizational knowledge.
11. Repeat Steps 7, 8, and 9 until the project is completed.

Time	Customers X		Customers Y	Project Team MGR		RN	PM	HR	TL	Suppliers D		E	Standard Work
							Task	1	1	1			not in place
5 days				Task			2		2	2			in place
				Task			3						in place
				4			Task						in place
3 days							Task	5	5	5			in place
1 day				6			6	Task	6				N/A
3 weeks				7		7	7	Task	7	7			not in place
3 weeks	8						8	Task		8			draft
	9					9			Tollgate Review	9			
							Inputs			Outputs			

Figure 4.18 Vertical value stream example.

Table 4.8 Example of Spread Plan Tollgates and Criteria

Tollgate	Passing Criteria
Launch preparation tollgate	• All Materials and equipment have been purchased • Resources to perform the work has been hired • Pilot location is identified • Subject matter experts are available on the required days for support • Standard work is written and posted • Unit 5S is complete
Project completion tollgate	• Kamishibai system shows 90% compliance to standard work audits • Corrective action and problem-solving system is in place and operational • Edits to standard work have been made and posted • Unit is meeting planned volume and cost projects and has sustained them for 90 days • Daily Huddles are being held and all staff is engaged in problem-solving

If you ensure you have met the tollgate criteria prior to going to the next phase of the project plan, you will minimize re-work later in the project. If you plan all the tasks necessary to meet the tollgate criteria, you minimize the number of steps needed to complete the project. The combined impact of these two design elements in your project plan can reduce the timeline for execution by 50% to 75%, while ensuring high-quality results at the end of the project.

One of the assumptions made in spreading known solutions is that there was a pilot area to design, test, and validate the improvements to deliver results. The pilot area is also accountable to create standard work, develop any supporting documents like tip sheets or checklists, and create visual management systems to monitor and incrementally further improve the process. Rarely do lean organizations create organizational-wide improvements. The pilot/spread approach has several benefits. These include having the ability to rapidly design and test changes in a focused environment. Allowing the organization to learn quickly from mistakes or challenges. Narrowing the number of participants engaged in the improvement minimizes the change management effort required to allow the team to adopt the changes. Another benefit is creating champions who can help sell the changes and the benefits to other parts of the organization. The challenge you might face would be the "not invented here" syndrome. Every unit and every specialty area thinks they have something special that makes adopting someone else's work unnecessary, difficult, or impossible. "We are different" is what you will hear as change comes. To overcome this, I recommend a small working session to adapt or adopt the standard work and visual management. There likely are some varying clinical issues that have to be addressed as solutions are spread across the organization. However, there is a substantial difference in modifying the work to meet clinical needs versus scrapping all the solutions that have demonstrated benefit in a similar unit or department.

Adding Additional Value Streams

Throughout this chapter, we have focused on accelerating our improvement by delivering and then spreading value stream improvement. In Step 2 of our roadmap for getting started, we discussed selecting and mapping our key value streams. If we retained the notes we made during value stream selection, we will find it simple to determine which value stream to select now. Going back to our data from Figure 4.1, let us assume we are continuing to improve staff and medical staff satisfaction for our organization.

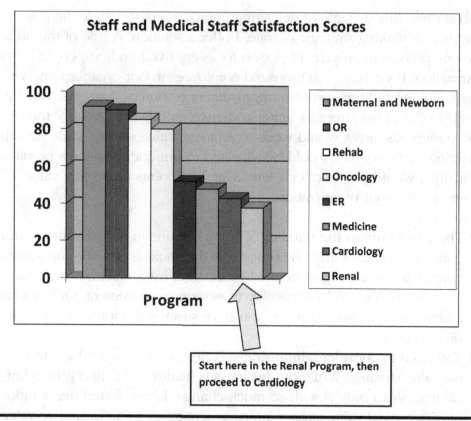

Figure 4.19   Pareto analysis of staff and medcial staff satisfaction by program.

As Figure 4.19 shows, the graph indicates we should start in the value stream of Renal Services. If we were going to add another value stream, which one would we select next? The chart would tell us that Cardiology would be the next candidate. But what if the rehab program was making a lot of noise about staff and medical staff satisfaction? A word of warning: It will be *VERY* tempting to deviate from the data and embark on the value stream mapping in an area of "high noise" for the organization. However, we must remain strategic in our deployment of lean. We need to stay focused on the areas that best help us meet our strategic outcomes. At times, the area of pain will impact your outcome measures, but often it will not – and if it does not, beware! You have an obligation to direct your critical few improvement resources on the most strategic areas. Many organizations struggle because they have a lot of lean improvement, but not all of it is strategic, and therefore it does not add up to anything meaningful in terms of results.

To address this struggle of delivering improvement to where the pain is today, versus making strategic change, I offer a solution. A rule of thumb is to have one process improvement person for every five hundred people in your organization. If we have five thousand employees in our organization, we will require ten full-time process improvement resources. I suggest you allocate 80% of your resources to strategic change, in this case eight of the ten improvement resources would work on strategic value stream work. And the remaining two resources would be allocated to imminent business problems.

Finally, I would like to offer a few other key points on adding value streams within your organization.

- There is a limit to the number of value streams in which your organization can engage at any one time. This threshold is based upon several criteria, including organizational headcount, infrastructure (improvement resources), and your ability to sustain improvement. Only add an additional value stream when you have sustained improvement in the previous one.

- You need to consider administrative value streams as well as clinical value streams. While our business is healthcare delivery, the clinical teams can only absorb so much change. I have found that a ratio of 75% clinical value stream improvement to 25% administrative value stream improvement works well. Administrative value streams such as recruiting and onboarding, supply chain management, and revenue cycle (for example) can impact the pace of change within the clinical value streams. So do not let your clinical improvement get too far ahead of your administrative improvement.

- Do not exclude any areas of your business from the value stream selection process. There is a lean way to deploy IT, perform help desk and call center operations, execute strategic planning and strategy deployment, create a new service, or design a room, clinic, unit, or entire facility. There is a lean way to perform parking services, volunteer services, and security services. One way to expand the breadth of lean improvement is to use lean in areas that might appear (to a novice) to not be applicable. How about improving centralized scheduling and staffing, developing, and implementing an evidence-based care map, improving foundation services (ending the waste in fundraising), and shortening the cycle for clinical research? Hopefully, you are getting the picture: Anywhere work is done, a lean approach exists.

Once you are spreading your improvements and increasing your improvement pace, you are on your way to becoming a lean organization! The improvement of multiple areas of the organization at the same time will help you achieve your strategic measurable outcomes.

Chapter Summary: Key Points from Chapter 4

- Phase 2 in the transformation roadmap entails beginning organizational improvement, delivering improvement, sustaining the improvements, and then spreading improvement across the organization.
- Improvement should be aligned with your corporate strategy. Ensure you are improving on the right value streams needed to make strategically aligned changes.
- Just like the organization requires some steering and governance. Each value stream will also require governance. Be sure to have a physician leader and an administrative leader for each value stream.
- It takes a lifetime to learn any one of the many improvement sciences. While all of the methodologies are based on the scientific method, world-class lean organizations use the A3 form and A3 thinking to deliver improvement.
- Visual management is cornerstone to sustaining lean improvement. Visual management systems are needed to monitor and improve process, results, and work environment. Visual management also helps create a culture of improvement because the transparency of process and results helps staff and clinical staff motivation.
- When standard work is in place, and visual controls are developed and utilized, it is possible to improve every day. This technique is known as managing for daily improvement.
- Leadership standard work and Kamishibai support visual management. These tools bring visual management to life through hands-on engagement of management and staff.
- Expect double-digit improvement in your key measures. Capturing savings is an integral part of the improvement process. Savings can be captured into three buckets: hard savings, soft savings, and cost avoidance.
- The improvement journey is best supported with on-going lean coaching and development. Lean improvement is not intuitive, and leadership and management will require ongoing support to create a culture of improvement. At a minimum, every organization will need to continue

to develop new skills and techniques to remove the different forms of waste that are uncovered.

■ When results have been sustained lean artifacts and lean thinking can be spread to other parts of the organization. Spread includes adding additional value streams as well as using lean project management (through the vertical value stream) approaches to migrate improvement through an organization.

Notes

1. Cascade Strategy, *High Reliability Organizations: Principles, Strategies & Examples* (High Reliability Organizations: Principles, Strategies & Examples (cascade.app), September 2023), accessed May 14, 2024.
2. David Mann, *Creating a Lean Culture* (New York, NY: Productivity Press, 2005), pg. 25.
3. David Mann, *Creating a Lean Culture* (New York, NY: Productivity Press, 2005), pg. 26.
4. David Mann, *Creating a Lean Culture* (New York, NY: Productivity Press, 2005), pg. 26.
5. Masaaki Imai, *Gemba Kaizen* (New York, NY: McGraw Hill, 1997), pg. 105.
6. Masaaki Imai, *Gemba Kaizen* (New York, NY: McGraw Hill, 1997), pg. 105.
7. Tara McGowen, Kamishibai for Kids, Kamishibai a Brief History, http://www.kamishibai.com/history.html, accessed April 2024.

Chapter 5

The Transformation Roadmap – Phase 3: Make Organizational Improvement the "New" Culture

For many organizations, phase 2 is both awesome and horrifying at the same time. The ability to generate organizational results runs from easy to impossible. For every two positive steps forward, there is one step backward. Fear not, every organization that has embarked on a lean transformation has gone through exactly the same experience. The difficulties associated with progress are present because the old culture and the new culture are now at battle. The systems that have been developed or evolved over a period of years are not going to leave your organization without a fight. Worse yet, it is not even possible to forecast where the resistance will come from. The key to transformation is to embrace the new culture and shut down the old systems as quickly as possible.

A question is often posed as to why organizations fail to change their culture. Why is change so difficult to make on a large scale? While there are many opinions on the root cause of these failures, I believe the number one reason for failure is that organizations cannot sustain operating two different systems. It is simply too difficult for the leadership and management to balance old systems and new systems. Since managing in the old system is more comfortable, change fades away. So how can an organization quickly shut down the old systems and embrace the new culture of improvement?

DOI: 10.4324/9781003532132-5

The key lies in hardwiring improvement into the organization to make the change last. Most healthcare organizations will start their improvement in a clinical area. This makes perfect sense because lean is about generating more value for our customers. In healthcare our customer is the patient. So, the early gap in changing your culture lies within your administrative and support processes which have not been addressed yet and are designed to optimize your existing culture. There are many support and administrative systems that have to be addressed to hardwire improvement. Several of these systems are shown in Table 5.1.

The core business of healthcare is taking care of your customers; your core business might be research, prevention services, primary care, acute care, post-acute care, home care, etc. The important thing to keep in mind is that without patients, none of the activities in Table 5.1 are necessary. If your core business is healthcare, then that is where your focus needs to be. All of the support areas exist to help the organization function. The function of the organization is healthcare; the support areas need to ensure that they are supporting the front-line staff and physicians, and their corresponding management, not the other way around.

By this time in the transformation journey, you will be seeing substantial improvements in quality, safety, access, and cost. But these results will not continue without the support organizations improving at an identical rate. Lean is not just for direct care; it is applicable anywhere work is done. Any support area of the organization that digs in and protects their turf defending processes that are no longer adequate to support a culture of improvement must be addressed. Aligning these processes in support of the clinical work will cement the changes in the organization. For an organization to transition into a culture that supports the improvement process, every single person in every department must be dedicated to improvement and creating a positive culture. One way to align all the departments to the new culture is to engage the administrative and support processes in lean improvement. This can come in a couple of different ways. One way is to launch the daily management system into the back shop processes. This will engage staff in local improvement aligned to your enterprise's true north measures. Another approach is to launch some administrative value stream improvement. One hidden benefit you get from administrative improvement is that once it is in place and sustained, there usually is an organizational-wide impact. For example, if we address and improve the process of staff recruiting, it will impact all programs.

Table 5.1 Non-clinical Processes and Systems That Will Need to Be Changed to Support a Culture of Improvement

Department	Core Process
Organizational Development	• Improvement capacity building for clinical and administrative staff, management, and physicians
Information Technology	• Help desk services • IT design, development, and deployment • Functionality changes to support waste elimination and redundancy
Finance	• Accounts receivable management • Account payable • Payroll • Budgeting • Month end close • Capital planning
Human Resources	• Recruiting • Onboarding • Job descriptions and competencies • Promotion criteria • Occupational health services • Lean management development • Scheduling and staffing
Materials	• Developing a lean supply chain
Operations or Marketing or Facilities	• New process or new service development • Construction services • Redevelopment • Project management
Senior Leadership	• Strategic planning • Strategy deployment • Improvement governance • Committee management
Medical Leadership	• Physician credentialing • Physician lead quality improvement • Physician engagement • Physician integration processes

Lean Capacity Building

A culture of improvement cannot be created with a handful of internal experts and a few leaders championing the change process, rather, everyone will need some skills in the science of improvement. Candidly, this is one of the most powerful attributes of lean organizations. Everyone can participate! Skills will need to be developed at all levels of the organization. Table 5.2 lists the levels in a typical healthcare organization and a summary of the skills that you should build.

Are you surprised that the highest levels of leadership require the most skills? In a world-class organization, the role of the senior leadership is to mentor and coach their subordinates. Mastery of lean tools and concepts must occur to enable the leadership to become mentors. It is not expected that everyone will take intensive training to become experts, but you can see from the prior table that everyone will need some capability. However, a capacity-building plan should be developed to ensure that the organization is constantly learning new skills about the application of lean and the management of a lean system. While the concepts are not difficult to understand, they also are not intuitive. In fact, the lean approaches go against the many years we have spent in management. Lean is full of contradictions of what we may have learned from prior management courses. For example, "doing things one at a time is better than doing work in a batch," "all work has a rhythm," or "you sometimes must go slow to go fast." If you work with a Sensei, you will come across these sayings from time to time. This is

Table 5.2   Capacity Building

Staff and Medical Staff Affected	*Skills Required*
Everyone (including physicians)	• **7 Wastes** • **5 Principles of improvement** • **A3 Thinking** • **Common tools to see and eliminate waste** • **5S**
Line management and physician leadership	**Everything above plus:** • **Managing for daily improvement** • **Basic project management skills** • **Problem-solving skills** • **Value stream management**
Middle management and senior leadership	**Everything above plus:** • **Strategy deployment**

actually part of the elegance of an improvement system that is derived from Samauri foundations.

I would like to share a simple analogy as a final thought on capacity building: Learning lean is like learning golf. It really does not matter how many books you have read, or how many videos you have watched. Golf is best learned by focused practice under the watchful eye of a professional. Golf is "learned by doing." Lean is also learned by doing. Any capacity building that occurs must be application based. Learn the tools, techniques, and approaches on real examples in the workplace. Lecture, classroom training, and simulations are all helpful, but the best learning occurs when the tools are learned and then immediately applied.

Lean Information Technology

Tremendous amounts of money are spent on IT. Integrated business systems that share databases for purchasing, inventory management, and accounts payable, and financial accounting are common. On the clinical side of the operation, capital is invested in electronic patient records, scheduling software, medication management, utilization management, and countless other systems. Data is captured and shared with the click of a mouse. Reports can be generated providing all types of statistics and trends, broken down by diagnosis, cost center, provider, etc. Nonetheless, there are differences of opinion on the value of IT systems within healthcare. A Harvard study in 2009 concluded that in an evaluation of 4,000 U.S. hospitals over a four-year period of time, the investment in installing and running hospital IT systems is greater than any cost savings.[1]

The financial impacts of an integrated IT system are debatable, but does IT make healthcare safer? Automatic pharmaceutical dispensing units that provide unit dose medications help with accuracy and obsolescence. Barcoding systems are used to verify the correct patient is being treated. Electronic patient medical records allow clinicians to quickly share information which could enable speeding up the time for decision-making. I think everyone would agree that the use of IT systems creates the ability to improve the quality of healthcare. What about clinical value? The integrated databases and corresponding reports definitely appeal to administrators, but what about physicians, nurses, and allied staff? In my travels, I have taken a straw poll on how well staff and medical staff like their IT systems. The responses vary greatly from indispensable to total waste of time. So, I summarize current healthcare IT spending as an investment with a questionable financial return, some quality improvement capability, and mixed reviews on the value from the clinician's perspective.

Regardless of my assessment, research firm BCC (Business Communications Company) estimates that the total clinical healthcare market is projected to grow from US$7.4 billion in 2011 to nearly US$17.5 billion in 2016.[2] The challenge is learning how to use lean thinking to deliver compelling value from the application of IT. Rather than debating the cost savings, improvement in patient safety and quality, and staff satisfaction associated with the use of the system, use the principles of lean thinking to eliminate waste, and move the true north measures to accomplish your strategic outcomes.

The biggest problem that I see organizations make when investing in IT is that they bend their processes to fit the IT system and not the other way around. Lean thinking organizations will follow the following steps when acquiring IT functionality (Table 5.3).

Many organizations determine what is desired for the solution first. For example, a new electronic scheduling system is needed, and they then proceed to jump to step 10. A lean organization would begin by asking, what is the problem we are trying to solve?" and then follow the steps in A3 thinking to get to the root cause and develop a countermeasure. By starting with the solution, the first four steps in A3 thinking are being skipped.

To close the section on healthcare IT, note that lean thinking not only applies in the acquisition and deployment of IT but also in the support systems of IT. Clinical informatics and decision support requests, as well as help desk services, can all be run in a lean way. Standard work should be in place, balanced to the customer demand for services. Output (services, and support) should be managed visually with a process control board. Results should be managed through the performance management system. Continuous improvement is expected in the areas of staff engagement, process quality, lead-time for responses and services, and cost performance. Not having high-performing IT systems will eventually have a detrimental impact on the ability to continuously improve in other areas of the organization. Since the initial writing of *Lean Leadership for Healthcare,* I have had the opportunity to collaborate with two wonderful lean minds, Kurt Knoth and Susan Schnedaker, on a book called *Lean Electronic Health Record.* This 2018 book is published through CRC Press via Taylor & Francis Group. This topic became so important that the two pages of documentation in this book, do not do the topic justice. I would invite you to review this literature if you want to explore a deeper dive into how lean organizations approach their IT systems.

Table 5.3 Acquiring IT for Healthcare

Step #	Activity
1	Initiate an A3 and select true north measures aligned to the organizational strategy.
2	Value stream maps the end-to-end process.
3	Using creativity before investing in capital, execute the rapid improvement plan and re-design the process by creating flow and pull, making the process defect free, and managing visually.
4	Determine if the improvement meets the strategic targets. If the new process meets the targets, you do not an IT solution.
5	When incremental improvement can no longer meet the organizational targets, consider capital investment.
6	Determine if incremental investment on your current IT platform will allow you to meet your improvement targets.
7	If IT investment is determined to be the best solution, map the future state.
8	Evaluate process alternatives that enable the organization to meet the future state.
9	Investigate which IT solutions enable the future state process.

10	Perform a stakeholder analysis to be sure the solution accomplishes the following:
	• meets the needs of patients and family members
	  • improves quality and access
	• meets the needs of staff and medical staff
	  • delivers clinical value
	  • reduces duplication
	  • minimizes errors
	  • is intuitive and doesn't require hours of training
	  • minimizes hand-offs
	  • minimizes transactions
	  • remote access if necessary
	• meets the needs of the organization
	  • does not increase the overall costs of the organization through entering transactions, keeping the system upgraded, etc.
	  • can be supported
	  • ideally is interoperable
	  • is supported by process
	  • compliance with statutory requirements
	  • mitigates risk

(Continued)

Table 5.3 (Continued)

11	Write the requirements document with the return on investment articulated
12	Get capital approval
13	Research alternatives
14	Select an alternative
15	Perform a vertical value stream analysis to develop the project plan
16	Deliver the project in the least waste way
17	Perform a post-project evaluation to evaluate the ROI and how well the project delivered value

Lean Finance

As part of their innovation series published in 2008, The Institute of Healthcare Improvement (IHI), created a white paper on the "Seven Leadership Leverage Points, for Organizational-Level Improvement in Health Care." Leverage point five is "Make the Chief Financial Officer (CFO) a Quality Champion."[3] The general context of this leverage point is that CFOs are finding significant opportunities to both improve patient care and margins by reducing and eliminating error and clinical waste.[4] An important step in making change the new culture is that process improvement work quickly shifts from an expense (funding teams and facilitators to make improvement), to an indispensable asset. Continuous improvement can and should create ongoing improvement in quality, access, and cost.

In a lean organization, the CFO is one of the biggest fans of continuous improvement. The CFO is a visible champion who can relay at a moment's notice the correlation between a culture of improvement and the corresponding favorable impact on the balance sheet and income statement. Since the CFO has major impacts on budget construction and reporting, and the allocation of corporate funds, having the CFO as a big fan is important. But being a lean organization and creating a culture of improvement goes beyond having a cheerleader. Lean leadership implies leading by example and a great lean organization deploys lean finance. Lean finance is about creating a system of continuous improvement within the core finance and accounting processes. Lean systems can be applied to the revenue generation cycle, accounts receivable, accounts payable, payroll, budgeting, month-end close, and health records management (billing and coding). Anywhere work is done, lean can be applied, waste can be eliminated, and improvement can be made. Finance and accounting are no exception.

For each of these areas, the value stream mapping and analysis tool can be used to create an improvement plan. A3 thinking can be applied to create continuous flow and pull; within each of these processes, waste can be eliminated, and lead-times can be shortened for services. Defect-free principles can be used to mistake-proof the data going into and coming out of the work, ensuring a high degree of accuracy. Standard work can be created to support the new processes, and this standard work can be managed visually with process control and performance boards. Double-digit improvement is expected year over year in the areas of quality, lead-time, and cost performance. As an example, a 650-person healthcare community service agency with an annual revenue of $250 million servicing 17,000 clients per month took a lean approach to the month-end closing process. The current state process took 22 calendar days to close the books. The data quality was highly questionable, and because the statements came out so late in the month, the results were rarely used for decision-making. The process involved bouncing data from accountant to accountant and between departments with little time for analysis.

To improve the month-end close process, value must first be specified. Who is the customer of the month-end close process? We could make the case that management is the customer since the data could be used for decision-making. This is not really the case, however. Month-end reporting is a financial requirement necessary to meet accounting requirements and reporting laws. As such, the close does not really help patients. So, it is pure overhead and ideally should be as transactional as possible. The analysis of the reporting can be quite helpful in understanding where wasted time and activity is entering the business. The value added to the business is in this analysis! Summarizing the current state, the process delivered financial data necessary for reporting requirements that delivered little management data. This is basically pure waste.

After creating a new process workflow, the month-end reporting and analysis workflow was reduced to seven working days with 1.5 days built in for managerial analysis. The transactional activities were improved to create accurate data and the new financial analysis delivered business value added. Six-month plans were put in place to reduce the close time to three days with the long-range goal to have a one day close. Would a one-day close benefit your organization?

Another example of lean finance would be an improvement in the revenue generation cycle. An urban teaching hospital with revenues of $1 billion and ~5,000 employees wanted to improve both their top line and their cash flow. This organization supports over 100,000 annual ER visits, 25,000 annual inpatient admissions, and 350,000 annual outpatient visits. Before applying lean to this process, the organization had a bad debt expense of 2.03%, and the accounts receivable outstanding at 52 days.

Finance leadership led a value stream improvement from the point a patient registers to the point where cash is collected. A series of kaizen events using A3 thinking followed in the following areas:

- Patient access (registration)
- Collection of co-pays
- Capturing preferred accommodations
- Transcription
- Coding
- Billing
- Accounts receivable

Each process was left with standard work that could be managed visually. An analysis of variation from the standard was conducted daily, supported by the team huddle. Problem-solving efforts were applied to close the gaps between actual and target. In the first year, on an investment of about $100,000, the project returned over $15,000,000. The $15,000,000 would scale to $30,000,000 in the second year as the solutions were spread to other programs. There were a few modifications to data fields and screens, but no major IT purchase was required. The improvement was the result of repeated applications of seeing and eliminating waste that changed the way work was done. The changes were supported by creating a culture of improvement to allow ongoing continuous improvement to the process led by the staff. In addition to the financial returns, the streamlined registration practices lead to a better patient experience and less waiting for the staff. The improvements in the health records cycle, transcription, coding, and billing, lead to enhanced physician satisfaction.

Lean Human Resources

One area of your organization that plays a key role in change and change management is human resources. The employment life cycle is monitored through human resources. I see the life cycle of an employee as follows (Table 5.4).

Table 5.4 Employee Life Cycle

Life Cycle Phase	Activities
Recruitment	Job descriptions and competencies
	Recruitment and sourcing
	Hiring cycle
On-boarding	Orientation
	Initial training
Retention and development	Ongoing training, education, and skills development
	Leadership and organizational development
	Personnel management – management of status changes
	Employer of choice programs
	Compensation and Benefits
	Promotions
	Employee evaluations
	Occupational health and safety administration
	Labor relations
Separation	Planned and unplanned separation from the organization

Any organization that wants to embed change as their new culture better be paying a lot of attention to the human resource practices and policies. Your organization sends signals every time an employee action is taken. Promoting the manager that does not follow standard work over the one that does, sends a signal. Leaving lean training out of orientation and on-boarding of new staff and medical staff sends a sign. Not having lean skills as a competency for new hires outside of the organization sends a signal. If you are having trouble getting physicians to participate in quality improvement, make the requirement part of the hiring process. Reward the team and team members that best follow standard work. Every human resource action related to staff and medical staff is an opportunity to change the culture of your organization.

The long-term sustainability of your new culture will be directly tied to your recruiting practices. Hiring people with multiple years of lean experience is a plus, but not a requirement. Hiring people that can work in a team, be open-minded to team-based change, and can follow standard work is necessary. The skills and competencies you require should be written into the job description and followed along with the job posting and corresponding interviews. Don't underestimate the amount of work it will take to update the dozens of job descriptions that exist in your organization. You can update the descriptions on an as-needed basis but start early.

Lean thinking should follow the employee through their life cycle. This can be accomplished in two ways. First, lean skills and attributes can be built into the various activities of the life cycle. For example, lean training can begin at orientation, and lean competencies can be integral to raises and promotions. Second, lean thinking can be used to optimize and complete the human resource department work. Can waste be taken out of the orientation training? Can waste be taken out of occupational health and safety practices? Can the hiring cycle time be reduced by 50 percent? Are the human resource practices executed with standard work? Are they managed visually with clear targets and action plans? Is A3 thinking evident and obvious?

Frequently, human resources have the lead in creating personnel-related policies for an organization. One example would be the absence management policy. I have frequently heard human resource department personnel say that the managers do not follow the absence management policy. Managers may skip steps in the administration of the policy or fail to document an absence in a timely manner. Certainly, the expectation is that everyone will follow standard work, managers included. Let's look at the application of lean from another perspective. This book is about leadership. Human resource leadership may be starting with the wrong problem. With regard to creating a culture of improvement, "clean up your own sandbox before you play in someone else's." Rather than changing someone else, a requirement to fix the absence management process is to start by changing yourself. Improve the hiring process and streamline labor relations. Optimize occupational safety and health services. Work with your own staff to create a culture of improvement and deliver value to the organization. When this is underway, the opportunity to engage others outside of your area of focus will be much easier.

Back to the absence management policy: I am not inclined to let management totally off the hook. However, as lean thinkers, we should use the tools to improve the process. Is it difficlut to find out who has been missing work and when? A3 thinking and problem-solving tools can be used to understand why the absence management policy is not consistently used. Develop countermeasures to resolve the root causes and test the solutions.

Engage management in the problem-solving process, and the chances of success will increase created of their increased ownership of the problem.

A community hospital, let us call them Meadowbrook, was having trouble sourcing and hiring nurses for the organization. With the global and national shortage of nurses today, this is actually a common problem most healthcare organizations face today. This hospital has approximately 150 beds and a staff of 1200 employees. The hospital is state-of-the-art, with competent management and leadership. The commute was not excessive relative to the "big city" competition, yet the hospital had a difficult time filling positions. Bob Broach, an experienced lean consultant once commented that "the best people are on the market the shortest period of time." This makes sense intuitively, as the best people are always hired first. And this statement also implies that a long recruiting cycle is not your friend. The best people will be off the market if a competitor can hire faster than you.

The organization decided to perform a value stream analysis on the recruiting cycle. The current condition had a lead-time for a new hire of 72 days. The timeline looked as follows (Figure 5.1):

A series of four-day kaizen events followed, spanning nearly nine months, which included: improving the posting of positions, streamlining the applicant screening process, reducing the interviewing cycle, improving the offer letter process, improving the employee physical process, and reducing the timeline and effectiveness of the orientation process. The final results reduced the recruitment cycle to 42 days. This improvement of nearly 30 days effectively solved this organization's recruiting issues. Qualified candidates could be entered effectively into the recruiting cycle and hired in a

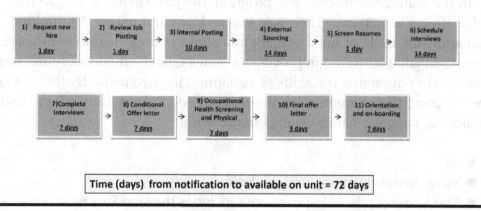

Time (days) from notification to available on unit = 72 days

Figure 5.1   Current conditions nursing new hire recruiting cycle.

timely manner. The net result for Meadowbrook was a reduction in agency/ temporary staff expense of nearly $1.8 million annually and a reduction in annual overtime premium of $680,000.

Another example of making a change in the new culture involves management development and promotions. In many organizations, the best charge nurse or team leader gets promoted to the next open supervisor or manager position. In industry, the saying goes if you take the best painter and make him/her your supervisor; I cannot guarantee you got a great supervisor, but I can guarantee you just lost your best painter. The same goes for great clinicians. The best clinician does not always make the best supervisor. Does this mean we cannot promote deserving people? Absolutely not, but a great lean organization has the best clinicians in a position to succeed when promoted.

An urban hospital in a metropolitan area of approximately three million people wanted to improve the skills of their management team. This organization, whom we will call Lakeshore Health, decided to establish some lean-based promotion criteria. Any staff member that wanted to be considered for management had to take a one-year position as part of the lean core team. This program, known as the lean management residency program, was designed to ensure that any new manager was an internal expert in lean thinking before assuming their new role. Candidates were required to interview for these positions, and not everyone was accepted. Applicants needed to be in the top 20% of their cohort, be listed on the promotable watch list, be open-minded to change, and have the ability to carry a room. After an extensive interviewing process, the top candidates were accepted into the management residency program.

In the management residency program, the participants were given a value stream to improve. Their role was to learn and master A3 thinking and apply the cycle of improvement to a series of areas within their value stream. In addition to the improvement activity, large amounts of time were dedicated to mastering the skills of sustaining improvement. By the end of the program, the residents were deeply exposed to lean thinking and had dedicated, targeted, hands-on experience with:

- 5S
- Value stream mapping and analysis
- The kaizen cycle of improvement includes the standard work for preparing, executing, and sustaining a rapid cycle improvement
- Standard work

- Visual management systems of both process and results
  - Managing for daily improvement
  - Kamishibai
- Improvement and sustaining project management skills
- A comfort with charts and graphs
- Experience with staff engagement
- Leadership standard work
- An understanding of true north measures
- Experience in working vertically and horizontally across the organization
- Linking local improvement to program and corporate strategy
- Driving double-digit improvement in the key measures

When the first class graduated, the residents initially returned to their home area to make contributions to the program/department from which they came. This created an incentive for managers to encourage staff to participate in the program. When a supervisor position opened up, the interested candidates applied and frequently were given new positions. The results were dramatic. A typical resident, when compared to their peers, outperformed their counterparts in all measurable areas. The average increase in performance versus their peers against the key measures was 12–65% higher in any measurable category. These key measures include quality and safety, lead-time and access, cost performance, patient experience, growth, and staff engagement. This is how you reward interested and highly qualified candidates with new roles and simultaneously improve the performance of the organization.

Having your promotable staff get experience as lean thinkers before taking on a leadership assignment truly holds great potential for your organization. The assignment on the lean core team taught the potential leader a new way to manage. Improvement became part of the culture of their new departments/programs. As a young manager, there is a tendency to fall back on the experiences you encountered as a staff member. Most people lead and manage as you learned from your predecessor. A period of time immersed in lean thinking will create new and better experiences to draw upon; this eliminates the many months of trial and error a new manager must experience when new to the role. By promoting candidates from the lean residency program, your organization is sending a signal that lean management is important.

Closing out lean in human resources, one can see that seeing and eliminating waste applies to not only clinical care but administrative processes as well. We will expect the same double-digit improvement in our core human resource processes by seeing and eliminating the waste associated with the administration of our human resource policies and practices.

Lean Supply Chain

A lean process is one where non-value-added activity is continuously reduced. In creating a culture where change is the new way of business, the supply chain holds great promise. One area of frustration for staff is the proximity and availability of supplies and materials. The good news for healthcare is that the notion of lean supply chain is well documented. A great lean healthcare supply chain can yield the following benefits:

- improved availability of materials and supplies
- shorter lead-times for replenishment
- materials and supplies near or at the point of use
- more frequent replenishment of supplies mitigating large amounts of storage
- less obsolescence of materials and supplies due to increased supply velocity
- better ergonomics associated with material and supply presentation
- improved inventory turnover
- reduced supply chain costs (lower cost of goods sold, reduced administrative costs, reduced shipping/receiving/materials management costs, and reduced carrying costs)
- safer care
- improved staff and medical staff satisfaction
- improved patient experience
- better supplier relationships

How effective is your supply chain? There are many third-party vendors within healthcare that provide kitting and distribution services in very short lead-times. Oftentimes this is supported with some type of supply chain management functionality. Materials and supplies, with the exception of some hard-to-acquire pharmaceuticals, most often can be ordered and received within 1 to 2 days. Shorter lead-times, assuming you frequently order exactly what is needed, should lead to higher inventory turnover. Inventory turnover is the ratio of how many times an organization's inventory is sold and replaced over a period of time. Generally speaking, there are two calculations of this ratio. The easier formula to understand is as follows.

$$\text{Inventory Turnover} = \text{Sales \$/Average Inventory \$ on Hand}$$

As an example, assume New River Hospital (fictional name) has annual healthcare billings of \$400 million and carries inventory on hand of \$70 million. New River's inventory turnover is as follows:

$$\text{Inventory Turnover} = \$400 \text{ million}/\$70 \text{ million} = 5.7 \text{ inventory turns}$$

5.7 turns implies that the inventory dollars of New River Hospital turnover roughly six times per year. It is generally known that inventory turns across all industries range from 8 to 12 annually.

Now, back to the healthcare supply chain. With the availability of supplies and materials in 1–2 days, we should expect inventory turns approaching 100. Why? Assume that there are 250 working days per year. Materials can be received every 1–2 days. Theoretically, we could turn over all of the inventory every 2 days. This would lead to 250 days/2 days average inventory on hand = 125 inventory turns.

My experience in working with North American healthcare organizations shows that the majority of organizations have typical turnover numbers of 4–12 annual turns for storerooms and 2–8 annual turns for surgical supplies. There is a big gap between 125 turns and 12. For a \$400 million dollar organization, 125 turns shows on-hand inventory of \$3.2 million, while 12 turns has an on-hand inventory cost of \$33.3 million. The difference of \$30 million might eliminate the need to borrow for capital improvements or prevent the delay of starting a new program.

In a lean supply chain, materials and supplies would be pulled into the organization at the rate of customer demand. The lean word for a pull system with minimum inventory designed to meet customer demand would be Kanban. Kanban loosely translates to signboard or signal and is a replenishment system based on signals that come from the true needs of the customer. This is significantly different from a forecasting system, or a min-max system, or a re-order point system. A Kanban system is an entire management system for operating the supply chain in the least waste way.

What does a world-class supply chain look like? I have been in a few of the lean, tier one automotive suppliers and a few automotive assembly plants that routinely get near 1000 inventory turns annually. This means the entire factory turns over all of its inventory dollars every 4 hours! While I am not sure of any healthcare supply chain approaching 1000 inventory turns, there are programs starting to approach 50 turns!

Supply chain practices exist to allow the organization to function. In and of themselves, the supply chain creates no direct value to the patient. They serve the staff and medical staff in their delivery of value-added services. Since supply chain practices consume time, space, and resources while failing to directly meet the needs of the patient, they are excellent candidates for the elimination of process waste. Lean leadership of supply chain practices implies that world-class rates of improvement should be strived for along with the key measures of human development, process and product quality, lead-time for supplies and materials, and productivity. While not a true north measure, the supply chain should add a measure of inventory utilization such as turns or reduction in working capital. It is not possible to provide world-class healthcare without a world-class supply chain. Lean organizations understand this and create the vision, align the resources, and inspire the supply chain team for greatness.

Lean Project Management, Lean Construction, and Lean New Service Introduction

As you may now recognize, there is a lean approach to all of the work done in an organization. Anywhere work is completed, and value is created for a customer (both internal and external customer), waste is present. A lean organization understands this and aspires every day to make the organization more waste-free. Significant organizational dollars are spent on introducing "new" things; earlier we discussed introducing new technology and IT systems. Project work is plentiful within healthcare. New quality procedures need to be put in place, new therapies are introduced, and accreditation standards must be met. New equipment and technology to support better and safer care are purchased and deployed. Additionally, new programs are introduced. New services and clinics are made available to patients. And facilities are re-developed, or new construction projects are completed.

Table 5.5 Lean New Product and Process Introduction

System and Organizational Management	Planning System	Execution and Delivery System
Business case	Quality function deployment	Concurrent engineering
System level architecture and standards	Voice of the customer	2P/3P design
Portfolio management	Vertical value stream mapping	Value engineering
Cost modeling	Obeyu concept (Big Room)	Design for X
Knowledge management	Net present value analysis	Quality systems (mistake proofing)
Strategy deployment	Project risk analysis	Failure mode effects analysis
Visual management	Kano	Cause and effect problem-solving

In a lean organization, regardless of the final value delivered either to patients or the organization itself, a similar approach is used: lean new product/process introduction. World-class new product/process introduction management involves meeting two simultaneous objectives: delivering compelling value to the customer and doing the work in the least waste way. Table 5.5 shows a small sample of the tools used in lean new product/process introduction.

The vertical value stream approach to project management, part of the lean planning system, was discussed in the deployment of IT projects earlier in the chapter. This project management approach can be used to manage any project. Lean project management is used to meet the customer specifications of any project in the least waste way. This approach has been used effectively in managing the following types of projects within healthcare:

- preparing for accreditation
- introduction of new therapies
- deployment of new medical equipment (diagnostic imaging, medical, surgical, etc.)
- facility redevelopment
- new construction

- month-end close (financial)
- optimizing the budgeting cycle
- spread of known lean solutions to other departments and programs
- introduction of new services (clinics and procedures)
- IT development and deployment
- acquiring new businesses
- capturing additional/new market share
- development and deployment of new training curriculums
- orientation of new employees
- integrating a new provide practice

There are countless other areas for the lean new product and process approaches to be realized. For those of you new to lean, I think you can now see that a comprehensive enterprise-wide lean management system is much more than a toolkit to improve patient flow, reduce cost, and improve the quality of care. Lean is an entire business system that permeates every process in your entire organization. Respect for people and the elimination of non-value-added activities become part of every staff member's everyday job. Making changes to the new culture implies continuously improving every system in your organization. From the list above, there are a number of lean tools and applications involved in new product/process introduction. Like all of the lean tools and applications, they take years to internalize. Unfortunately, this set of tools and techniques is much more technical in nature and cannot be learned in a single session. A good Sensei will be able to teach your organization the new product introduction process or direct to someone who can.

The lean new product and process introduction system comes from the Toyota Production System approaches used to introduce new vehicles. Toyota can bring a new vehicle to market in about 60% less time of many of its competitors. It has developed this system over 50 years by refining its new product introduction process that continues to evolve and improve today. As an example of a new process introduction, Crescent Moon Hospital launched a new service that provided short-stay rehabilitation services to adult medicine patients. Crescent Moon is a very small community hospital with approximately 100 in-patient beds supported by ~800 employees and ~200 volunteers. The hospital had challenges discharging patients from their acute care beds since the community services had a gap in their offering negating the area's ability to provide the appropriate level of care. There were long-term care choices, complex continuing care choices, and home choices, but no short-term rehab offerings within fifty miles of the hospital. Thus, the leadership team and medical program decided to offer a 16-bed short-stay rehab program.

The improvement process began with the creation of an A3 to develop and deliver the required services. The improvement plans on the Short Stay Rehabilitation Unit A3 called for a thorough understanding of the voice of the customer and a Process Preparation (2P) design kaizen event to create the new service. The project closed with a vertical value stream to acquire and deploy the people, equipment, and construction to launch the new service. A brainstorming process was used to identify the voice of the customer and define the process requirements. An example of the brainstorming format used is shown in Figure 5.2.

Once the voice of the customer was defined, the next major step involved designing the process. In a lean organization, the entire process is defined *before* any work is done. Process definition includes defining the following seven workflows:

1. Identification of the people required to do the work
2. Defining the work methods
3. Defining the materials and supplies needed to do the work
4. Defining the equipment needed to do the work.
5. Defining the information requirements to accomplish the work tasks

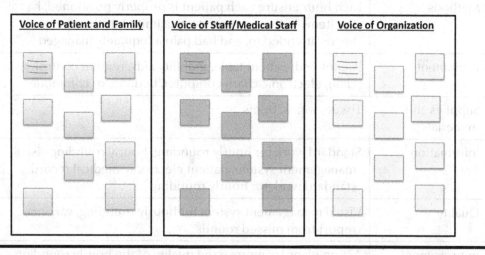

Figure 5.2   Voice of the customer.

6. Defining the quality control systems to know the work has been done properly
7. Defining how quality and improvement systems will be used

The 2P (Process Preparation) kaizen event is tailor made to define these seven workflows. In addition to defining the process, the 2P kaizen event is used to develop breakthrough improvements in the introduction of a new product or process. This specific event looked at several of the core processes that would occur within the unit on a regular basis and defined their corresponding seven workflows. The core processes included unit admission, medication administration, development of an inter-professional plan of care, discharge planning, meal delivery, rehabilitation treatment and scheduling, rounding, and charting. Obviously, there are other processes that occur on a daily basis in a rehabilitation unit, but these were considered to be the trouble areas for the organization that needed to be well defined prior to the build and opening of the new unit.

Providing a further illustration of the seven workflows, Table 5.6 shows the seven flows for the hourly rounding process that was developed and

Table 5.6 Seven Flows for Hourly Rounding

Product	Hourly Rounding
People	Unit nurses, physiotherapists, physiotherapist assistants, multi-skilled attendants
Methods	Each hour ensure each patient is properly positioned, has all the items in the appropriate proximity, has their personal needs attended to, and had pain adequately managed
Equipment	Patient bed, patient table, mobility aids, remote control, patient chair, electronic chart, computer, bedpan, or commode
Supplies and materials	Tissue, wipes, briefs
Information	Standard work for hourly rounding, hourly rounding visual management system, patient electronic medical record, standard work for hourly rounding
Quality	Visual management system for hourly rounding, variance report from missed rounds
Improvement	Action plans to improve the quality of the hourly rounding process Visual management of results of the performance of the rounding process

deployed on the new unit. Before producing the final product, the 2P kaizen actually develops multiple ways to meet the customer requirements; a minimum of seven different ways are explored and evaluated against the customer requirements before settling in on a solution. The solution is then performed in a mock simulation to verify its effectiveness.

Of note on this core process, upon opening the rehab unit, the patient satisfaction data was the best in the hospital and has been sustained in the 98th percentile against peer units. Additionally, as a result of the hourly rounding, the call bell requirements were reduced by 85% over other peer units. These types of breakthrough results are anticipated and expected from 2P improvement work.

This particular project closed with a vertical value stream analysis to develop the implementation plan. An example of a lean project management plan is shown in Figure 5.3.

There are several steps associated with creating a lean project management plan. At a high level, these steps include:

1. Assemble the team of people that will be doing the work
2. Document the project name and due date

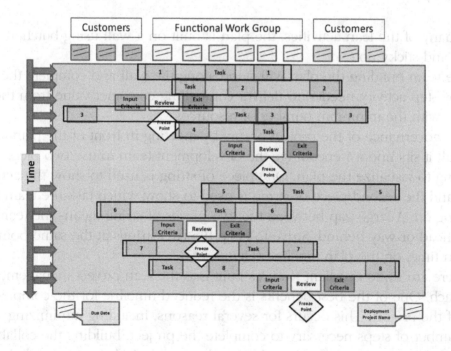

Figure 5.3   Lean project management plan.

3. Identify the key milestones
4. Document the information necessary to answer the questions needed to meet the milestones (inputs)
5. Document the evidence that the questions have been answered (outputs)
6. Define the work tasks necessary to answer all of the inputs and deliver the outputs
7. Assign the tasks to a lead function
8. Determine who will be needed to collaborate on the tasks to compress the timeline and free up resources
9. Define the timelines to enable concurrent design
10. Document who needs to attend the milestone reviews and when
11. Develop the standard work for the collaborative tasks. Complete the task work
12. Hold the milestone reviews to make sure all questions have been answered before proceeding to the next milestone and to review the process for continuous improvement and updates to the standard work
13. Repeat steps 11–13 until all milestones have been met
14. Perform a final review of the process and make adjustments for future work

Like many of the lean activities, the plan is built on a wall using butcher paper and sticky notes.

The team building the plan will stand along the wall and complete the step-by-step activity needed to deliver compelling customer value from the project with the minimum number of resources.

The governance of the project occurs by meeting in front of the plan at the wall it sits upon; I encourage the development team to use two pieces of string to visualize the plan. One piece of string is used to show the actual date, and the second piece of string is used to show which task the team is working on. A large gap between the two pieces of string means the team is way ahead or way behind. Strive to keep the two strings at the same point, and on time, on the plan timeline (Figure 5.4).

There are some excellent features built into the lean project management approach. One of the best benefits is the reduced timeline for the completion of the project. This occurs for several reasons, including minimizing the number of steps necessary to complete the project, building the collaboration upfront so time is not lost chasing down technical experts for their

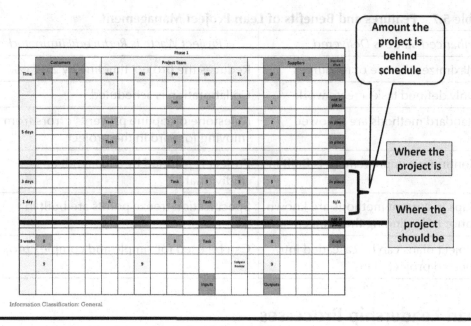

Figure 5.4   Managing the project schedule timeline.

opinions and feedback, holding the discipline of the milestone reviews to prevent incomplete tasks to creep into the next milestone creating rework, and standard methods are followed building on the organizational knowledge and best practices. Table 5.7 summarizes some of the additional benefits.

In many organizations, there are often multiple project management approaches. The IT team follows a project management discipline from the IT sector, Facilities/Construction follows a project management discipline from the construction sector, and Quality follows a project management discipline from the continuous improvement sector. A lower-level manager now has to be moderately competent in at least three different approaches. In a world-class lean enterprise, there is a single standard project management discipline followed: The vertical value stream approach to project management is the only approach used across the entire organization. This helps simplify the language and the concepts utilized for the entire organization. As a leader, it takes courage to create an organizational standard that breaks down the technical complexities of project management. This necessary step will help create a shared vision for the organization and align the resources on the journey to world class.

Table 5.7 Features and Benefits of Lean Project Management

Enhanced Value is Delivered	Project Waste is Reduced/Eliminated
Maximizes the use of resources	Reduces the project timeline by 25–75%
Only defined tasks create work	Collaboration is scheduled
Standard methods are followed	Milestone discipline prevents errors from moving forward in the project
Continuous improvement is built in	Project is planned by a team not an individual
Gaps in current methods are known prior to beginning the project	Specification freeze points are built in
Project plans can be cascaded into nested project plans	Can be used for simple and complex projects

Lean Leadership Processes

Senior leadership in your healthcare organization will be heavily involved with many of the processes already discussed in this book. A valuable lesson learned is that regardless of the competency of the lean core team, the strength of the middle and line management staff, and the strength of your profit and loss statement, if the senior management team practices do not change with the organization, then your specific leadership behaviors will drive the organization back to status quo. Senior leadership actions and behaviors are the single largest factor for successful lean transformation. Leadership processes include not only your organizational core processes but also processes completed and executed by the senior team.

Many of the leadership practices will change by addressing the core processes discussed eariler in this chapter. Capacity building will require leadership to develop lean thinking skills. HR policies will lead to the hiring of lean thinking managers and physicians. Financial systems will use lean thinking in budgeting and financial reporting. Great lean organizations eliminate the annual budgeting requirements and move toward a three-month rolling budget. In Chapter 2, the approach lean organizations use toward strategic planning and deployment of the strategy were discussed in great detail. All of these processes will impact how leadership works within the organization.

There is one additional leadership process that is worthy of mention, committee management. Healthcare is full of committees, with three to five times as many committees as what I see in other industries. There are board committees, medical management committees, best practice committees, quality committees, professional practice committees, pharmaceutical and therapeutic committees, and a host of other standing and ad-hoc committees in practice. There is nothing wrong with committee work. A focused group of committed individuals coming together as a team can get a lot accomplished. The challenge is that on many committees both the focus and the commitment are lacking. The process is further complicated by no clear committee goals, no standard agenda to follow, poorly run meeting etiquette, and less than stellar attendance. Additionally, homework between meetings is frequently not completed or poorly completed, leading to a lack of progress and a lot of wasted management hours. These management hours compete for the time we want managers and leaders to spend in Gemba problem-solving and driving lean thinking. Take a minute to look through your leadership calendar this coming month. How much time is spent in standing meetings and committees? In a great lean organization, this time will be no more than 30%. In most healthcare organizations I work with, this time tends to be closer to 70%.

Lean organizations use A3 thinking to manage the committee process (Figure 5.5). Every committee must work from the A3 form to deliver on their goals. Imagine if every committee answered these four questions:

A-3 Theme:	Pharmacy Committee		Date:	27 Sept August 2024 Revision #: 0		
Team Members: Bill Smith, Jean Mangum, Elliott Wilson, Samantha Todd, Jennifer Jones, Russell Kline						
Reason For Improvement: Live the corporate value: Improve the Quality of Care Be Fiscally Responsible Improve Access to services						
Current Performance and Reflections on Current Performance: Pharmacy Spend is equal to $8,000,0000 Costs have gone up each year for 11 consecutive years No defined formulary utilized No formal process to introduce new medicines no process in place to practice anti-microbial stewardship		Target Performance: Reduce overall spend per patient visit establish a well-defined formulary that is followed by physician group Have a well defined to medicine testing and introduction process anti-microbial stewardship is in place introduce new drug therapies to reduce LOS				
		Dimension	**Measure**		**Current**	**Target**
		Quality	reduce infection rates by 2015		.022	.011
		Delivery/Access	Reduce I/P LOS		5.1	4.4
		Cost	Reduce Rx spend		$8 Million	reduce 10%
		Anticipated Hard savings: $800,000 in drug expense Anticipated Soft Savings: Reduce infection rates by 50% in four years				

Figure 5.5   First three boxes of an A3 for the pharmacy committee.

1. What is our reason for improvement?
2. How would we describe our current condition and what reflections do we have on our current conditions?
3. What is our desired condition?
4. How do we measure success?

Completing these four questions would enable the committee to document the first three sections on the A3 form. Following A3 thinking, the next step would be for the committee members to quantify the gap between current and target conditions. Closing the gap would allow for solutions to be generated, which would constitute the working actions and small experiments of the committee members. This converts the committee work from a meeting to organizational value-add. Validated solutions would be rolled out to the broader organization through the follow-up plans; the effectiveness of the solutions would be validated through measurement tracking. Progress of the committees would be reported simply by updating and reporting from the actual A3 document.

Rising Sun Hospital had each of their committees go through A3 thinking and create improvement plans for their individual committees. In their current state, the hospital has 84 committees. Seven committees were standard committees required by their by-laws and seven were ad-hoc committees added to resolve a specific hospital problem or to manage a project. Upon completing their A3 forms, the senior team had an opportunity to review the documents and the status of the committees. As an example, it became readily apparent that the four committees shared similar goals and measures. The decision was made to immediately consolidate the four committees and create a single committee in its place. 30 other committees were dropped when the improvement potential was quantified, and it was deemed that the ROI for the committee work was insufficient for the investment in time and resources. The net result was a reduction from 84 committees to 50 (42% reduction), resulting in 9500 hours of annual committee time returned to management and physician leaders. Additionally, standard work was created for managing the committee agendas, thus reducing the meeting length from 1 to 2 hours to a standard meeting length of 45 minutes. The standard agenda made the committees much more effective, and 37 of the 50 work groups met their annual targets for improvement or met their project timeline. This improvement saved management and physician leadership an additional 2500 hours per year! Could your organization benefit from an additional 12,000 hours of management time?

Leadership processes should evolve over time. Lean thinking organizations are constantly looking for ways to eliminate non-value-added activity. Since leadership processes generally do not directly meet the needs of a customer, they are candidates for improvement. Those that do not deliver value should be eliminated, and the processes that do deliver value should be executed in the least wasteful way; no part of the organization can be skipped if you desire to become a lean enterprise. Leadership engaged in improving their processes inspires the organization for greatness through leading by example. This applies to committees, standard meetings for project updates, staff meetings, board meetings, etc.

Medical Leadership Processes

In a lean healthcare organization, it is a requirement to have physicians that are engaged and inspired in their daily work. While physician engagement does not guarantee transformational success, **failure to engage physicians guarantees transformational failure**. Due to their specific role within the healthcare system and the wide scope of practice, physicians are in a unique position to stop quality improvements in their tracks. Physicians can create medical orders whether they are evidence-based or not. Physicians can choose to follow organizational clinical pathways or choose to deviate from them. I am not implying sabotage to organizational best practices, but physicians have both more leeway and more responsibility than other members of the care team.

The process becomes even more complicated when we look at how the medical staff is employed and managed. Some physicians are employees of the hospital/healthcare system, and some are independent consultants with or without admitting privileges. Some physicians are part of a group that is hired to fill a specific medical role in the hospital such as diagnostic imaging or emergency services. The leadership of the medical staff is also distributed. Once you move beyond the board and the chief medical officer, there might be program chiefs, medical directors, and department chiefs; each organization has a different degree of accountability within their management framework. Some organizations have unionized physician groups adding another layer of complexity to the management of the system.

A lean organization works with some "knowns" and develops a plan to operationalize these "knowns." The following conditions must be satisfied to create a culture of continuous improvement:

1. Standard work needs to be defined and followed by all staff and medical staff. Systems that are based on individual physician practice will never be able to transform. Culturally, individual phsycian based practice has been the norm for physicians, so this transition to standard work is difficult.
2. Physicians need to take accountability for developing and following their own standards. The lean office (kaizen promotion office) can assist with the facilitation of the improvement work in the same way this office facilitates improvement across the rest of the organization.
3. The measures and targets for the organization and the medical staff need to be aligned. In many organizations, the physician compensation structure drives the behaviors of medical practice. Administration and medical staff need to share aligned measures along the true north dimensions of staff development, quality, safety, access, cost, and growth.
4. Physicians also need to participate, full time, on the kaizen improvement teams and use A3 thinking to deliver results. Like the rest of the organization, the skills of improvement and the change of the culture are built using A3 thinking learned in the structure of a kaizen event. Most organizations immediately default to going around the physicians or offering them a part-time presence on the team; these shortcuts will prevent your organization from transforming.

The organization, thus, needs a plan to ensure all of these conditions are satisfied. The physician engagement plan needs to include the following items:

- plans to create system level physician standards, created by physicians, and implemented by physicians.
- an accountability framework to ensure standard work is followed by the medical staff (I have found this to be extremely rare within healthcare organizations)
- aligned measures and targets for administration and medical staff
- plans to ensure physicians can participate on the improvement teams in a full-time capacity

What world-class healthcare organizations find is that when the physicians take the lead in a meaningful way, rapid progress in transforming the system can occur. Additionally, like all people, we tend to support and follow our own ideas. So, solutions generated by physicians have a much higher likelihood of being followed by physicians. There are many stories that exist about the time a change was made without physician input and how the change was perceived and followed by the medical staff. We want to avoid this phenomenon from happening during an enterprise-wide lean transformation.

One of the approaches used by lean healthcare organizations is to take advantage of the physician credentialing and privledging process to hire and credential physicians with a framework to help engage the physician group in lean quality improvement. All healthcare organizations have hiring criteria for new physicians and an accountability agreement (or physician compact) that governs their employment. The best lean organizations build the lean behaviors and time commitments directly into the agreement. How much farther along could you be in process improvement if improved if your physician agreements included one or more of the following statements:

■ participates, full time, on a kaizen event team once per year.
■ follows department standards including standards for quality, clinical pathways, and order sets. Provides feedback for further enhancements.
■ assists in the development and deployment of physician department standards.
■ monitors personal performance against the true north measures of the department. Takes personal action and accountability to ensure measures are met.
■ participates in team-based quality improvement and patient safety.
■ leads one quality improvement initiative for the department using A3 thinking each calendar year.
■ assists in peer audits of physician standard work.
■ demonstrates behaviors that encourage teamwork and continuous improvement of the department.

This list is not meant to be exhaustive, but rather to stimulate thinking on what can be done in your organization to change the new culture. Lack of physician engagement is second on the list of why organizations fail to create a culture of improvement, right behind, senior leadership involvement. Building the physician behavior and physician engagement needs directly into the hiring specifications process can help ensure the organization is making change part of the new culture.

Many organizations, while sincere about wanting to engage physicians, have a difficult time understanding where to begin. I offer the following suggestions for consideration in helping you get started.

1. Begin by standardizing clinical quality. Engage physicians in the development and deployment of consistent approaches to evidence-based care. Patients deserve the best possible care.
2. Standardize process. Develop plans for department-wide consistency and accountability. As an example, define standard work start times, standard work end times, consistent charting and documentation standards, standard rounding times, etc. What type of consistent information do you require from and provide to the inter-professional team? What time of day do you need or provide this information? Variations in physician and staff practice in this area lead to significant levels of lost productivity and frustration from both parties. Build discipline and repeatability into the department processes.
3. Develop solutions using the following approaches:
   a. Use creativity before capital. Do not default to more staff, more resources, more equipment, and most importantly more technology. These investments should be last.
   b. Be consistent with lean principles. Solutions should create continuous flow, utilize pull, move toward defect-free environment, and be managed visually.
   c. Use lean tools. Specifically follow A-3 thinking. Avoid jumping to solutions.
   d. Solutions should be non-personality based. World-class healthcare is not created by individual practice and preference. World-class healthcare is created by developing a system that is repeatable and independent of the professional.

Taking Lean Beyond Your Four Walls

Healthcare is a system. You might be concerned that many of the activities that help make a change in the new culture are within your organization's four walls. At some point, patients and caregivers will transition into or outside of your organization. To truly become world-class, you will need to bring lean quality improvement to your customers and suppliers. It is easy to pull suppliers in and demand they improve performance. You own the agreements and the contracts. This is just the same as making it easy for your customers to pull you in and demand you improve your performance.

Both of these behaviors are not a partnership. World-class lean organizations work together with suppliers and customers to take waste out of the system. This creates a win-win for all parties. Simply demanding one party improve their performance is potentially a win-lose situation. Taking waste out of the system creates the best possible outcome. When non-value-added activity comes out of the process, the customer wins. System quality improves leading to better outcomes and higher customer service, lead-times for services decrease, and the total cost of the system goes down. These are wins both sides of the relationship can readily support.

Earlier in the chapter, the approach to creating a lean supply chain was discussed; the lean supply chain is a customer-supplier relationship that extends beyond your four walls. The focus of this next section is on the transitions of care. These transitions of care are also customer-supplier relationships between the sending party and the receiving party, but not to the patient. The patient expects that there will be no gap in performance and no gap in communication. Transitions of care happen frequently within healthcare. Emergency medical service patients transition to the emergency department. The emergency department patient transitions to an in-patient unit. In-patient unit patients transition to home health or rehabilitation services. Primary care patients transition to specialty care; the list is endless.

It is understood in healthcare that the handover of a patient from one professional to another or from one organization to another represents a time of increased risk. To be sure, patient consent and privacy legislation create some well-intentioned difficulties in the handover process. The medical complexity of some patients and variations in electronic medical records also create additional challenges. A lean look at the transition process, however, can bring new insights to a currently daunting challenge. Looking at the value-added activity from the patient's perspective cuts across all the organizational policy and funding barriers that make the transition process difficult. Lean leadership needs to provide the vision for the organization, and if seamless transitions become the goal, then leadership needs to allocate the resources for success and inspire the organization for greatness.

As an example, one post-acute care provider organization realized that their admission process was a significant barrier to patient transitions. In the current condition, the rehabilitation hospital would only take admissions on Tuesday and Thursday afternoons. This led to many conservable days being accumulated in their acute care partners. Their joint lean efforts led to an admission process that could happen 7 days a week within a 12-hour window. In addition to the reduction in conservable days, the rehabilitation hospital admission rate went up seven percentage points improving access.

The greatest lean healthcare organizations routinely include patients, suppliers, and customers in their improvement efforts. By taking waste out of the system, for the benefit of the customer, all three parties get improved performance. When taking a traditional suppler-customer relationship approach, waste is often simply shifted from one party to another. This is not improvement, although one organization might show better performance numbers. This would be offset by the other organization showing worse performance numbers, or increased cost. Unless the non-value-added activity is totally eliminated, and not simply shifted around within the value stream, real improvement in performance does not occur.

This type of improvement is a bit more complex than improving within your own organization, which is why I left it for last in this chapter. High levels of trust must exist for improvement to be realized between organizations. Additionally, there needs to be a way for both organizations to share in the rewards including fiscal improvement. This can only work with transparency of costs that are sometimes difficult for parties to expose. If the real passion is on improving the patient/client experience, then this activity will become easier. It will take lots of leadership to truly accomplish your vision. But taking lean outside your four walls is the pinnacle of making change in the new culture. Those organizations that take leadership in this space are often held in high regard by both their supplier, their customers, and their community.

Chapter Summary: Key Points from Chapter 5

- Transformation is difficult because the new lean culture and the current organizational culture are at odds with one another.
- The organization to make change last. New changes to standards, processes, and workflows need to be hardwired into the organization to make change last.
- Processes and systems across the organization need to be updated to support lean thinking. This is not intuitive and will meet resistance from leadership. The majority of these processes will fall under administrative and support functions. Key areas needing to be addressed will include:

- Human resource policies
- Creating a lean supply chain
- New process introduction, project management, and construction services
- Senior leadership processes include strategic planning, Hoshin Kanri (or strategy deployment), governance of strategic objectives and improvement work, and committee management

■ Support processes exist to allow the clinical and medical staff to better serve patients and caregivers.

■ Lean capacity building at all levels of the organization is a requirement to make improvements to the new organizational culture.

■ As your organization culture changes, you will be ready to take improvement beyond your four walls to suppliers and service partners. This is a necessary step to continue to remove waste from the health-care enterprise.

Notes

1. Lucas Mearian, Harvard Study: Computers Do Not Save Hospitals Money, 2 December 2009, www.computerworld.com/s/article/print/9141428/Harvard _study, accessed March 2024.
2. Thu Pham, 2012 Health IT Spending and Trends, On Line Tech, 28 December 2012, http://resource.onlinetech.com/2012-health-it-spending-trends/, accessed March 2024.
3. J. L. Reinertsen, M. Bisognano, and M. D. Pugh, *Seven Leadership Leverage Points for Organization-Level Improvement in Health Care,* 2nd ed. (Cambridge, MA: Institute for Healthcare Improvement, 2008), pg. 20.
4. J. L. Reinertsen, M. Bisognano, and M. D. Pugh, *Seven Leadership Leverage Points for Organization-Level Improvement in Health Care,* 2nd ed. (Cambridge, MA: Institute for Healthcare Improvement, 2008), pg. 20.

Chapter 6

Leadership Behaviors and Actions for Success

Leading by Example

Virtually every organization that I have worked with or talked with has a vision statement, a mission statement, and a set of core values. The statements and values are created with the intent to guide the thinking and behavior of the organization. Since care for patients and clients is at the center of healthcare services, many of the vision statements read somewhat the same.

A sample healthcare vision might read:

- "To be the greatest community hospital in the state/province"
- "To be the worldwide leader in healthcare research and quality"
- "Providing the right care, at the right place, at the right time."

The core values frequently have a common set of themes as well. Core values might include:

- Patients and families first
- Teamwork
- Integrity
- Safe care

 DOI: 10.4324/9781003532132-6

- Collaborative care
- Meeting patient needs along the continuum of care
- Respect

Having spoken with dozens of different healthcare leadership teams and their boards, each can articulate the vision and values of their organization well. However, in speaking with the different layers of the organization, first to middle management and physician leadership and then to line staff and medical staff, the clarity of the vision and core values frequently varies. Some organizations do an excellent job of continuously communicating their vision and values. The message of what the organization is trying to become and the values the organization will live to get there are discussed frequently. Other organizations rarely speak of their mission and values, and the communication is only demonstrated in some vision and/or values posters scattered about the organization, and perhaps in a few slide presentations. The values are further degraded when the true actions of the organization, specifically the behaviors and actions of leadership, run counter to the values. For example, the core value of "patients first" in your organization is trumped by the strong desire to meet program/unit targets that drive access improvement at the expense of patient experience. One other consistent shortcoming is the ambiguity of the vision or goal. Imagine this phrase: "To be the leader in healthcare by year 2028." This has so many different interpretations that the phrase becomes valueless. Does this mean that the organization implements a nationally recognized cancer center, or do we open local primary care clinics that reach out into every area of the community? Or do we do both? That depends on our definition of being a leader in healthcare. When the vision is unclear there will be no unity of purpose for the staff and medical staff. The statement is actually powerless and unfair to the organization. So how do we move our organization toward our vision? It is in getting to our well-articulated and clear vision that our organization is transformed.

A few key leadership behaviors adopted at the highest level of your organization will go a long way in ensuring your organization lives the right lean values. Table 6.1 summarizes the leadership behaviors necessary to create a culture of improvement. In order to inspire the team to do their best, leadership needs to walk the walk, not just talk to talk. In leading by example, or leading from the front, as the military would say, you demonstrate that change begins with me. This is the most powerful statement that leaders can make in an organization. As we previously emphasized, "The tongue in

Table 6.1   Lean Leadership Behaviors

Leadership Behavior	Why Necessary
Participate full time in a three-day value stream analysis and a four-day kaizen event	• Demonstrates commitment to the approach • This is the best way to learn the tools • This is the best way to learn how the kaizen experience changes the culture while compressing the timeline for results
Learn the tools	• Everyone in the organization needs the ability to not only think lean, but to actually use the tools to see and eliminate waste
Walk the value streams • Perform gemba walks	• Changes the role of the leader from "manager" to coach • Best lean approach to develop subordinates • Gives leadership visibility in "gemba" to show importance to staff and medical staff • Gemba is the source of all facts. Going there eliminates jumping to conclusions and problem-solving in the conference room
Commit the appropriate resources to be successful	• Shows commitment to continuous process improvement • Reprioritizes less important activity, allowing management wiggle room for process improvement activities
Hold individuals and teams accountable (staff, management, and physicians) • Address antibodies	• Shows respect for people • Ensures standard work is followed. Implementing and following standard work is the way organizations improve and sustain. • Ensures consistency in how staff and medical staff are treated • Makes visible those who choose not to participate in process improvement activity • Separates personality-based actions and process-based actions
Redeployment versus unemployment	• Shows respect for people • Demonstrates that team members will not lose their job as a result of participating in process improvement activities
Demand and monitor results	• Aligns with the lean pillar of continuous improvement • Shows respect for people by stretching their capabilities • Helps develop management and staff by staying involved with the process and results
Believe	• Greatness is available to everyone, but comes faster to those who expect it

your shoe speaks more loudly than the tongue in your mouth," implying go spend time in the gemba.

Participate

There is no better way to learn the improvement tools, the change management approaches, the impact of meaningful, empowering improvement to the staff than to participate in the improvement activities like a value stream analysis or a kaizen event. Now comes the true challenge to senior leaders: you must leave your rank and title at the door. Lead with humility. This is a prerequisite to success and provides a sign of respect. Obviously, the improvement team will know you are the CEO, but you could be an approachable CEO that welcomes honest feedback during the week. Imagine the chill of the team if a CEO expresses anger with a recommendation. The team's forward momentum will stop. The humility of a CEO being able to attend as a team member has a far-reaching impact on the organization. The thought of a paradigm shift in the organization now has teeth. Participation means to be a fully functioning team member. Being present part of the time and then skipping out for meetings and phone calls is not sufficient and demonstrates the wrong behavior. (Nor is sitting in the room but spending a generous portion of time scrolling through your smart phone or laptop.)

As a team member, learn to see waste by using the actual tools and then use the improvement principles to eliminate waste. At the senior leadership level, a commitment of one full improvement week per year would be a great start, and more is even better. The entire leadership team needs to participate, including the CEO, Vice Presidents, COO, CNO, Chief of Staff, and CFO. It is preferred to have the leadership team participate in an event early in the improvement journey as this demonstrates commitment to the transformational efforts. One great joy from this attendance is when other senior leaders or employees of an organization give the standard reply of "I don't have time for an improvement event." The comment "really; the CEO found time" leaves a strong retort to be considered. Additionally, the impact of attending an event on each individual senior leader's commitment to future lean events is immeasurable.

Learn the Tools

Learning the improvement tools is part of lean capacity building as was discussed in the previous chapter. I can't name a single organization that ever transformed into a culture of continuous improvement where the entire leadership team was not fully competent in the application of the lean tools. Using lean tools and lean thinking shapes organizational culture. When you learn the tools, you will start to use them in daily operations. The use of tools to see and eliminate waste leads to better decisions and different and better management actions. The collection of management actions is what shapes organizational behavior, and the organizational behaviors are what defines your culture. As I discussed before, you cannot delegate lean leadership, and changing the culture of an organization is not something that can be micromanaged.

The use of leadership and management decision-making, without a thorough understanding of lean tools, will actually drive a wedge in your transformational efforts, splitting lean thinkers from non-lean thinkers. Traditional approaches and management efforts will conflict with lean management approaches. Great lean organizations reduce command and control structures, a pillar of traditional management approaches. Information is transparent and variation in expected performance leads to real-time problem-solving. All staff and medical staff are engaged in process improvement using lean thinking. To lead this effort, every leader must become a lean thinker and be competent in the scientific method (A3 thinking), as well as all the supporting tools used to see and eliminate waste. When beginning improvement, one of the best single indicators of how successful an organization is in transparency is this: "does good and bad news travel at the same speed and accuracy throughout the chain of command"? Bad news typically travels at hyper speed but good news not so much. Once you have transparency and a great culture, "bad" becomes an inaccurate tag. The news may be unpleasant at first, but the lean organization will embrace the feedback as an opportunity to improve, not to be swept under the carpet. And good news will soon have the same velocity as "bad" news.

Beyond participating in improvement events, either within your organization or at someone else's organization, there are a couple of other ways lean organizations advance the learning of the tools and their application at the leadership level. Such methods include teaching the lean tools to the organization and their application, reading, and studying lean literature for self-development, and facilitating improvement to cement the technical aspects of improvement with the cultural aspects.

Rotate Teaching the Core Lean Tools

In the best lean organizations, the leadership teams take the time and effort to participate in teams and learn the tools for improvement. This shift is not easy. Many senior leaders want to delegate this activity. One of the keys to being a great lean leader is to have the ability to ask the right questions. It is difficult to impossible to ask the right questions without having a grasp of the fundamental lean tools to see and eliminate wasted time and activity. Asking the wrong question leads to frustration by the improvement teams and can move your culture back to the status quo.

To overcome this, the leadership team can teach the organization specific improvement tools. This ensures and hardwires some level of mastery in lean knowledge and lean thinking. Typically, a handful of tools and techniques are identified, and the leadership teams invest time to master each of the highlighted techniques. A starting point might include 5S, problem-solving, A3 thinking, pull systems, managing for daily improvement, and one item flow. On a rotating basis, the leadership team holds workshops or lunches and learns with the organization to transfer this knowledge. In teaching the content and answering questions on the topics, a mastery of the subject matter is developed. This mastery can be transformed into asking great questions ensuring the lean process is followed.

Use a Book of the Month Club to Continue with the Academic Understanding of Improvement

Another approach used by lean organizations is to continue the academic understanding of lean. Each month, or every other month, a book on a lean topic is identified and the leadership is required to read this publication. On a monthly basis, a de-brief session is scheduled and the reflections and learning from the book are shared. Key takeaways can lead to changes in standard work and can be tested in experiments using A3 thinking. The ongoing exposure to new lean thinking and new lean approaches helps to not only learn the lean tools but to learn different applications of the tools. A lean organization is first a learning organization. Seeing and eliminating waste is a never-ending challenge. Forming a book of the month club re-enforces the concept of continuous learning.

Become a Lean Facilitator

There is no better way to learn the tools than to be put in front of a kaizen team and lead the team through a cycle of improvement using A3 thinking. The great lean organizations that transform their cultures all have leadership that can apply the common tools used to see and eliminate waste. The common tools to see and eliminate waste are shown in Table 6.2.

The benefit of leading a team is not only a deeper understanding of the tools, techniques, and behaviors required to improve but also a further grasp of the team dynamics that occur in an improvement workshop and an immense appreciation for the change management required to move a team to a better place. I would not coach you to start by leading a team. I would begin by participating on several teams and slowly learning the tools and techniques of a kaizen event. After about 3–4 events, you will feel confident

Table 6.2 Common Tools to See and Eliminate Waste

Tool	Application
Takt time	Calculation that shows the relationship between the available time to complete work and the volume of work to be done. Shows the rate of inputs and outputs to a process.
Time observation	Direct observation used to quantify waste in units of time
Cycle time/Takt time bar chart	Tool used to determine staffing levels by showing the relationship between the cycle time to complete the work divided by the takt time
Flow diagram	Process map used to show flow, connections, and waits
Spaghetti mapping	Tool used to show the waste of motion and transportation
Communication circle	Tool used to show information hand-offs
Standard work	Form used to show the recipe for standard work by showing the work sequence and time associated with each task along with key points ensuring the work is done correctly the first time
Process control	A visual management tool that shows the work plan and the actual work completed. The plan is based on standard work and meets the takt time calculation. Variation from the plan allows for management by exception and enables an immediate intervention.

in leading (co-leading) portions of the event, and at about event 12, you can take the training wheels off and lead a team independently.

Walk the Value Streams

Regular leadership rounds are another requirement. In lean, these rounds are known as "gemba walking." Gemba walking is different than patient safety rounds, or patient communication rounds, or medical rounds, as they are designed to develop people. Keep in mind that a lean leader is first a coach and mentor. Fortunately, participating on the teams and learning the tools will make you a better mentor and coach! Gemba walks are based on a master-apprentice model of learning. Just like in martial arts, the master (Sensei) first leads by example, showing the student what to do. The next step is to have the apprentice practice. The third step is to have the master observe and provide feedback. This feedback is a combination of critique and encouragement.

In an actual gemba walk, the leader or manager will first walk the area and show the subordinate how to see waste, lead problem-solving activities, hold a daily huddle, manage visually, etc. Next, the subordinate gets a chance to practice. In an experienced lean organization, gemba walks will occur weekly. In an organization new to lean improvement, gemba walks can occur in time increments from weekly down to as frequently as daily. Finally, in a future gemba walk, the leader observes the subordinate and provides feedback on the performance. The feedback should include opportunities for improvement as well as encouragement for the successes. Opportunities for improvement should be documented and managed visually. The action items that come out of a gemba walk should become part of the improvement plans documented on the visual management performance system. The gemba walks can leave lasting impressions. Asking a simple question to the front-line staff: "if you could change one thing in your process, what would it be"? You will find the responses illuminating, the front-line staff will feel "listened to" and respected. The idea when implemented will deliver local level improvement.

In addition to gemba walks, leadership models the proper behavior simply by walking the value stream. This behavior shows support for the improvement process while allowing you to challenge the team when performance is off or not being sustained, and to recognize the team when a job is well done. Pay attention to the visual management systems and the results boards. What is important to you is also important to your team.

When you show your team that you are interested in the visual management systems, they will take notice. The real beauty in this effort is when the walks become a regular practice, you not showing up will result in immediate feedback as to why you did not "round." At this point, the basic premise of responsibilities going both ways has been established.

Commit the Resources to Be Successful

In addition to participating and showing commitment through involvement, leaders can also show support by committing the appropriate resources required to be successful. A successful improvement experience requires investment in three areas: facilitation, team resources, and improvement supplies. This can be considered your "seed money" opportunity. On rarer occasions, you will need to consider capital to improvement. This should always be a last resort.

Facilitation

Many organizations underestimate how much time it takes to improve. The preparation activities, the actual improvement team activities, and the sustaining activities all require some skilled facilitation – which subsequently require some full-time resources to be done well. One full-time facilitator is necessary for each value stream to be improved. This person can be a dedicated resource or a seconded resource – but either way, he or she should be full-time. A consistent shortcoming of this requirement is that organizations have no problem providing a person that is fully qualified for this role, but the organization has a HUGE problem allowing this individual to release prior responsibilities ... in other words, the organization now forces two jobs upon this individual. A sure indicator of burnout and sub-optimal outcomes. The responsibilities of the improvement facilitator are summarized in Table 6.3.

The data collection activities and the suite of sustaining activities require extensive amounts of time. Part-time resources are ineffective in completing these two specific activities well. Ineffective data collection leads to less-than-optimal results caused by having a faulty premise upon which to see and eliminate waste. Ineffective sustaining activities can lead to slow results and, more frequently, project failure. The sustaining activities are completed by the area management and area medical management. One failure point is the improvement facilitator does all the sustaining activities. What will happen here is the improvement facilitator will one day leave the area to go

Table 6.3 Improvement Facilitator Responsibilities

Carries the title of "internal expert for lean improvement by demonstrating a mastery of the tools, techniques, and application of lean thinking	Trains support staff and medical staff on lean principles, practices, and process
Monitors the preparation activities to include logistics, membership selection, measurement baselines and targets, improvement scope, and data collection	Facilitates improvement activities using A3 thinking
Assists in improvement sustaining activities to include auditing, data capture, visual management monitoring, and training of support and medical staff in standard work	Assists in the development of line management through the teaching of visual management and leader standard work
Teaches the three dimensions of visual management to the organization: process, results, and enabling a high-performing work area	Assists in managing the breadth and depth of the improvement (also known as the pace of change)
Develops and mentors team leaders and new facilitators	Assists in the population of the improvement scorecard
Assists in managing the improvement plan at the value stream level. Participates on the value stream steering committee	Assists in the development of visual management systems

to another part of the organization for improvement. When this happens, everything falls apart. The role of the facilitator is to teach the area being improved to sustain and to build the artifacts; the visual management, standard work, audit systems, etc. to allow the area leaders to sustain and then incrementally improve. **Sustaining activities are 80% of the work in a project**. Most organizations are hyper focused f on the improvement kaizen, but this is the easier part of the improvement cycle. Plan for 15% of the time to be used for preparation activity, 5% to be used for the design session to see and eliminate waste grounded in standard work and visual management, and 80% of the energy to be used in sustaining the changes. This energy is why lean organizations have full-time facilitators.

Team Resources

In addition to an investment into full-time facilitation resources, investment will need to be made in improvement team resources. Lean is a process of the people, and it is desirable to have everyone participate. Getting a team together to work through an A3 project or to work through a kaizen event means that team resources must be made available. Having the right team, working on the right project, with the right targets, is a fundamental requirement for success. Plan to allow staff and medical personnel time to be available to work on improvement. An improvement team will require between six and ten people to ensure that all key stakeholders are involved.

Middle Management Expectations

Additionally, middle management will need some "wiggle room" to improve. They need to have some dedicated time to focus on change management and building a lean culture. They also need to be given the freedom to "fail." Learn from each failure and improve … give them the freedom and confidence to TRY. Evaluate the priorities of your middle management. Typically, line management has two responsibilities, administration of the department, such as scheduling, managing time off, attending meetings, payroll, etc., and improvement. What percentage of time do line leaders spend on administration versus improvement? Go into one of the manager's calendars and check. I am guessing the results will be very telling. One thing we know is if you want improvement, you must spend time on improvement. Good leaders keep those directly reporting to them focused on the right things. De-emphasizing the least important activities can go a long way toward ensuring success. After the presentation of a recently completed rapid improvement event, the Chief Operating Officer of a major hospital system stated to the lean team: "We believe in lean, we are willing to help you free up time. Please let us know what specific activities you feel can be removed from your 'plate.' Bring your recommendations to me so we can discuss and make the decision." This is the leadership we are looking for allowing management some elbow room to work on improvement.

Giving management elbow room only works if the managers both know what to work on and have the discipline to work on the right things. One of the tools we can use to assist in focusing on improvement is leader standard work. Think of leader standard work as a daily, weekly, and monthly checklist of things that need to be accomplished to improve the department, oneself, and the organization. I have frequently seen two managers of equal talent and motivation in their daily work. One is extraordinarily effective, and one is not. The difference is what the two managers chose to focus on each day. Why not create standard work to get the managers, middle managers, and executives to focus on the most important things?

Figure 6.1 is an example of leader standard work for a manager.

Leader standard work (LSW) allows for a shift in daily focus from just results to process and results. We know a good process is the result of a good recipe. What is our leader's recipe for success? Additionally, leader

Manager Standard Work Checklist

Name: Georgia 2N

Daily: Start of day activities

❏ check VM for call ins
❏ review Email for critical messages
❏ check in with CN for staffing coverage issues

Daily Activities:
❏ Tier 1 huddle 6:45a
❏ Tier 2 huddle 8:30a
❏ Round on 5 patients
❏ Kamishibai audits 1130a
❏ Bed meeting at 930a

Multiple times per Day

Activities:
❏ check process control systems 10a
❏ check process control systems 230p
❏ review clean and dirty utility for 5S opportunities
❏ work on action plans from huddle

Weekly Activities:
Monday
❏ payroll by noon
❏ order office supplies
Tuesday
❏ Program meeting at noon

Wednesday
❏ safety meeting at 3p

Thursday
❏ value stream steering at noon
Friday
❏ Unit council meeting at noon

Monthly Activities:
❏ review financials and develop plans on the 10th of the month
❏ meet with pharmacy on the third Friday each month at 10a

Daily: End of day activities:
❏ final walkthrough at 5p
❏ check in with CRN for night shift plan
❏ prepare for next days huddle
❏ turn off office lights

Tasks/Meetings – Things to do today

Projects/Improvement Activities

Daily Notes & Observations

Notes for Next Meeting

Figure 6.1 Leader standard work for a manager.

standard work shows leaders what to do and what *not* to do. Use LSW as an opportunity to design wasted time and effort out of the leader's daily work. In our LSW we want to do two things. First, we want to allocate time to managing the visual controls. If you have been paying attention, at this point we have many visual controls in place, like process control boards, the managing for daily improvement boards, 5S controls, kamishibai audits, and value stream performance system controls. Be sure and allocate sufficient time to audit these systems, make interventions in real-time, and improve these systems, this takes time, effort, and persistence. This does not happen in a series of one-hour weekly meeting. Secondly, we want to execute the daily accountability process. This activity involves project managing the action items coming out of the management system, the process control system, A3 improvements, etc. These follow-up actions will require problem-solving efforts and these activities can be solved by the leader or delegated as appropriate, but again take focused time. It should be noted that some of the activities in LSW are sequenced to time. For example, a daily huddle happens at a certain time of the day. Many organizations have tiered huddles to review and escalate key issues affecting safety, quality, risk, operational barriers, etc. We do need to include some of the administrative work into our LSW. As an example, payroll is due on Monday morning every other week. This work is essential and should be included in the LSW. One opportunity for leaders is to stop being slaves to email/text messages. I watch leaders virtually addicted to their smart phone and each email/text sets about a flurry of activity that is not always important or urgent. My recommendation is to schedule time each day to review and act on email. This will allow time to focus on improvement.

Supplies

Regarding providing resources toward improvement, you will want to allocate some funds to cover the supplies and materials needed to improve. Office supplies are necessary to complete the improvement activities, and other supplies are needed for the visual management systems. Floor tape and label-making equipment are needed for your 5S system. 3' by four' (or larger) dry-erase boards are ideal for process control systems, although electronic systems are becoming more prevalent. These can be acquired on demand so there is no need to purchase them in advance. However, you should plan ahead by establishing a budget to cover the cost of these supplies. Do not underestimate this step. I have seen teams "spin" for three days because no one in management knew who was going to pay for a $25 file folder rack.

While not an exhaustive list, here is the supply list I believe every lean improvement facilitator should have access to:

- Projector and screen or a TV monitor that you can project to for training
- Computer to deliver training files from
- Printer for on demand printing needs
- One big roll of 48-inch-wide butcher paper. This is used for process mapping.
- Five packs of the multi-colored 3" by 3" post-it notes (must include some variant of red or pink for wastes)
- One to twelve pack of fine-point sharpie markers (black)
- One to four pack of multi-colored flip chart markers (ensure you have a red and green marker in the set for value-added and non-value-added identification)
- Two pads of flip chart paper and a stand. You can also use the sticky flip chart paper
- Three rolls of 1" wide masking tape or painters' tape (assuming we can tape on the walls)
- Two rolls of scotch tape
- Clipboards are helpful for time observation
- Some form of watch with a second hand is required for time observation. Stopwatches used to be used, but this has been replaced with the stopwatch function on smartphones.

External Resources

It's also important to consider the resource of improvement expertise. Just as you are likely to consult a personal trainer to help you get in shape, or an accountant to help with your taxes, consider hiring a lean expert to help you with improvement. Bringing in some outside expertise to help with training, leadership development, infrastructure development, and team improvement is a wise investment for many organizations. External lean expertise comes in many forms, from a lean expert with expertise in one field, to a lean Sensei who has expertise in many business areas. A good external resource will shorten your lead-time for results, accelerate the breadth and depth of your improvement, minimize your organizational risk, and assist in your development of management and leadership. Additionally, an outside resource is not tied to your political structure and organizational structure. This is a tremendous asset when it comes to the impartial ability to focus on process, instead of designing an improvement system based on personalities and organizational politics.

Should you wish to seek expertise outside of the organization, you must find experts who have practical experience in management development. Not the theory of lean management development, but a resource that has led lean management development in a lean organization, preferably more than one. Understanding the lean tools, while overwhelming at first, is the easiest part of improving. The most difficult aspect of creating a culture of improvement is changing the way management thinks, acts, and behaves. You will see a wide variation in lean expert capability when you move beyond tools and into management/leadership development. Be cautious if the promises are "too good to be true," such as "we can complete a lean transformation in a year" minimizing the true responsibilities associated with transformation. This promise is a clear indication that they probably have not led a successful lean enterprise transformation which takes many years. Ask about their experience and ask for current references that you can contact. One of the powers of healthcare is the sharing of information. If honesty is what you seek, your peers at other healthcare systems will give you the true "scoop" of the effectiveness of their lean "experts."

By providing appropriate resources for improvement including facilitation resources, team member participation, "wiggle room" (dedicated time and flexibility) for middle management grounded in leader standard work, and a budget for improvement supplies, you will greatly enhance your chances for success. Additional benefits can be gained by the use of outside lean expertise, particularly with respect to lean management development at all levels.

Hold People Accountable

For lean to be successful, there needs to be accountability for all people involved. In many organizations, a healthcare team consists of a collection of individual contributors working at their own pace and achieving different outcomes. A great lean system begins by creating team-based, standard work and then making sure that everyone consistently follows that standard. Ideally, everyone should follow the standard because they believe in the standard and are committed to the new process. Regrettably, that is not usually the place where you will begin. Inevitably, approximately 85% of the people will follow the standard, but the other 15% will require "encouragement." A general rule of thumb is that in every lean event you will have 5–10% of the group be the "builders" or totally dedicated to making lean succeed, 5–10% of the group will be the "destroyers" who strongly desire to see lean fail. The remaining 80–90% are the "fence sitters" that wait to see which side will win.

In addition to getting staff to follow standard work, we need to address resistance in management. The "frozen middle" is a term often used in lean circles that refer to middle management and their lack of willingness to embrace organizational change. The majority of front-line staff is excited about participating in the change process and being listened to. This group likes to be able to bring forth ideas that are embraced and implemented quickly. Senior leadership is pleased with lean improvement because it brings about a sense of excitement in the organization and it delivers meaningful results in a shorter period of time the previously realized. But middle management is caught in the middle of the change process. In a lean environment, all the existing management systems and personality-based processes are being eliminated. This is very threatening to middle managers who have not yet developed their new lean management systems and do not yet trust lean tools and approaches. Additionally, once visual management systems are in place, the manager's operation is completely transparent for everyone to see. Not everyone is comfortable with this visibility. An unpleasant phrase (to some) accurately describes one aspect of the lean process when properly applied: "when the lean flashlight shines in an area, the cockroaches run for darkness." A statement of fact is that some will not be able to accept lean. They have done it "this way" for years and by golly, "I'm not changing." This is when the dedication of middle and senior management will receive their "test." Everyone in the organization will be watching intently … "what will they do." This is the crossroads that must be crossed often. There will always be the few that will challenge lean and even after retraining and allowing for respectful input; they refuse to comply. Then the question becomes: "Do we have organizational change and improvement expectations, or may everyone do it their own way?" In a lean environment, many of the systems and tools used in management are replaced by new lean processes, standard work, and visual management systems. When the old systems are dismantled, managers feel uncomfortable. What happens, often unintentionally, is that managers tend to hold on to the old systems and tools. This behavior is counterproductive in an improving environment where we ask managers and leaders to embrace new tools and processes to guide decision-making and inform improvement. Human behavior will have us revert to the known, vice the unknown. This is often the case even when the "unknown or new" carries the promise of tremendous improvement.

Leadership needs to be supportive of middle management during the change but also needs to let go of the old systems and encourage subordinates to let go of the old systems as quickly as possible and embrace the new methods. While leadership needs to provide middle management with training on the new system, middle management also needs to be held accountable for both the process and the results. I have used middle management frequently in this section. Middle mangement includes clinical management, administrative managementm and physician managment. In the early part of the improvement journey, accountability to the process is even more important than the results. If we are not getting the desired results, we can change the process to direct to the proper results. But if we are not following the process, we will never even get to a baseline to evaluate if the process will generate results. Just as we expect the staff to follow standard work to ensure waste is eliminated from the system, we expect management to follow the lean management processes to ensure the correct results. These processes are management's standard work.

We also expect the healthcare organization to hold physicians accountable. While physicians certainly have much more autonomy than the rest of the staff, there are standards that should be met by the entire medical staff as well. These include (as a small sample) start and stop times, standards for the quality and timeliness of documentation, adherence to evidence-based best practices, and adherence to infection prevention and control practices. I have seen *MANY* great improvement efforts fail because the organization and the medical leadership would not hold the medical staff accountable in following standard work. Subsequenly, the organizations thay do this best, consistnely achieve the best results.

I have one last thought on accountability; while we prefer the improvement experience to be a positive one for patients, medical staff, and staff, at times it can be a difficult or even unpleasant experience. In the spirit of providing the best possible patient experience and outcome, sometimes improving means changing work hours or moving work from one resource to a different one. As leaders, we need to *always* do the right thing in service of the patient. On rare occasions, the staff might decide they do not want to follow the new process. If you are honest with yourself, you know some of the staff is not following the work standards in place today. Evidence-based care is not used, documentation requirements are skipped, etc. It is your job as a leader to inspire your staff to follow the standard work. On even rarer occasions, an individual will need to be disciplined for not following the new process. While I do not want to anticipate the need for disciplinary action, I would be remiss if I did not acknowledge this possibility, or even likelihood. As I tell managers, "There's a reason you're a leader." One of those reasons is your requirement and ability to hold staff and medical staff accountable to maintain standards.

To summarize this key point: if you are *not* going to have a culture of accountability, then you can stop with lean improvement, or any improvement for that matter. You have *no* chance of being successful if the staff, medical staff, and management do not consistently follow standard work. If there is no standard, there is no improvement. In simplest terms, a standard is a basis for comparison. If you cannot compare one activity against another, then you cannot validate improvement; great lean organizations understand this point. Once your organization understands that standards are no longer optional, you will see everyone start to accept accountability. The visual management systems make it readily apparent if standards are being followed. But your organization reflects how you behave and if your organization does not hold staff and medical staff accountable today, you have some work ahead of you. As I mentioned before: some will refuse or not be able to adjust to the lean "change."

Address Antibodies

One of the challenges you will face as an organization is how to deal with people who want no part of the change process. These people may be overt resisters and be extremely vocal about their displeasure or they may be passively opposed to change and simply uncooperative. These people can come from any part of your organization: staff, physicians, managers, directors, or even members of the senior leadership team. Experience shows that 5% to 20% of the organization will resist change. This is not an insignificant number, and you must deal quickly and effectively with this population, otherwise you will fail to change the culture. Lean organizations call these resistors of change "antibodies." The analogy is as follows: In the human body, when an infection invades your system, antibodies become active to preserve the status quo. The antibodies have a specific purpose to return your physical system to its normal state. The same is true when you try to change the culture of your organization. When change is infused into your organization, the antibodies will become active to preserve your existing culture and status quo. Is this a bad thing? Not with respect to the healing process but for a change initiative, the answer is yes, but follows with a brief explanation. Not every antibody has ill intentions. Some antibodies become active out of great concern that the changes will be harmful to the patients, themselves, and the organization. We need to take great care and communicate frequently the benefits of the changed processes to all our stakeholders. One of the reasons we test solutions, before we spread them, is to identify and answer unintended consequences from our standard work that may lead to undesirable results. If this has been done, then many times the concerns of the "anti-bodies" is unwarranted. Most anti-bodies, however, do not come from the goodwill population. And unfortunately, if not addressed, antibodies multiply. If you do not appropriately deal with the antibodies when they first become active, they will influence other people in your organization. Left unchecked, this group can totally derail the change process and end your attempt at creating a culture of continuous improvement. The question is, "how do we deal with the antibodies"? The first line of defense is to make expectations clear when you begin improving. Leadership must be crystal clear on the reason for change, what's expected from staff and medical staff, who will be affected, and the consequences for those who choose not to participate. This message needs to be tailored for the distinct levels of the organization. An "elevator speech" can be prepared for staff, medical staff, and management to address the concerns of each of the layers. This speech should be delivered early in the change process. The next way to address antibodies is to get them involved in the change process. Are you more likely to accept your own ideas or someone else's? People like their own ideas and the more people that can be involved with an idea, the less resistance you can expect. The majority (80%) of your antibodies will completely change their position once they have participated in either a kaizen event or an A-3 improvement project. This change in people can often be very dramatic. On countless occasions, I have seen a staff associate formerly labeled a troublemaker become a great lean champion following an opportunity to participate in improvement. Is this not a great win for your organization? To take someone deemed "difficult" and turn them into a believer and practitioner of continuous improvement is a great feat!

On rare occasions, participation is not sufficient to turn an antibody. In these cases, you will need to apply situational leadership, dealing with the staff or medical staff associate on a case-by-case basis. The organization needs to be consistent in how it addresses antibodies. You do not want different standards for different layers or departments within your organization.

There is a phrase you will hear in lean circles, "the fastest way to change the people is to change the people." Sometimes you must separate an individual from your organization who not only fails to participate in improvement, but also fails to follow standard work, and who negatively influences others. Let us hope this is not a frequent occurrence, but I would be remiss if I did not make you aware this does happen.

In summary, antibodies become active to preserve the status quo of your organizational culture. Antibodies need to be addressed quickly and fairly to prevent them from negatively influencing other staff members. Anti-bodies typically show up by intentionally not following standard work, being vocal about not following or supporting standard work, or both. The best way to address antibodies is through clear communication and by getting them involved in the process.

Redeployment versus Unemployment

The primary focus of lean is to generate major improvements by seeing and eliminating wasted time and activity, and simultaneously create a culture of improvement. To foster this improvement culture, we need to create an environment where the staff, medical staff, and management trust the organization. One of the key areas of trust begins with job security. As wasteful activity is eliminated from your organization, you can anticipate that personnel resources will be freed up. If there is no meaningful work for these resources, it can be tempting to downsize the organization through layoffs, particularly if the financial position of the organization is not strong.

The organization's staff deserves the assurance of continued employment from the first utterances of the lean enterprise transformation coming to the organization. Rumors of workforce reductions will start early on, and the organization can nip it in the bud by ensuring that clear communication of the following message, "No employee will lose employment due to lean efforts. An employee may be required to change jobs due to improvements, or change shifts, work hours, etc., but your employment is not at risk." The fastest way to destroy your continuous process improvement journey is to lay off an employee following an improvement activity. In good faith, we bring staff and medical staff together to eliminate wasted time and activity from the organization. In doing this we simultaneously improve staff morale, patient quality and safety; we increase access, and we lower costs. We cannot "reward" our staff for this effort by asking them to find another job elsewhere. The first time you lay someone off because of an improvement, your chances for further improvement using an empowered staff are *zero*. No one is going to improve themselves out of a job. Why would they?

Lean organizations meet staff needs and organizational needs by offering employment security, not job security. If we identify a need for 12 registration clerks following an improvement, and 16 registration clerks are currently on staff, what do we do with the surplus 4? Lean organizations use a term called redeployment. We want to redeploy these staff members to other open positions. Admittedly, those positions might not be in registration, they may require a shift change or other adaptation, but they allow the staff to be retained. Think redeployment, not unemployment!

Why is redeployment essential? The answer is simple. By far, most of your organization's expenses are related to staffing. Let us reflect on that statement. Your staff members certainly need salaries and benefits, which show up on the income statement, but what are the other costs? Employees also need telephones, computers, parking spaces, personal lockers, and desks. They use materials and equipment, consume office supplies, and need break rooms, microwaves, and refrigerators. Many of these items require ongoing operational expenses. Take a look at your budget; try to connect each line item to your staff and you'll likely be amazed to discover how much of your budget goes to supporting your personnel. This is much different than the common phrase in healthcare that 65% of our expenses are related to staffing. Sixty-five percent of expenses might be directly attributed to salary and benefits, but what about all the other personnel-related expenses? Lean organizations estimate that up to 80% of overal expenses are directly related to the number of people you employ.

As leaders, we have a responsibility to use our resources wisely. If we can avoid adding resources by eliminating wasteful time and activity, we have a requirement to take full advantage of that opportunity. Likewise, if we free resources up we should make them available to the rest of the organization through a redeployment strategy. This practice allows staff members the security in having a job while meeting the needs of the corporation in filling an open position. In lean organizations, this practice is followed even if the position requires significant re-training.

We can consider many alternatives to laying off staff, which I call the "redeployment hierarchy." Be mindful, we are after a hard dollar cost savings in labor, we just want to accomplish this without a formal workforce reduction. Here is a list of possible redeployment strategies:

1. Reduce or eliminate temporary or agency staff
2. Implement a strategy to not replace any attrition

3. Allow employees that have been redeployed the ability to complete training for an open, posted position
4. Reduce or eliminate overtime
5. "Insource" services that have been outsourced
6. Add new services and programs with the resources that have been freed up.
7. Run temporary improvement teams with the resources you have freed up to accelerate improvement.

It may, however, be too late for you to avoid reducing headcount. Perhaps your financial position indicates that you have no choice. Can you still deploy a lean management system? Absolutely, but you need to address the personnel situation *first*. Any staffing changes need to be finalized before you begin to improve. In this situation, the challenge you will face is that you must resource the improvement teams with a smaller staff. In some organizations this can be a difficult proposition. However, if we want to show respect for all people, then we need to address our staffing issues in a fair and up-front way. It is disrespectful to people to use lean continuous improvement to lay off staff to meet fiscal concerns. There are other approaches that demonstrate respect for people more appropriately using a redeployment approach. You may be asking one additional question regarding redeployment: Whom should we redeploy? Should we redeploy the worst staff member, the best staff member, go by seniority, or leave it up to the process owner? If you are working in a unionized environment, the answer is straightforward. Any change in staffing will need to take place in accordance with the language in your collective agreement. In a non-union environment, I suggest you use a new paradigm. Great lean organizations always redeploy their *best* performer. I realize this may come as a shock! Believe me, as a former manager, I used all kinds of strategies to retain (actually to hoard) my best people. You may be asking (as I did), "now you want me to give up my best employee willingly?"

Lean organizations celebrate redeployment as a tremendous organizational success. When we redeploy, we reward our best performer by giving him/her an opportunity to go and learn a new skill! We do not want to give this opportunity to just anyone. Our best and brightest should get the opportunity to advance and develop. The remaining team will survive in our lean organization. Through the lean improvement that preceded the redeployment, you created a new process with standard work and visual management. As a result of standard work, *everyone* will be able to improve their performance. And with visual management, you have control of both the process and the results. There will never be a better time to release your best performer for their next exciting opportunity.

Monitor and Demand Results

This leadership lesson is about expectations. When you satisfy your curiosity and participate on a team, you will quickly learn that 95% of the work done is non-value-added activity. In lean, we want to eliminate and reduce non-value-added activity. When you see this for yourself, your expectations of what is possible should change. Using lean, you can *expect* double-digit improvement in performance. Remember, we are trying to eliminate the non-value-added activity, which accounts for 95% of the activity. A well-run team should improve the key dimensions of staff morale, quality, access, and cost by more than 10% with each kaizen cycle of improvement. If you are just beginning to improve, I expect that your results will be even better, because you will be eliminating even more waste. As a leader, you have the right to demand results using a lean improvement system. Create a sense of urgency in the teams. Take interest in the daily, weekly, and monthly performance. Expect improvement by monitoring and demanding results and excellence!

Believe

Throughout your transformation journey, never stop believing! As a leader, you also need to monitor and demand results. If you do, your achievements will be significant. A lean leader can take your organization to a place it has never been. It is a place where both staff and medical personnel are excited to come to work, where patients get world-class care, and where access increases so that essential healthcare services can be offered to more people in your community every day. It is a place where these essential services can be delivered in a cost-effective way, so that your healthcare organization can maintain excellent fiscal health, year after year. Every organization has the capability to be great using lean improvement approaches. Creating the shared vision, aligning the resources, and inspiring people to achieve the vision deliver the leadership required to make this greatness possible. You will know when you have crossed the tipping point when employees come to you and never say we need to "fix" a particular problem. They come to you and say that we have an improvement opportunity.. They will know how to perform the improvement and what is possible when the problem is solved.

Chapter Summary: Key Points from Chapter 6

- Creating a culture of improvement begins with leadership changing the way they think, act, and behave.
- Demonstrating proper leadership behavior brings the organization's vision, mission, and values to life which is essential for transforming your organizational performance and culture.
- The key lean leadership behaviors include:
  - Participating, full-time on improvement teams
  - Learning the lean tools to see and eliminate waste
  - Walking the value streams and performing gemba walks
  - Committing the appropriate resources to be successful
  - Holding yourself, individuals, and team accountable for results
  - Addressing "Antibodies"
  - Having and following a re-deployment philosophy to absorb freed up human capital
  - Demand and monitoring results
  - Believing in the greatness your organization can achieve

Chapter 7

Mitigating Transformation Risk and Avoiding Common Mistakes

Being Successful and Avoiding Failure

I would like to start this chapter with a topic most people would rather avoid failure. There are a wide variety of statistics out there, but the general consensus is that most transformational efforts fail. For those of you that have been around the block a few times, I am sure you can relate. The new organizational structure failed to deliver the intended results. The new IT system did not lower costs. The new piece of laboratory or diagnostic imaging did not meet its productivity targets. This does not imply that improvement was not made, or even that improvement was not sustained, but rather that the project did not hit all its projections. Failure from a lean enterprise transformation perspective implies that the organization failed to create a culture of continuous improvement. In all organizations, some type of improvement work is taking place. Simply keeping up with new and changing accreditation standards, current evidence-based treatments and procedures, and new insurance requirements requires some type of ongoing organizational change and improvement. Change in process, often dictated by regulation, and change in process delivered by intentionally seeing and eliminating waste leading to standard work and visual management are

DOI: 10.4324/9781003532132-7

not the same thing. Several promient health systems out front with results using lean improvement approaches less than 10 years ago have completely eliminated all of their improvement resources and abandoned their transformational efforts. I purposely wrote this book to try to change the number of healthcare organizations that have failed on this journey, or discontinued their journey.

A successful lean enterprise transformation implies that *all* staff and medical staff are engaged daily in eliminating wasted time and activity. With each iteration of removing wasted time and activity, the entire organization becomes more patient centered. Improvements, aligned to the organizational strategy, are met and newer targets are established. In a transformed organization the key measures of staff engagement, quality/safety, patient/family satisfaction, access/lead-time, cost, and growth are *always* improving, forever. Delivering daily improvement becomes how the organization functions. Focus on improvement is embedded into all the activities of the organization. Leadership, management, staff, and medical staff all understand that every process can be improved. Status quo is never accepted, even when change is difficult or unpopular.

Getting to this place is living in "very rare air." My Sensei used to tell me only one to three percent of all organizations that embrace lean as a transformation strategy gets to world class. That implies that 97–99% of organizations never reach world-class status. So, should we give up? The odds of getting to world-class status are not very good. The short answer is absolutely not. While only a few companies get to world-class level, the odds of getting to great are better, and these odds are almost guaranteed if you follow the roadmap described in the previous chapters. In creating a culture of improvement, the goal is to continuously get better. A great lean organization understands that eliminating any non-value-added activity is good for the customer and all stakeholders, and each wasteful step eliminated gets the organization to "better." Always aim high but celebrate all the improvements that you have captured and realize along the way.

As a leader you will want to do everything in your power to give your organization the best chance to succeed. Seeing improvement in how care is provided is reason alone to transform. But when you also see the changes to management, staff, and medical staff culture and behavior, any leader quickly becomes a believer in a lean management system. So, what are the actions that a leader can take to mitigate the risk of failing to transform, or prevent excessive stumbling through the transformation journey? Many of these points have been discussed earlier, but I will consolidate and repeat some of these key topics and add a few new thoughts as well. An early stumbling block organizations face when starting on a continuous improvement journey is that they fail to realize how much work is truly involved.

Developing an A3, selecting the right team, measuring the right things, and using the right tools and approaches make up 5% of a sustained project. The common mistake organizations make is failing to gather the appropriate baseline measures. Without the baseline measures, it is impossible to show an improvement. There is no data to compare past performance against current performance. A key point here is to ask and evaluate the following statement: do the selected measures *DRIVE* the *PROPER* behavior? The routine causes for this include selecting the wrong measure(s), reliance on IT captured measures, and failure to resource the data collection efforts. Many times, the best way to gather the best information is to spend time in the gemba performing time observations. Even skilled facilitators often do not like this part of the job. Time observations are not glorious, but enable your organization to not only see waste but see the sources of the waste and lost time associated with the waste.

The next 15% of the improvement efforts come from designing and testing solutions leading to improvement. Completing the A3 cycle of improvement either from a kaizen event or a project will take about 40 hours of team effort. Recall we want to see and eliminate waste, follow A3 thinking, and generate interventions with which we can experiment. Once we can validate the experiments to solve the problem we can define the standard work and the visual management support systems to ensure the waste remains gone. If you have been through a kaizen or an A3 project, there are times when it feels like more than 15% of the total project work, but this effort really is small when you consider what comes next.

The remaining 80% of the work in lean improvement is in deploying and sustaining the change. Why is sustaining change so difficult? It is because the existing culture of the organization will always pull the system back to status quo. Your staff, volunteers, managers, board, etc. will all behave in ways that promote the status quo. Your systems and processes will all drive your changes back to status quo. These can be overcome, but it will take a lot of work and effort. The roadmap for transformation and the lean leadership behaviors were all developed to allow change to stick. Every step is choreographed to break the pull of status quo allowing your organization to develop a culture of improvement. Recall that the roadmap covers preparing to change, accelerating the change, and making change the new culture. The leadership activities detailed in the roadmap are not "hard" to accomplish, but they are time-consuming. How much time do you currently spend in the "Gemba?" How difficult will it be to refocus your workday to enable you to accomplish your leader standard work? Are you prepared to work through the personnel issues with the "antibodies"? Can you dedicate the time and attention to the lean steering committee to govern the transformation? Each of these activities takes focus, time, and attention. But each activity is necessary to create the culture of improvement everyone is striving for. I compare sustainment to starting and staying on a diet. Starting a diet is hardest at first. The initial week is an unpleasant experience. But after that initial week, some success can be seen. When sticking to the plan, the second week is a bit easier, and the results are more apparent. After the first 30 days, it is easier to continue because the results are both gratifying and apparent. Staying on this path allows success to continue to grow. We can liken sustaining quality and process improvement to going on a long-term diet plan.

There are a few common stumbling blocks organizations frequently encounter when embracing lean improvement. We have already discussed the first of these, underestimating the amount of effort it will take to be successful. Other common mistakes include the following:

- Do not waste the first 6–9 months
- Failure to monitor the breadth and depth of the change
- Failure to get everyone involved
- Eliminate two systems as soon as possible

Do Not Waste the First Six to Nine Months

Many organizations want world-class results without doing the heavy upfront lifting. In an effort to change the culture, these organizations rush out and hire internal or external experts and jump into some type of lean improvement. The initial burst of energy is refreshing, and individual projects hold great promise. But then change becomes more difficult and sustainment from the first few projects is very weak. Results are either not being generated or are not being sustained or both. What is common at this juncture in your journey is that the action plans simply do not get accomplished. One reason is that you are in the midst of a confluence of two methodologies... the old and the new. As discussed previously the inertia to maintain the status quo will be present and shutting down the old systems and embracing the new systems will enable the best path forward for the organization.

It is somewhere in the six to nine month point that organizations realize they have not built the proper foundation to improve and have to reset their improvement efforts. There are no shortcuts to transformation. Each infrastructure creation activity and each improvement team deployed is a building block for future success.

Table 7.1 shows the key steps required to transform your organization. Most organizations skip the initial steps and jump in at the step "deliver improvement." I emphasize this step by using bold and italicized font. I did

Table 7.1 Transformation Roadmap

Phase 1 *Preparing to* *Transform*	*Phase 2* *The Acceleration Phase* *Improve, Sustain, and* *Spread*	*Phase 3* *Make Organizational* *Improvement the "New" Culture*
Find your change agent	Ensure you have selected the right value streams on which to focus	Build organizational lean improvement capacity
Get informed	Establish value stream governance	Develop lean IT processes
Get help	Set up your value stream performance system	Develop lean financial processes
Establish a steering committee	***Deliver the improvements*** using A3 thinking	Develop lean human resources systems and practices
Train your internal experts	Sustain the improvements and manage visually	Develop a lean supply chain
Develop and deploy a communication campaign	Capture the savings	Develop lean processes for project management, new product/process introduction, and construction services
	Spread lean thinking across the organization	Create lean leadership processes
	Support change with ongoing coaching and training	Create lean medical leadership processes
		Take lean beyond your four walls to suppliers, customers, and service partners

not bold and italicize "using A3 thinking" because most organizations fail to do that activity as well.

If all the steps in phase one and earlier steps in phase two are skipped, then somewhere between six and nine months, the process will deliver much less than optimal results. The key to sustainability is embracing and following leader standard work supporting visual management systems. By skipping all the previous steps, the foundation to sustain will not be in place. Many times, the reason the initial steps were skipped is because leadership failed to make the time and effort commitment to complete the activities. Essentially, the two most common mistakes organizations make are failure to understand the leadership time and effort needed and skipping the initial steps on the transformation roadmap, which are closely related. Regrettably, for many organizations, this initial failure is enough to halt a transformation effort. In other cases, organizations significantly reduce their effort or funding which leads to a slower pace of change or underfunded improvement effort. Lean is not a magic wand, but it is significant hard work.

I believe that every organization can overcome this loss in the first six to nine months, but it will not happen by delegating all the initial leadership activities to a lower-level position in the organization. Leadership has to set the vision, align the resources, and inspire the team for greatness. Lead by example. Commit the time and effort to build the infrastructure and be prepared to align the resources to sustain the improvements. Ensure that all the layers of management can focus their attention on leader standard work and visual management. Remember, sustaining is 80% of the work in a transformation, and being able to sustain your improvement is always the deciding factor in transforming your culture. If you are not seen on the floor and actually involved in the process during the sustaining efforts, you have just significantly reduced the sincerity the employees see in your and the organization's commitment to lean. The "antibodies" know it is only a matter of time.

Managing the Breadth and Depth of the Change

The focus of healthcare is patients. There are hundreds of diagnoses and medical conditions with hundreds of tests and treatments to support these conditions. Virtually all organizations begin their lean improvement in a clinical area. This makes sense, as the core business of healthcare is well ... healthcare. But how many different areas of healthcare should we be improving at the same time? There are dozens to pick from: emergency services, cardiology, primary care, pharmacy services, etc. And when should we branch our improvement efforts off into the administrative areas? Again, there are dozens to pick from, such as billing, scheduling, hiring, financial close, supply chain management, etc. A common mistake organization make when engaging in an enterprise-wide transformation is that they fail to monitor the breadth and depth of their improvement efforts. There is no magical formula to follow when managing the breadth and depth of organizational-wide change, but there are some guidelines that can be followed. One of the approaches you can take is to look at all your programs and core processes and evaluate which ones have the most impact on your strategic measures. A very small example of an analysis of programs and core processes is shown in Table 7.2.

We can move from a subjective feel approach to decision-making and migrate to an objective approach to decision-making. As long as you start somewhere in your top ten, your organization should be in good shape. As you can see in the Pugh analysis example above, the core process of cultivating advanced practice professionals (APPs) listed as APP strategy has a leverage score of 405 which makes it number one on this list for improvement.

A general rule of thumb is to be active in one value stream for every 500 full-time people you have in your organization. So, if your hospital has 3000 staff, you can handle up to six active value streams at any point in time. Engaging in more value steams than your staff population divided by 500 will stress your support resources. Engaging in less than that number will cause your transformation timeline to be really long, like more than 20 years to get to the entire organization.

Once you have selected your initial value stream, begin by creating a model "cell." A cell is a work area where the five improvement principles are all in place. You want to create one area in your organization that has one item flow, pull systems in place, zero defect systems, visual management of process and results including 5S, and leader standard work. This area will be the place you send other areas of the organization when you want to highlight what "good looks like" from a lean perspective.

Following the model cell, the next step is to create a model value stream. A model value stream would have a series of "cells" that help create end-to-end flow within the value stream. As an example, let us review surgical services as a model value stream. Within this value stream, the following cells were created:

■ Clinic Visit where the decision to operate is made
■ Surgical Scheduling

Table 7.2 Pugh Analysis Example

Dimension	Measure	Weight	Patient Expereince of Care		Referral Management		Physician Compensation		Patient Engagement		Physician Practice Acquisition		Professional Services Contracting		APP Strategy		Strategic Planning and Growth		Risk/Quality and Safety	
			Rank	Contribution	Rank	Contribution	Rank	Contribution	Rank	Contribution	Rank	Contribution	Rank	Contribution	Rank	Contribution	Rank	Contribution	Rank	Contribution
HD	Staff Huddles	5	1	5	1	5	5	25	0	0	0	0	0	0	3	15	0	0	5	25
Q	Composit of 5 ACO22	30	0	0	3	90	4	120	5	150	2	60	0	0	4	120	0	0	0	0
SQ	LTR for Provider and Practice	15	5	75	4	60	1	15	4	60	0	0	0	0	4	60	0	0	2	30
D	3rd Next Available Appointment	15	1	15	3	45	3	45	1	15	0	0	1	15	5	75	0	0	0	0
C	PNO Total Cost/Visit	30	0	0	1	30	3	90	1	30	2	60	3	90	4	120	3	90	1	30
G	% of Non-Traditional Visits	5	0	0	0	0	5	25	5	25	0	0	2	10	3	15	2	10	0	0
	Leverage		95		230		320		280		120		115		405		100		85	

- Pre-Admission Testing
- Pre-Operation (day of surgery)
- Anesthetic Blocks
- Case Kitting (kit build, sterilization, and case cart build)
- Room Turnover
- Phase 1
- Phase 2
- Sterile Processing (Rinse and Wash)

For this value stream, the model cell was the pre-admission testing process. In this cell, standard work was created for chart preparation, registration, nursing assessment and education, allied assessment, and education as appropriate, lab and diagnostic imaging testing, and anesthesia consult. The patient went to a single room and almost all of the services came to the patient, diagnostic imaging was the exception. The visit length was reduced from 3.5 hours to a single hour and the productivity improvement yielded an increase in visits from 16 per day to 26 per day with 2 less staff. Following the completion of the entire value stream improvement plan the following results were generated:

- Sixteen percent decrease in the OR cost per case
- Increased OR cases by 21% over budget
- Increased prime time Pre-op, Day Surgery, PACU, Post-Op Day Surgery capacity by 30% thereby reducing overtime expense
- Improved OR on-time start times
- Redeployed and reutilized 4 FTEs
- Cases that had been outsourced were returned to the organization

Following the completion of one pass through the surgical value stream, surgical services completed a second value stream mapping and analysis exercise. Multiple cycles of value stream improvement in the same area is what is meant when lean organizations talk about going "deep." Going into other organizational value streams is what is meant when lean organizations talk about going "wide." Getting to world class will require a strategy that includes both going deep and going wide in your improvement efforts (Figure 7.1). A rule of thumb that is a challenge for some to understand is that the life span of a value stream analysis is one to two years. After one year, so many improvements and changes have occurred that it simply is not the same value stream. It is time for the next future state vision to be completed (yes, in the very same area). Believe it or not, you may receive more

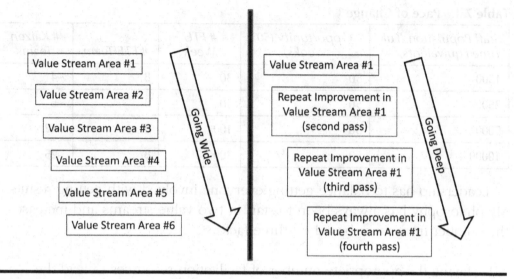

Figure 7.1   Going wide versus going deep.

benefit from the improvements in the second iteration than the first effort. In lean organizations, over multiple years, it is not uncommon to do a value stream analysis on the same areas for up to six iterations. Often, the most significant benefit will come from that sixth effort. The reasons are many, such as the team is now lean savvy, the measures are fully understood, and the process has fewer secrets that the team is not familiar with.

The trick is to find out at what pace your organization wants to go wide and what pace your organization wants to go deep. For your organization to get to the tipping point, everyone will need an opportunity to be on a kaizen team. Assuming there are fifty available weeks in a given year for improvement activity, you can divide your staff and medical staff population into the 50 weeks to get a feel for how many team members are needed each week to get to the tipping point. Table 7.3 illustrates how this number can be easily obtained.

The flaw in this analysis is that it assumes that every participant on every team is a different employee. In reality, about one-third of the team will have been on a team before and only two-thirds of the team members will be newly exposed team members. You will want to be aggressive in getting everyone involved, but not so aggressive that managing the suite of organizational change creates chaos, or even worse, your organization cannot sustain the changes as they unfold. Never confuse activity for productivity; just because you are working on improving in 4 or more value streams simultaneously doesn't mean change is being sustained.

Table 7.3 Pace of Change

Staff Population (Full Time Equivalents)	Opportunity (50 Weeks)	# FTE/ Week	# FTE/Team	# Kaizen Teams
1500	50	30	8	~4
2500	50	50	8	~6
5000	50	100	8	~12
10000	50	200	8	~25

Leadership has to balance getting everyone involved with getting results. My philosophy has always been to start in two value streams and increase the number from there based on three factors:

1. Having the appropriate number of facilitation resources to lead the improvement activities. Assume one full-time resource per value stream engaged.
2. Ensuring the results are sustained all along the improvement process.
3. Maintain the following ratios of improvement activity:
   a. Ten to twenty percent of the value stream improvement work should be on their second pass of improvement. (go deep)
   b. Eighty percent of the work should be in the clinical areas. Twenty percent of the improvement work must come from the administrative areas of the organization.
4. No more than two value streams should be engaged per executive level sponsor. When managing more than two improving value streams, the ability of the senior sponsor to focus and remove barriers becomes very challenging.
5. Previous action plans are on track and the expected outcomes have been achieved.

If you do a careful analysis of the number of teams required to get everyone involved using Table 7.3, the number will likely appear quite daunting. Very few organizations start off at that pace of improvement. I encourage organizations to start small and create the model cell and model value stream, and then increase the number of value streams based on the factors discussed above. In the first year of improvement, leaders will get a feel for both the pace of change and their ability to manage and sustain change. The goal is to ramp up to everyone being engaged while sustaining the improvements along the way. This number will change as you get more experienced. The breadth and depth of change is a topic to be governed by the executive steering committee (Chapter 3).

Leadership, Management, Clinical Staff, Support Staff, and Medical Staff Engagement

One of the roles of senior leadership in creating a culture of improvement is to remove the organizational barriers to enable improvement teams to make rapid change. Management's key role in the change process is to manage visually through leader standard work, to hold staff accountable to following standard work, and to problem solve any barriers to standard work. The key role of the staff and medical staff in the change process is to follow the steps of A3 thinking to quickly see and eliminate waste and develop a new standard that can be managed visually. The staff and medical staff, through the management system, will then monitor and improve the standard on a daily basis to create a culture of continuous improvement.

In order to get to this elusive culture of improvement, everyone must participate in the improvement activities. The common mistake organizations make when embarking on a lean enterprise transformation is they fail to engage all the stakeholders in the change process. Senior leadership will better be able to remove the organizational barriers if they understand A3 thinking, and have participated in both a value stream and a kaizen event. Management will be better able to follow leader standard work and manage visually following active participation in the improvement activities and targeted coaching. The staff and medical staff will be much more supportive of change and following standards after they have been given the opportunity to participate directly in lean improvement through a kaizen event or working through an improvement A3. The most effective results come from when the executive sponsor determines the expected goals for their value streams. This is especially true after the first pass of a value stream when executives become more confident in what can happen through lean change.

Engagement is so important that I recommend you track your engagement numbers as an organization. Table 7.4 can be used to track event participation.

In a lean enterprise transformation, participation does not necessarily equate to engagement, but it is a great place to start. Participation in improvement teams creates a structured environment for staff and medical

Table 7.4 Sample of Event Participation Tracking

Role	# of People on 0 Events	# of People on 1 Event	# of People on 2 Events	# of People on 6 to 11 Events	# of People on 12–35 Events	# of People > 36 Events
Senior leadership	6	3	1	0	0	0
Management	62	81	42	21	0	0
Staff	2100	1100	540	62	14	0
Medical staff	400	75	8	2	0	0
Volunteers	800	240	63	4	0	0
Internal experts	0	0	0	6	2	3

staff to engage. Tracking participation numbers also helps the organization understand where the lack of participation by a certain role will potentially create a barrier to improvement in the future. The area of most concern is physician participation. We have many different professionals in the health-care system: nurses, physicians, respiratory therapists, occupational therapists, and physiotherapists. We also have social workers, pharmacists, laboratory technicians, and imaging technologists. With all these professional people engaged in healthcare, why are we singling out the physicians? Physicians are in the unique position of being able to personally choose whether to follow or not follow organizational standards. Physicians can deviate from standard order sets and clinical pathways, they can add or subtract diagnostics, they can add or subtract medication treatments, and decide if and when to discharge. No other staff function within the healthcare environment is in the unique position to unilaterally practice with this autonomy. Is this a bad thing? Absolutely not! However, it is essential that physicians are engaged in our improvement work. By engaged, I do not mean popping into a room on occasion during an improvement activity. What we desire is a healthcare system that is physician-led! Who is in a better position to lead improvement than our medical staff? Clinical healthcare needs physician champions. We need to synthesize the continuous improvement in practice, therapeutics, medicines, surgical procedures, and diagnostics to deliver, (even invent) better evidence-based, best-practice care. Ask any physician if they have any "waste" in their typical day, typical surgery, or typical patient visit. Without exception, the answer is "of course I do." Lean can help physicians be more effective in their chosen profession and improve quality outcomes for the patient. Lean gives physicians back their biggest currency, time. On many occasions, I have seen an inter-professional team collaborate with a physician to develop a clinical pathway. Such a pathway uses the latest technology, protocols, order sets, and treatments, and is evidence-based. After the team reaches alignment in both process and format, the pathway is documented in a manner consistent with the requirements of health medical records. The work is piloted on a few patients with favorable results in outcomes. When presented to the physicians working in the department, what do you think the reception is? Typically, the pathway is received with skepticism, criticism, and an offer to make many changes. Rarely is the pathway adopted and followed. The question is why? The likely reason is that physicians were not sufficiently invested in the change at the beginning of the process. The behavior of rejecting change is not specific to physicians. In any area of professional specialization, change is always easier to accept when you are invested in the change and part of the change. This becomes an opportunity for lean organizations. Rather than "managing around" physicians, how do we inspire and engage physicians to lead quality improvement? Great organizations have a strategy to engage physicians. This strategy may include creating a value proposition specifically for physicians (i.e., explaining to physicians the value of engaging in administrative improvement work, for example), holding special training and education sessions, leveraging the medical leadership, and in some cases providing some amounts of funding to allow for full participation. Experienced lean organizations even build improvement requirements for physicians into their physician agreements. I encourage you to engage the physician group early in the lean improvement process so that you can build this strategy collaboratively.

Inability to Operate Two Systems

In chapter five, I briefly mentioned why many organizations fail to change their culture. My hypothesis is that organizations cannot sustain operating two different systems. A lean healthcare enterprise runs fundamentally differently than a non-lean healthcare enterprise. What management, staff, and medical staff focus on, how they spend their day, the relentless pursuit of perfection, and the constant elimination of non-value-added activity do not resemble the traditional lean healthcare system. It is likely that your culture is not currently one of continuous improvement. Because of this, the many systems and processes in place today will always be pulling your culture back to status quo. The common mistake organizations make when embracing a lean enterprise transformation is they fail to realize this dual system phenomenon is creating havoc on the change process. It will require tremendous leadership and courage to take on the old systems.

These battles will not just be fought within the improvement teams. These battles will also occur at the senior levels of the organization. Finance will want to put in new controls that will add three days to the turnaround time for purchased equipment, negating the entire kaizen event team activity that was intended to streamline the approval process for new equipment. The new HR employee review system will now require an additional 2 hours per week per manager to execute, competing directly with "gemba" time for the manager. This list goes on and on. As the organization becomes more lean, traditional solutions to problems cannot be used as an overlay to previous lean solutions, but it will take time to get to that point.

The larger your organization, the more bureaucracy there will be in your organization. The value streams that your organization is trying to improve will be bombarded with changes from other parts of the organization that do not yet have a lean thinking mindset. The conflict of interest caused by these changes is demoralizing for the team and management and must be resolved at higher levels in the organization. These discussions are difficult to have. No senior leader likes having their corporate-wide project put on hold, or having an exception created for a single value stream. If consensus is reached, the resulting solution often takes the organization back closer to status quo, thus delaying the change process and the corresponding cultural transformation.

So how does an organization reconcile the differences? The best way is to transform the organization faster. The more lean thinkers and lean processes that exist in your enterprise, the less chance a non-traditional solution will get implemented. This solution might be at odds with the earlier chapter discussion on managing the breadth and depth of change. Again, you only want to go as fast as you can sustain. But all things being equal, changing at a faster pace shuts down your old system sooner. If going faster in your transformation is not an option, then I would ask you to consider running exceptions for your improving area. Maybe they go last on the timeline of corporate-wide process changes giving the area valuable time to get to sustainability. There also might be some lessons learned from the deployment of these initiatives and the end result will get you closer to a lean solution than what is currently on the agenda. Most importantly, do not gloss over this issue. In my opinion, it is the single greatest cause of transformational failure. Anticipate the conflict and have meaningful dialogue in the lean steering committee to identify issues and produce mitigation strategies.

Common Errors to Organizational Change Efforts

Change management expert, John P. Kotter had his book *Leading Change* published in 1996. Following 15 years of analysis of dozens of failed corporate initiatives, Kotter wanted to articulate why transformation efforts failed.[1] The summary of this analysis is that there are eight common errors in organizational change efforts including[2]:

■ allowing too much complacency
■ failing to create a powerful coalition
■ underestimating the power of vision
■ under-communicating the vision by a factor of ten
■ permitting obstacles to block the new vision
■ failure to create short terms wins
■ declaring victory too soon
■ neglecting to anchor the changes firmly in the new corporate culture

I thought it might be valuable to map the activities in the transformation roadmap described in Chapters 3, 4, and 5 to see if they provide solutions to these problems and help in avoiding the eight common mistakes organizations make (Table 7.5).

You can see that following the transformation roadmap will help assist your organization in avoiding the eight common mistakes organizations make in undertaking an organizational change effort. Many of the activities used in a lean enterprise transformation, like visual management and leader standard work, will actually address several of the common mistakes, leveraging even further their effectiveness in developing a culture of continuous improvement. Take a moment and reflect on the list. Would your organization be at risk from any of these possibilities?

There are many other risks associated with embracing a lean enterprise transformation. Various members of the senior team could oppose the changes as a distraction from your mission, or a union could become active. Another key risk is that a change agent will depart from your organization. Good change agents are in high demand and will be sought by many

Table 7.5 Avoiding Common Mistakes in Organizational Change

Organizational Mistake	Lean Transformation Roadmap Risk Mitigation Activities
Allowing too much complacency	• Establishing True North measures with double-digit improvement • Visual management • Managing for daily improvement • Kaizen rapid cycle improvement • A3 thinking
Failing to create a powerful coalition	• Enterprise transformation steering committee • Value stream steering committee
Underestimating the power of vision	• Deploying Hoshin Kanri • Communication strategy • Value stream analysis
Under-communicating the vision by a factor of 10	• Communication strategy • Measurement capture • Physician engagement strategy • Value stream and kaizen report outs • Lean capacity building
Permitting obstacles to block the new vision	• Executive sponsor • Enterprise transformation steering committee • Value stream steering committee • Daily team leader meetings during kaizen events • Leadership standard work • Visual management • Managing for daily improvement • Enterprise-wide engagement • Gemba walks
Failing to Create Short term wins	• Value stream rapid improvement plans with quick wins • Kaizen rapid cycle improvement • A3 thinking • Managing for daily improvement • Measurement capture
Declaring victory too soon	• True north measures • Deep versus wide pace of change • Visual management • Managing for daily improvement • Value stream mapping and analysis
Neglecting to anchor the changes firmly in the new corporate culture	• Chapter 5, "make organizational improvement the new culture," addresses how to prevent these common errors.

organizations and recruiters, particularly change agents with demonstrated lean expertise. Another key risk to the change effort is that the CEO or another key member of the senior leadership team retires. If one of these things occurs and derails your efforts, this is a clear indication that lean is not yet the organization's preferred way of doing business. I have seen many great initial transformation efforts get off track when an important leader departs the organization. And this can happen inside of a fiscal quarter. But if I listed all the potential reasons why organizations fail to create a lean enterprise, I would need a much longer chapter. I also like to differentiate between reasons and excuses. Every organization has the capability of becoming a lean enterprise, but not every organization has the will to succeed. Many organizations give up because the lift is heavy, and the effort required is deemed excessive. Rather than address the issues, many of which have been identified in this chapter, you will begin to hear a litany of excuses. What happens next is far too frequent, organizations jump on the next flavor of the month, and lean thinking, staff engagement, focus on the patient, etc. fade into the distant past.

However, I have also seen the opposite. I have seen where organizations have followed the key steps in the transformation roadmap having avoided skipping steps and taken their organization to a place where most everyone is engaged in seeing and eliminating waste to provide a healthcare system focused on the patient. They provide a system of care that is safe, outcome-focused, evidence-based, cost-effective, and timely. Their healthcare system is not complacent and new opportunities are constantly being discovered. As these opportunities are addressed, these organizations continue to create a great future for their patients and families, for their staff, medical staff, and volunteers, and for their suppliers and service partners. In a lean environment in concert with the two pillars of lean, continuous elimination of waste and respect for all people, everyone wins. Following the transformation roadmap will assist your organization in avoiding the common mistakes that organizations make and shorten the lead-time for success while mitigating the risk of failure. Your organization can do this! Many before you have been down this road within healthcare and outside of healthcare. Stay diligent, keep focused on the customer, and engage your staff and medical staff in solving problems using a structured approach with A3 thinking, standard work, and visual management. Once you get to scale, the lift becomes easier.

Chapter Summary: Key Points from Chapter 7

- Most organizations fail to get to world-class status.
- Any organization embarking on a cultural transformation can get to better and many can get to great. The reward for trying to transform exceeds the risk.
- Organizations make common mistakes when trying to deliver on a lean enterprise transformation. These mistakes include:
  - Wasting the first 6–9 months by skipping the beginning steps in the transformation roadmap
  - Failing to monitor the breadth and depth of change
  - Failing to get everyone involved
  - Failing to shut down the traditional healthcare system in favor of the new lean healthcare system
  - Tracking event participation is a proxy for engagement in the first few years of your journey.
  - Following the transformation roadmap will help your organization avoid the common errors to organizational change efforts identified by John Kotter in his work entitled *Leading Change*.
  - Every organization has the ability to become a lean enterprise, but not all organizations have the will to succeed.

Notes

1. John P. Kotter, *Leading Change* (Boston, MA: Harvard Business School Press, 1996), pg. ix.
2. John P. Kotter, *Leading Change* (Boston, MA: Harvard Business School Press, 1996), pg. 16.

Chapter 8

Closing Thoughts

The book began with the age-old discussion of the differences between leadership and management. Management is a set of work processes that keeps an organization operating effectively. Leadership is the set of processes that create organizations and then help organizations change to meet the ever-evolving business conditions. Lean transformation, which is creating a culture of continuous improvement leading to world-class rates of improvement in performance and culture, is a leadership process. The key aspects of leadership include creating and sharing the future vision of the organization, aligning the financial and human resources of the organization to achieve the vision, and then inspiring people to realize the new vision.

Transforming healthcare will require significant amounts of leadership. I envision creating an entire healthcare industry where world-class healthcare quality, patient safety, and customer service are the norm; a workplace that can be transformed into one where staff and medical staff are engaged in their work and inspired to do better and be better every day. Using lean approaches, you can help shape a healthcare system that not only delivers more "value" to patients, families, and their surrounding communities but also creates a place to work filled with joy and fulfillment. The answer is not in the previous flavors of the month, nor is it in the next hot software application. Artificial intelligence and machine learning surely will do things not imaginable today. Without a doubt work will be simplified and hopefully safety, quality, and patient outcomes will be dramatically improved with its use. But these applications are not systems, and they cannot look across the entire landscape of healthcare and transform people and workflows by eliminating wasted time and activity in all work performed by clinical, administrative, and medical staff.

DOI: 10.4324/9781003532132-8

I offered a roadmap for transformation in this book. Using this structured approach, you can change the performance and culture of your organization. Unfortunately, there is no "how to" manual to transform. Each organization will have to find its own way. The key leadership and management practices described in the earlier chapters can serve as a reference for you to use on your journey. My one piece of advice is that although the steps may vary in their timing, try not to skip steps in pursuit of a "faster" or "easier" transformation. I can assure you there is no easy button to change an organization's culture.

The ingredients of true commitment to the lean effort – persistence, consistency, and tenacity – will all be needed to get your organization to escape the pull of your current culture. Carefully consider each of the activities contained in the roadmap and work them into your transformation plan toward becoming a world-class healthcare organization. I have found it easier to manage the activities proactively rather than reactively. Each of the tools, techniques, and approaches in the roadmap will avoid common mistakes organizations make when trying to change their culture. Learning from these valuable lessons will shorten your lead-time for success and minimize the risk of failure.

Lean healthcare is a system where:

- All work is constantly scrutinized to eliminate wasted time and activity and deliver more value to your patients.
- The staff and medical staff continuously improve the quality and safety of care, approaching a defect-free system, reducing wasted time, and freeing up capacity for other work, decreasing lead-times for services, and lowering the cost of the delivery of these services.
- Healthcare is delivered with accurate and timely information shared seamlessly amongst the care team and patients.
- The medical staff and clinical staff collaborate to provide patient-focused, evidenced-based care with seamless transitions between specialties, subspecialties, and levels of care.
- A system where the patients, families, and communities participate in the design of the services leading to healthier communities with preventative strategies driving lower and lower costs.
- Care is delivered with outstanding customer service leading to an enhanced customer experience.
- Both patient and staff satisfaction and morale are continuously improving.

If you work in healthcare, then you or your organization is already aspiring to be in this place. Lean leadership will require you or your organization to establish and communicate your vision of becoming a lean enterprise. The transformation roadmap provided offers leadership approaches toward establishing the infrastructure and improvement framework along with aligning the resources toward achieving the vision. Also, the roadmap offers leadership tools, techniques, and approaches to inspire the team, by getting everyone involved, to realize your vision.

I would like to close this book with exactly the same closing comments I used in my first book. This statement applies equally to lean leadership.

> Fortunately, more and more healthcare organizations today are discovering the beauty of lean: a management system of simple principles, and methods that can be implemented in any organization to generate measurable, lasting results of improvement. You have taken the first step by simply reading this book. Now I encourage you to move forward with lean in your organization. Inspire others and lead positive change. Watch how "lean thinking" revitalizes your organization and sets the stage for great achievements ahead. So much is possible when you apply the lean approach to everything you do.[1]

In closing, I leave you with this, *"You can make this happen. Go be great!"* May God bless you on your journey.

Note

1. Ronald Bercaw, *Taking Improvement from the Assembly Line to Healthcare* (Boca Raton, FL: CRC Press, 2012), pg. 147.

Glossary of Lean Terms

2P – This is the short form of the term Process Preparation. 2P is an approach used to develop a new process or product. 2P begins with a voice of the customer activity, develops seven ways to operationalize each key task in the process, analyzes the seven ways using a Pugh analysis, and ends with the seven flows to define the new process.

A3 – Both the process and thinking for problem-solving based on the scientific method. The A3 is frequently used to document problem-solving exercises, status reports, and business cases. Named the A3 as the report is associated with the size of paper the report is documented upon. There are several types of A3 forms. The most commonly used are the A3 plan and the problem-solving A3.

Andon – A visual or audible signal that identifies when an abnormal condition has occurred. Typically combined with a stop the line mentality, where a process stops following an abnormality until its source can be detected to prevent recurrence of problems.

Antibody – A term used to define a person resistant to change.

Batch – An approach where large quantities of items (batches) are processed and then moved to the next operation.

Cause and Effect Diagram – Also known as a fishbone diagram or an Ishakawa diagram. The cause and effect diagram is used to develop possible causes of a know effect (problem). Key areas for brainstorming are developed around a standard set of categories. Typically the 6M's (manpower, measurement, methods, materials, mother nature, and machinery) and or the 4P's (people, process, policy, place).

Communication Circle – A tool used to show the waste of transactions and hand-offs of information.

Continuous Improvement – A mindset adopted by organizations to repeatedly identify and eliminate waste.

Current State – Workflow of the operation as it currently performs. Used as part of value stream mapping.

Cycle Time – The time it takes to complete a process, as observed through direct observation.

Cycle Time/Takt Time Bar Chart (Ct/Tt bar chart) – Also known as a loading diagram. This tool visually displays how each staff person is loaded against the takt time. Shown on the tool are the process takt time, the manual cycle time of each person in the process, and the minimum staffing calculation. Minimum staffing is equal to the sum of the cycle times divided by the takt time. The Ct/Tt bar chart is used to highlight wasted manpower and bottlenecks; and is a key in improving productivity.

Defect – Work that needs to be redone or clarified. An error that finds its way to the customer.

Direct Observation – The lean approach used to best identify waste. Direct observation involves going to an area and observing the process to identify waste. Direct observation is often combined with capturing time elements of the process to "quantify" waste.

Failure Mode Effects Analysis – A quality tool used to identify key risk factors in a process and take action to mitigate the risk.

Flow – Processing one unit of work through a series of steps in a continuous manner, at the rate of customer demand, in a standardized way. Ideally only value-added tasks are linked together.

Flow Diagram – A lean tool used to document a process. The flow diagram is used to show workflow and highlights process stops and starts, hand-offs, and disconnects.

Five S – Five terms, beginning with the letter S that are used to develop a high-performing work area.

Seiri – Remove unneeded or unwanted items from the workplace (equipment, tools, supplies, materials, information).

Seiton – Neatly arrange the remaining items. A place for everything and everything in its place.

Seiso – Thoroughly clean the workplace and return the area to like new condition.

Seiketsu – Create standard conditions to keep the workplace standardized and organized. Create work practices that enable standard work and proper workflow.

Shitsuke – Personal discipline to main the first four S's.

Five S Event – A team-based rapid cycle process used to implement 5S in a work area, while simultaneously training the staff.

Five Why's – An approach used to identify the root cause of a problem. Beginning with the problem you see (the direct cause), ask why the problem occurred and give an answer that directly addresses that question. Repeating the process five times will get you to the root cause of the problem. This approach is used to develop people.

Future State – Workflow created as a vision for what the new workflow will be. The future state is developed using the lean design attributes of flow, pull, defect-free, and visual management. Used as part of value stream mapping.

Gap Analysis – The quantification of the "gap" between the current and the target state. Generally this includes the wastes and their corresponding root causes preventing realization of the desired outcome.

Genchi Genbutsu – Japanese term for "go and see." This philosophy to solving problems implies that in order to truly understand a situation, one must go and see the situation at the place where work is done and value is created.

Gemba – Japanese term for "real place." Used to describe the place where work is done.

Gemba Walk – A management approach used to develop a subordinate. Following the master/apprentice model, the experienced leader walks through the work area with the subordinate to teach how to identify waste, and develop and evaluate plans for improvement. The mentor teaches the subordinate to practice kaizen (see and eliminate waste)

Heijunka – The leveling of volume and mix of work over a fixed period of time. A concept used to reduce batching while efficiently meeting customer demand.

Heijunka Box – A tool used to level the mix and volume of work.

Hoshin Kanri – Also known as Hoshin planning or policy deployment. A management approach to identifying key strategic goals and developing plans to realize these goals. The process concludes with a monthly review of both process and outcomes.

Inventory – Materials and information that accumulate between process steps.

Kaizen – A process used for continuous improvement to eliminate waste and create more value.

Kaizen Event – Team-based approach to rapid cycle improvement. Spanning 2–5 days depending on the scope of the activity, the scientific method is followed during this activity to deliver an improved process in a portion of a value stream ending with standard work, visual management, and process control.

Kanban – Japanese term loosely translated to mean "signboard" Kanban is a scheduling system based on the principle of pull used to determine what to make, when to make, and how much.

Lean Project Management – See vertical Value Stream Map

Line Balancing – A method used to even work content and time between workstations after waste has been eliminated. Ideally, each staff member will be loaded equally with a work amount equal to or slightly less than the takt time.

Loading Diagram – See Cycle Time/Takt Time bar chart

Managing for Daily Improvement (MDI) – An improvement technique designed to maintain and incrementally improve standards. The two core elements of Managing for Improvement include the MDI board which displays charts and graphs, and the daily huddle that engages staff in the improvement process through experimentation. This is also sometimes known as the Daily Management System (DMS)

Mistake Proofing – Work methods designed into the process that prevents the person doing work from making an error. (Also known as error proofing.)

Motion – Operator movement in excess of that required to complete a task.

Non-value Added – An activity that takes time, space, or resources but does not directly meet the need of the customer. (Also known as waste.)

Operational Review – A weekly and/or monthly process that monitors improvement activity from the A3 plan. Key elements of the review include reviewing trended outcome measures, discussion of past and future improvement activity to deliver on improvement and mitigation of risk and barriers to enable improvement to occur.

Over-processing – Doing work-related tasks in excess of value as defined by the customer.

Over-production – Producing/doing more, sooner, or faster than the next step in the process.

Performance Board – A tool used to show results from a process. The performance board differs from the process control board in that it details outcome results in lieu of process measures.

Plan, Do, Check, Act (PDCA) – A cycle of improvement, based on the scientific method. Used to propose a change in a process, implement the change, measure the result, and then take action to standardize or stabilize the change.

Poka Yoke – Japanese term for mistake proofing. Poka Yoke is a quality control method that designs the work in a way that makes it impossible to create a defect.

Process Control – A tool used as part of visual management to discern abnormal conditions in the output of a process. The common design shows both the plan and the actual output and sources of variation are documented in real-time.

Process Control Board – A tool used to visually display process control. The board shows plan and actual performance of the process.

Pugh Analysis – A quantitative technique used to evaluate multiple options against a set of criteria.

Pull – A signal used to link areas of continuous flow together. A method to control work by having downstream activities signal their upstream requirements. Used to reduce/eliminate the waste of over-production.

Sensei – In lean circles, a Sensei is an experienced person who has mastered lean approaches to both lean improvement and lean management.

Sequence of Operations – The recipe for a process. Step-by-step detail of the standard work. The sequence of operations makes up one-third of the requirement of standard work.

Seven Quality Tools – A name given to seven common approaches to analysis often used in solving quality-related problems. The seven tools include: the cause and effect diagram, the flow chart, the check sheet, the control chart, the histogram, the scatter diagram, and the Pareto chart.

Seven Wastes – Forms of waste found in operations. These wastes include over-production, over-processing, waiting, motion, transportation, inventory, and defects.

Standard Work – Work procedures used to define how an operator will complete a task or process. Standard work is based on three elements: sequence of operations, takt time, and standard work in process.

Standard Work Combination Sheet – A worksheet used to document standard work. The sheet provides a format to document the sequence of operations, and the takt time. The sheet also provides task times including manual task times, automatics task times, and walking.

Standard Work in Process – The amount of inventory needed between two processes necessary to maintain continuous flow.

Steering Committee – A body designated to govern lean improvement. The steering committee can be at the value stream or the enterprise level of the organization.

Spaghetti Map – A diagram used to show the path and distance of travel for a person, supply, or machinery. The map highlights the waste of motion and/or transportation.

Target State – A part of the problem-solving A3, where the attributes of the desired state of an improvement are documented. Critical here is to not list solutions as solutions are generated after the gap analysis.

Takt Time – A theoretical calculation used to provide the rhythm of output for a process in time units. The calculation consists of taking the available time to do work divided by the volume of work to be done.

Time Observation – See Direct Observation

Toyota Production System – A management system for excellence based on providing customers the highest possible quality, in the shortest time, at the lowest cost by removing wasted time and activity.

Transportation – Unnecessary movement of people, materials, equipment, etc. Transportation is also known as the waste of conveyance.

True North Measure – Operational excellence comes from five key areas: Staff morale (human development), Quality, Delivery (lead-time), Cost, and Growth. A high level strategic measure of one of the five areas of operational excellence is known as a true north measure. These measures become the compass for the organization to align effort and direction.

Value Added – An activity that directly meets the need of a customer.

Value-Added/Non-value-Added Analysis – A technique used to identify in each task step whether the step adds value or doesn't. Typically a value-added task is given a green dot and a non-value-added task is given a red dot. A typical process is nine parts non-value added to one part value added.

Value Stream – The activities completed to deliver value to a customer.

Value Stream Mapping – A tool used to show waste in a value stream and develop a plan for improvement.

Vertical Value Stream Map – A planning approach used for projects used to simultaneously deliver the correct value to the customer in the least waste way. The process begins by defining the milestones and then backward plans the tasks needed to meet the milestones thus ensuring the majority of the project is value added. This process is also known as lean project management.

Visual Management – A management system that makes normal from abnormal conditions transparent to allow problems to be identified at a glance so they can immediately be corrected.

Waiting – Customer delays caused by the absence of supplies, equipment, information, resources.

Waste – Any activity that consumes time, space, or resources, but fails to create value for a customer.

Zero Defects – A mindset based on the premise that while humans are prone to errors, these errors need not make it the customer thus becoming a defect. It is possible to achieve a zero-defect system.

Index

Printed in the United States
by Baker & Taylor Publisher Services